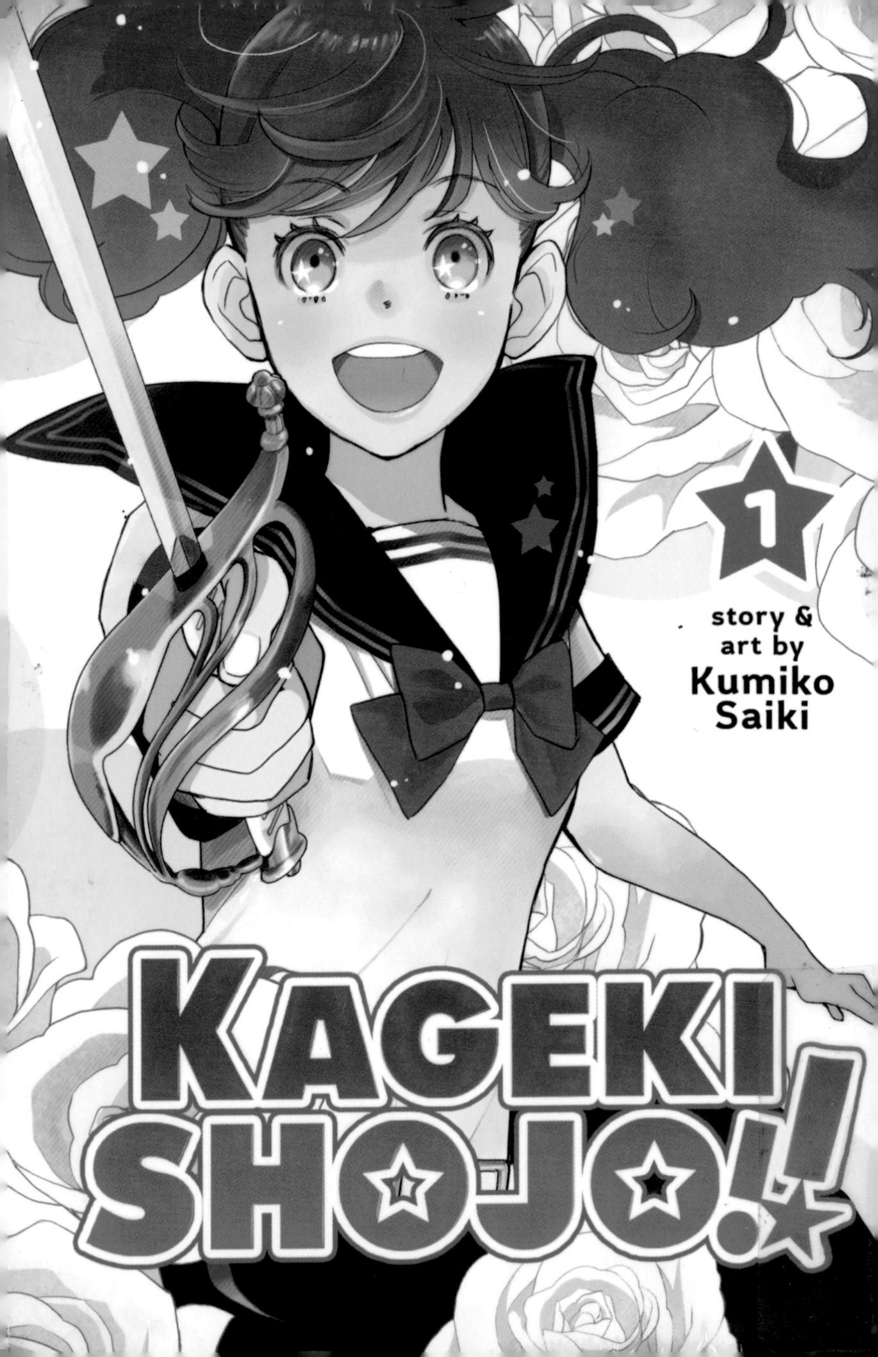
1
story & art by Kumiko Saiki
KAGEKI SHOJO!!

KAGEKI SHOJO!!

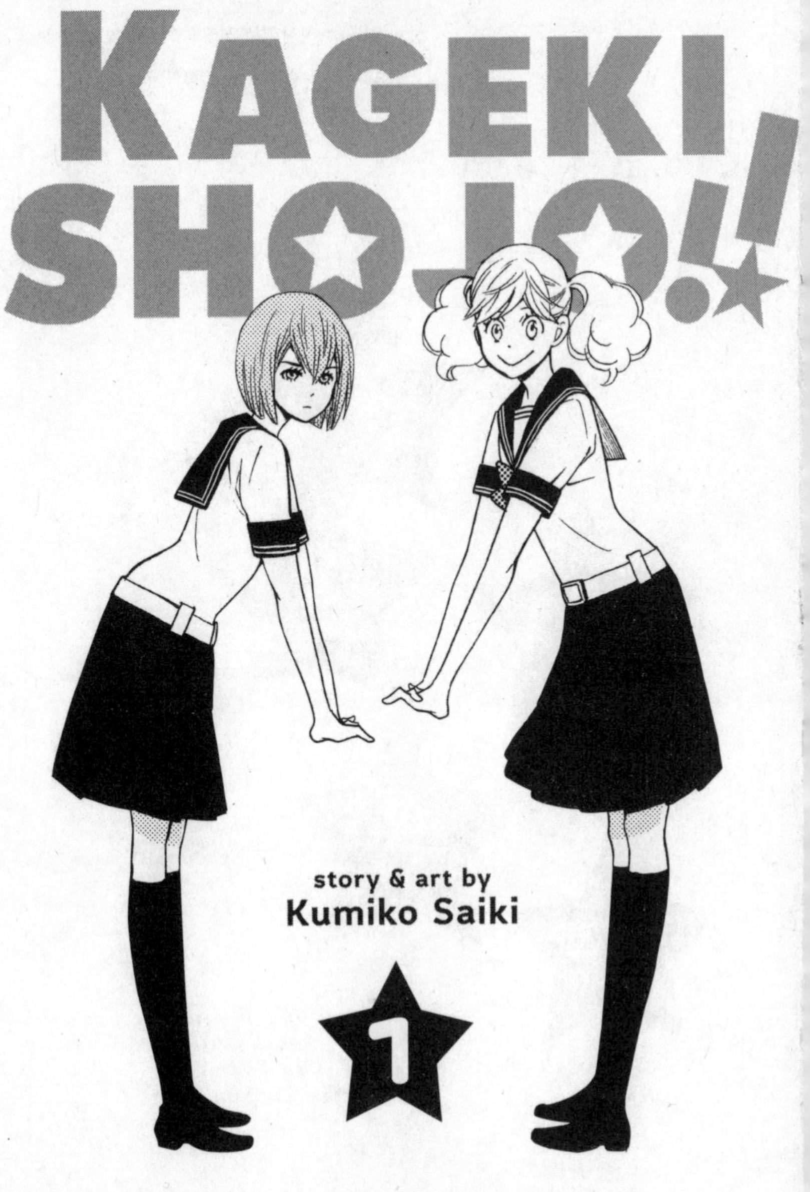

story & art by
Kumiko Saiki

1

Contents

Don't miss the prequel series *Kageki Shojo!! The Curtain Rises*

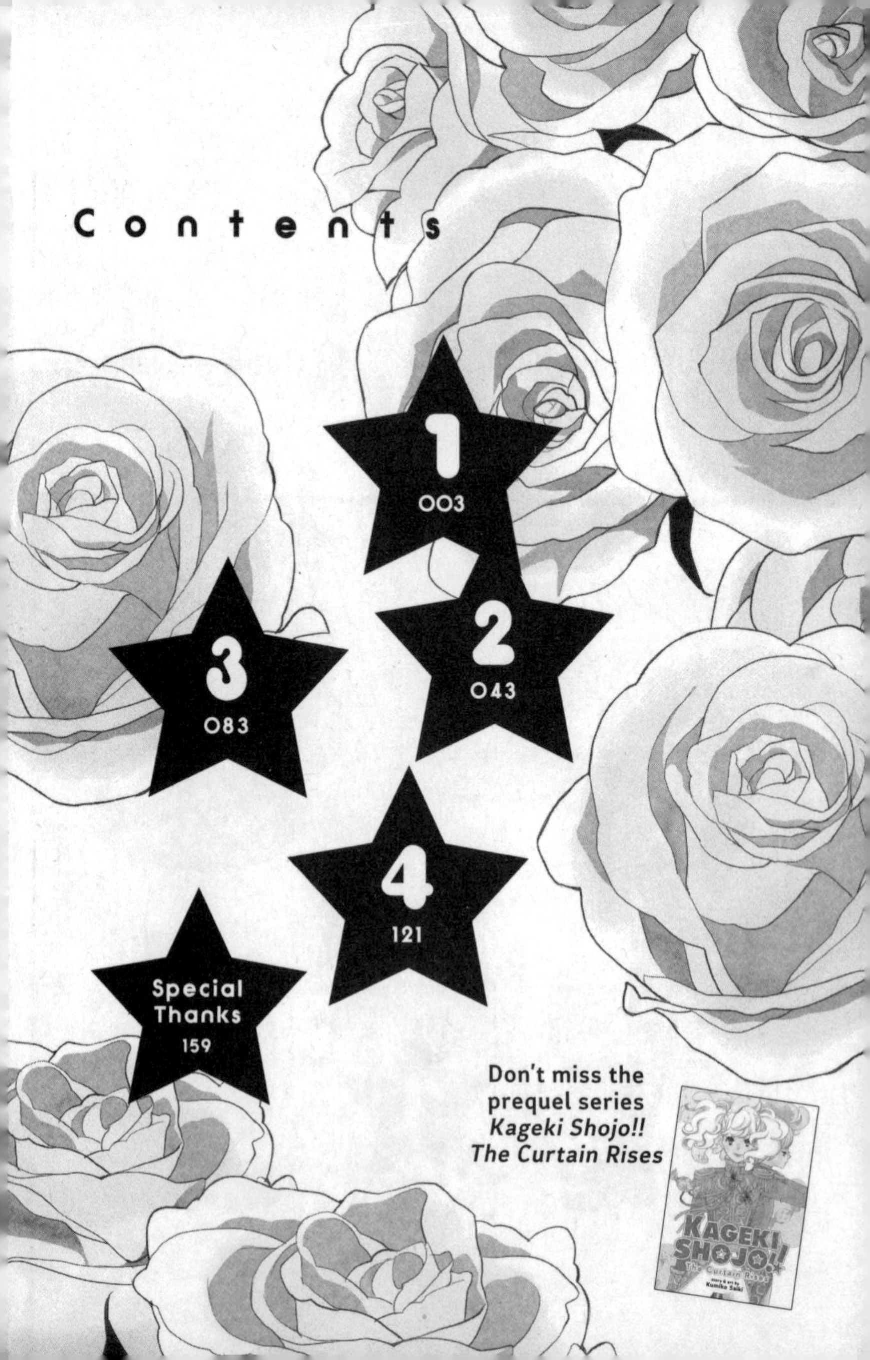

KAGEKI SHOJO!!
The Curtain Rises

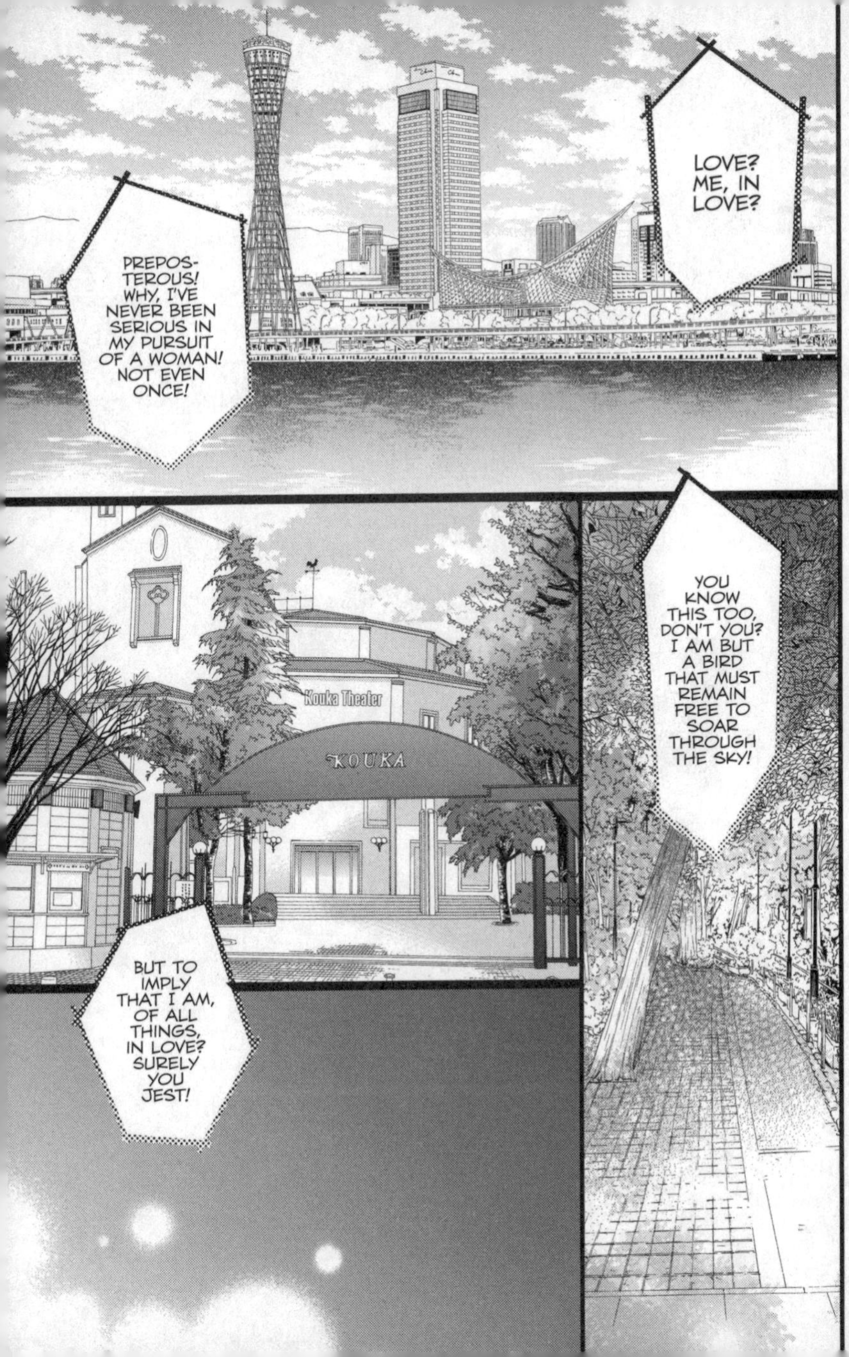
LOVE? ME, IN LOVE?
PREPOSTEROUS! WHY, I'VE NEVER BEEN SERIOUS IN MY PURSUIT OF A WOMAN! NOT EVEN ONCE!
YOU KNOW THIS TOO, DON'T YOU? I AM BUT A BIRD THAT MUST REMAIN FREE TO SOAR THROUGH THE SKY!
Kouka Theater
KOUKA
BUT TO IMPLY THAT I AM, OF ALL THINGS, IN LOVE? SURELY YOU JEST!

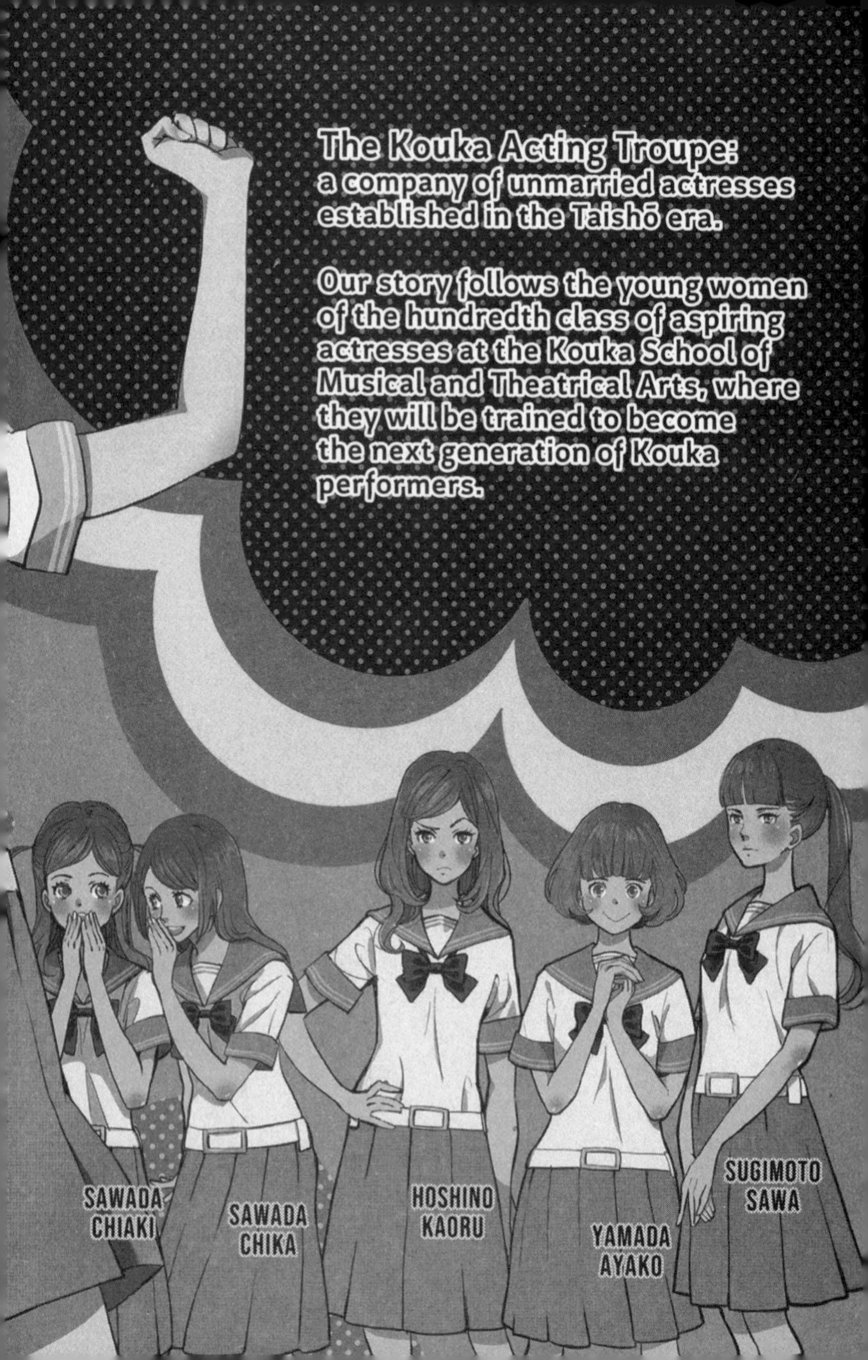
The Kouka Acting Troupe:
a company of unmarried actresses established in the Taishō era.
Our story follows the young women of the hundredth class of aspiring actresses at the Kouka School of Musical and Theatrical Arts, where they will be trained to become the next generation of Kouka performers.
SUGIMOTO SAWA
YAMADA AYAKO
HOSHINO KAORU
SAWADA CHIKA
SAWADA CHIAKI

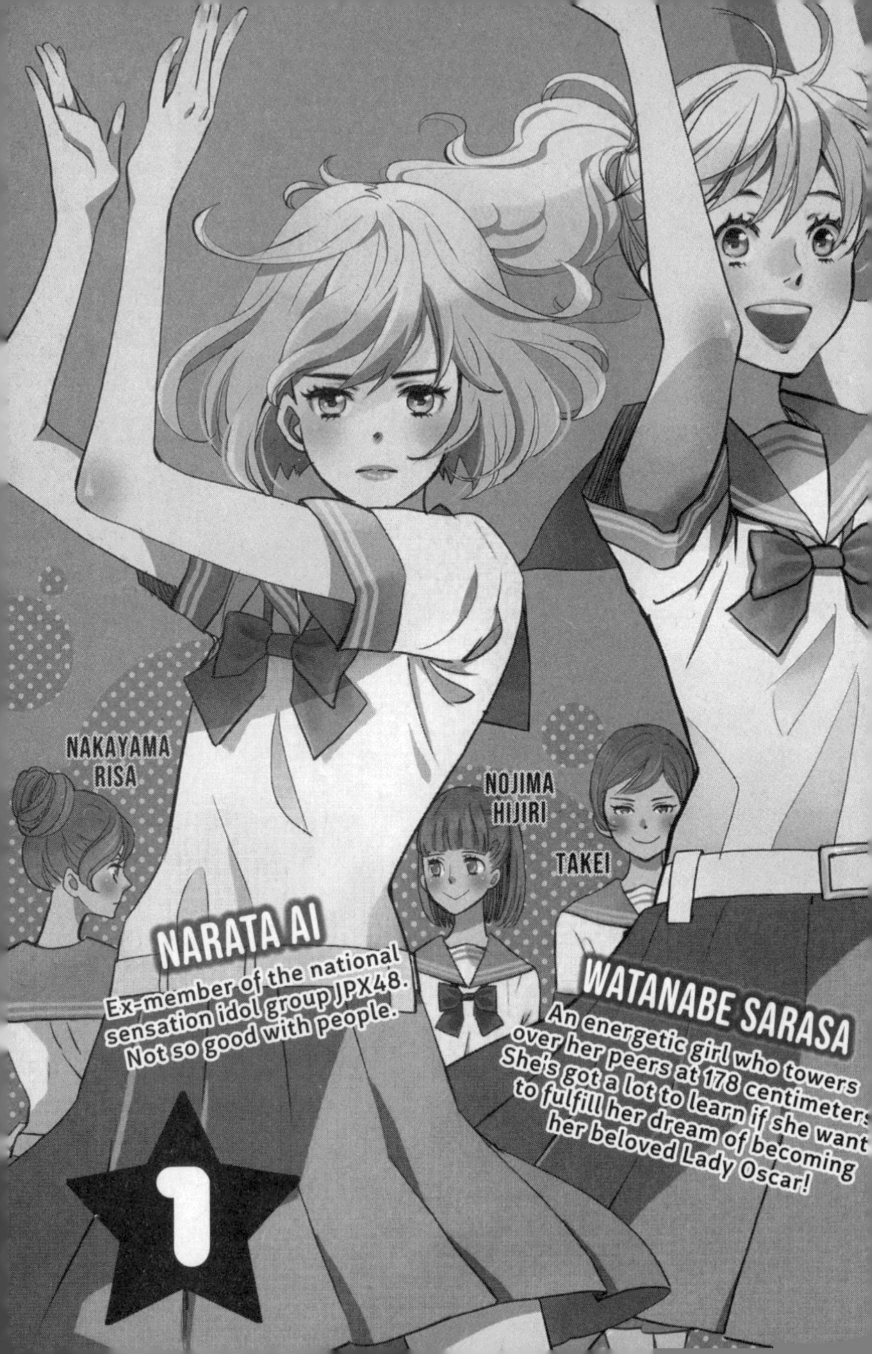
WATANABE SARASA
An energetic girl who towers over her peers at 178 centimeters. She's got a lot to learn if she want to fulfill her dream of becoming her beloved Lady Oscar!
TAKEI
NOJIMA HIJIRI
NARATA AI
Ex-member of the national sensation idol group JPX48. Not so good with people.
NAKAYAMA RISA
1

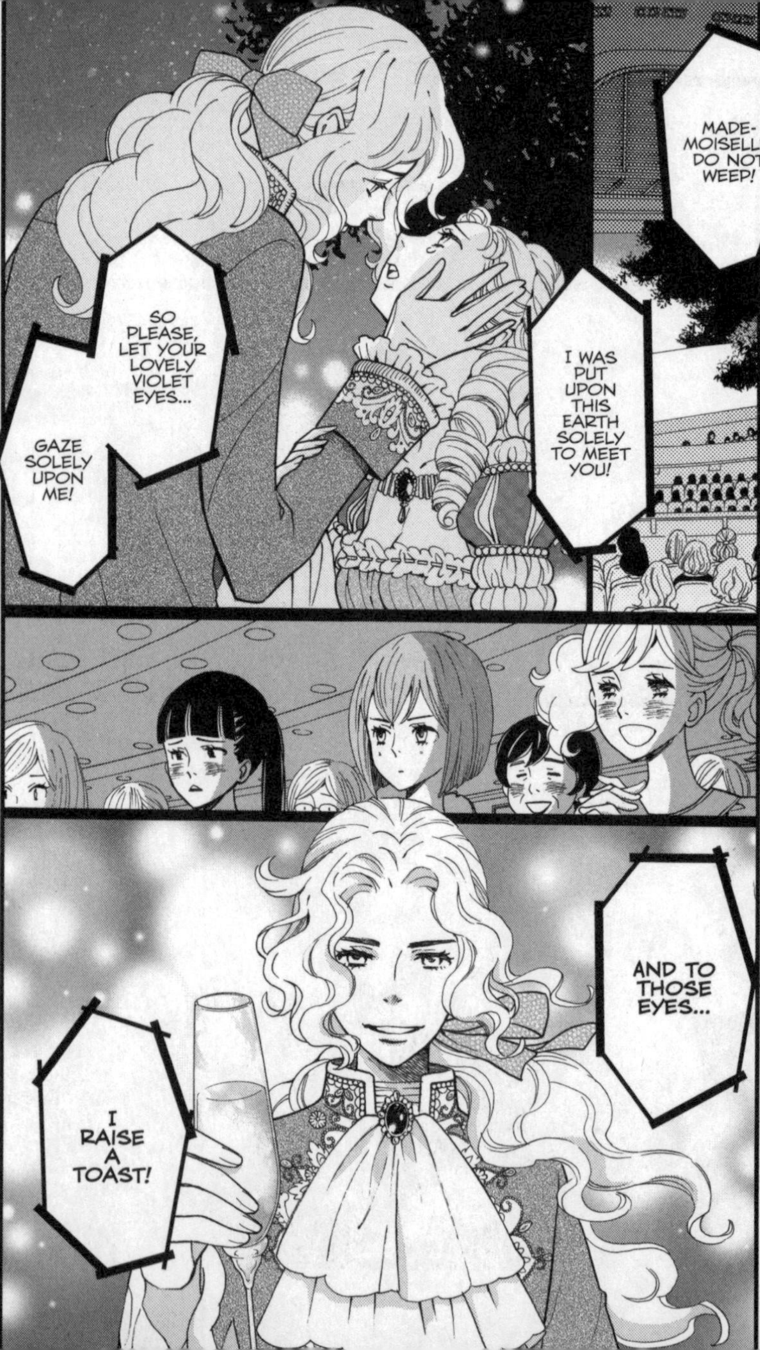
MADE-MOISELLE, DO NOT WEEP!
I WAS PUT UPON THIS EARTH SOLELY TO MEET YOU!
SO PLEASE, LET YOUR LOVELY VIOLET EYES...
GAZE SOLELY UPON ME!
AND TO THOSE EYES...
I RAISE A TOAST!

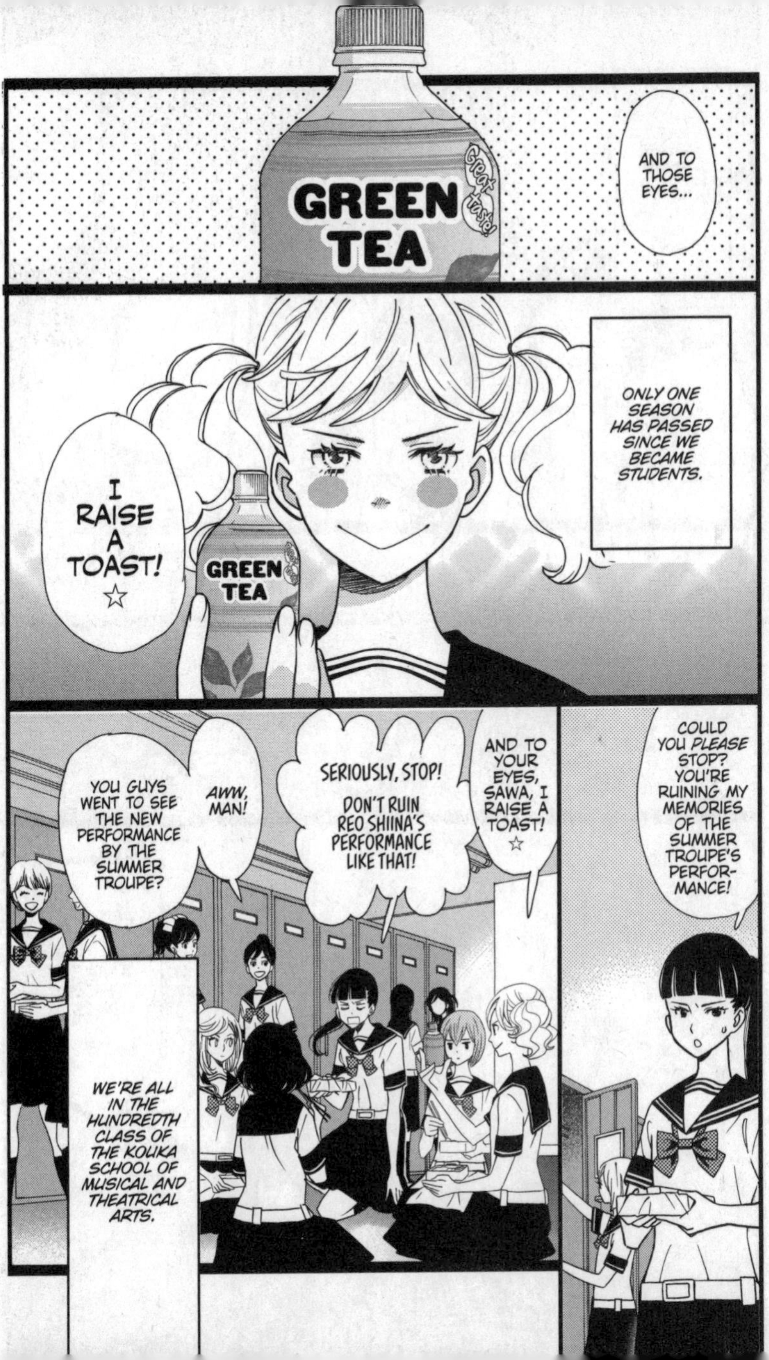
AND TO THOSE EYES...
GREEN TEA
Great taste!
ONLY ONE SEASON HAS PASSED SINCE WE BECAME STUDENTS.
I RAISE A TOAST! ☆
GREEN TEA
COULD YOU PLEASE STOP? YOU'RE RUINING MY MEMORIES OF THE SUMMER TROUPE'S PERFORMANCE!
AND TO YOUR EYES, SAWA, I RAISE A TOAST! ☆
SERIOUSLY, STOP! DON'T RUIN REO SHIINA'S PERFORMANCE LIKE THAT!
AWW, MAN!
YOU GUYS WENT TO SEE THE NEW PERFORMANCE BY THE SUMMER TROUPE?
WE'RE ALL IN THE HUNDREDTH CLASS OF THE KOUKA SCHOOL OF MUSICAL AND THEATRICAL ARTS.

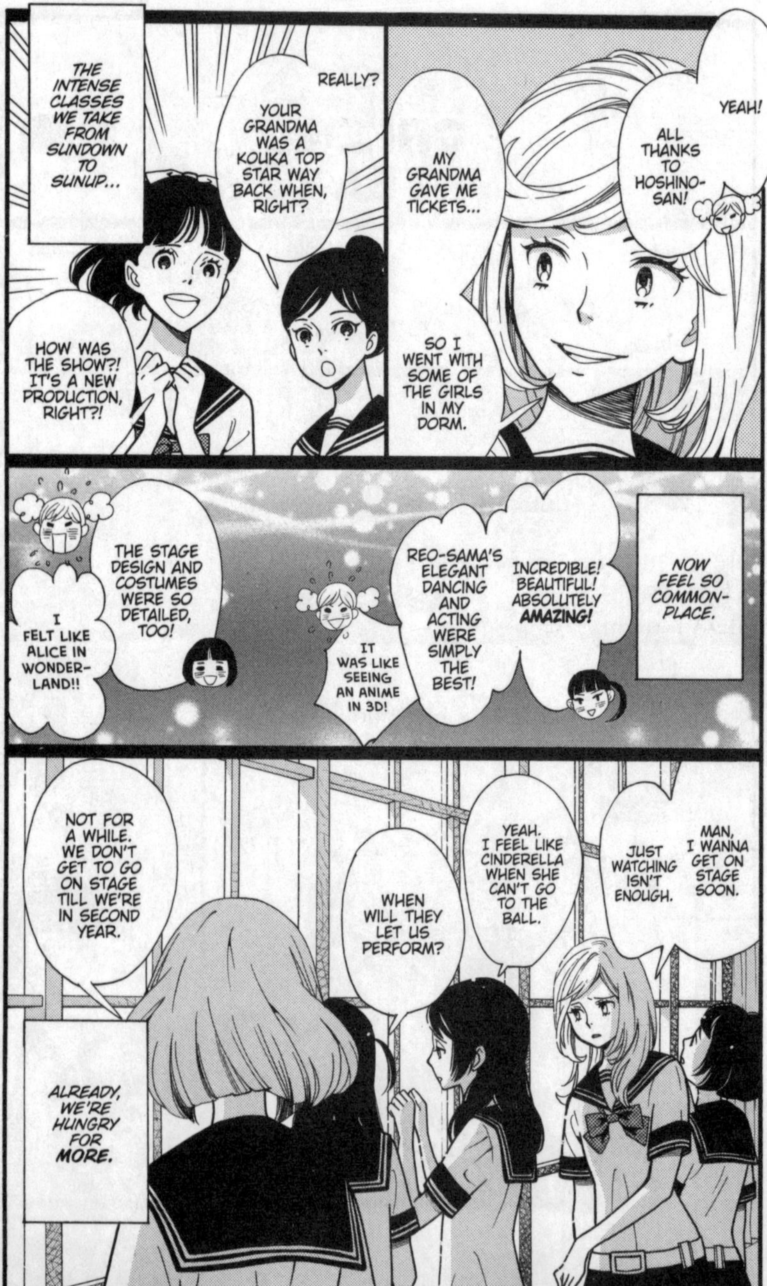
YEAH!
ALL THANKS TO HOSHINO-SAN!
MY GRANDMA GAVE ME TICKETS...
SO I WENT WITH SOME OF THE GIRLS IN MY DORM.
REALLY?
YOUR GRANDMA WAS A KOUKA TOP STAR WAY BACK WHEN, RIGHT?
THE INTENSE CLASSES WE TAKE FROM SUNDOWN TO SUNUP...
HOW WAS THE SHOW?! IT'S A NEW PRODUCTION, RIGHT?!
NOW FEEL SO COMMONPLACE.
INCREDIBLE! BEAUTIFUL! ABSOLUTELY **AMAZING!**
REO-SAMA'S ELEGANT DANCING AND ACTING WERE SIMPLY THE BEST!
IT WAS LIKE SEEING AN ANIME IN 3D!
THE STAGE DESIGN AND COSTUMES WERE SO DETAILED, TOO!
I FELT LIKE ALICE IN WONDERLAND!!
MAN, I WANNA GET ON STAGE SOON.
JUST WATCHING ISN'T ENOUGH.
YEAH. I FEEL LIKE CINDERELLA WHEN SHE CAN'T GO TO THE BALL.
WHEN WILL THEY LET US PERFORM?
NOT FOR A WHILE. WE DON'T GET TO GO ON STAGE TILL WE'RE IN SECOND YEAR.
ALREADY, WE'RE HUNGRY FOR **MORE.**

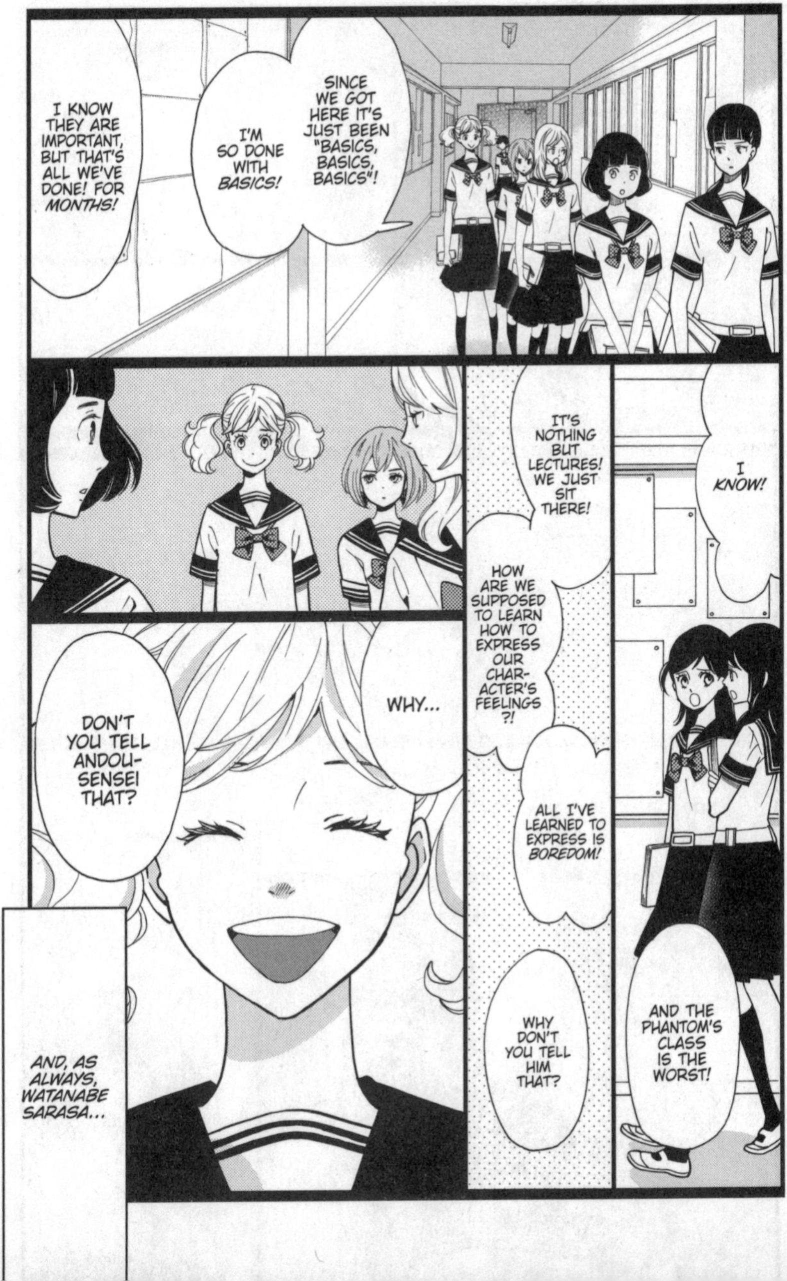
SINCE WE GOT HERE IT'S JUST BEEN "BASICS, BASICS, BASICS"!
I'M SO DONE WITH *BASICS!*
I KNOW THEY ARE IMPORTANT, BUT THAT'S ALL WE'VE DONE! FOR *MONTHS!*
I *KNOW!*
AND THE PHANTOM'S CLASS IS THE WORST!
IT'S NOTHING BUT LECTURES! WE JUST SIT THERE!
HOW ARE WE SUPPOSED TO LEARN HOW TO EXPRESS OUR CHARACTER'S FEELINGS?!
ALL I'VE LEARNED TO EXPRESS IS *BOREDOM!*
WHY DON'T YOU TELL HIM THAT?
WHY...
DON'T YOU TELL ANDOU-SENSEI THAT?
AND, AS ALWAYS, WATANABE SARASA...

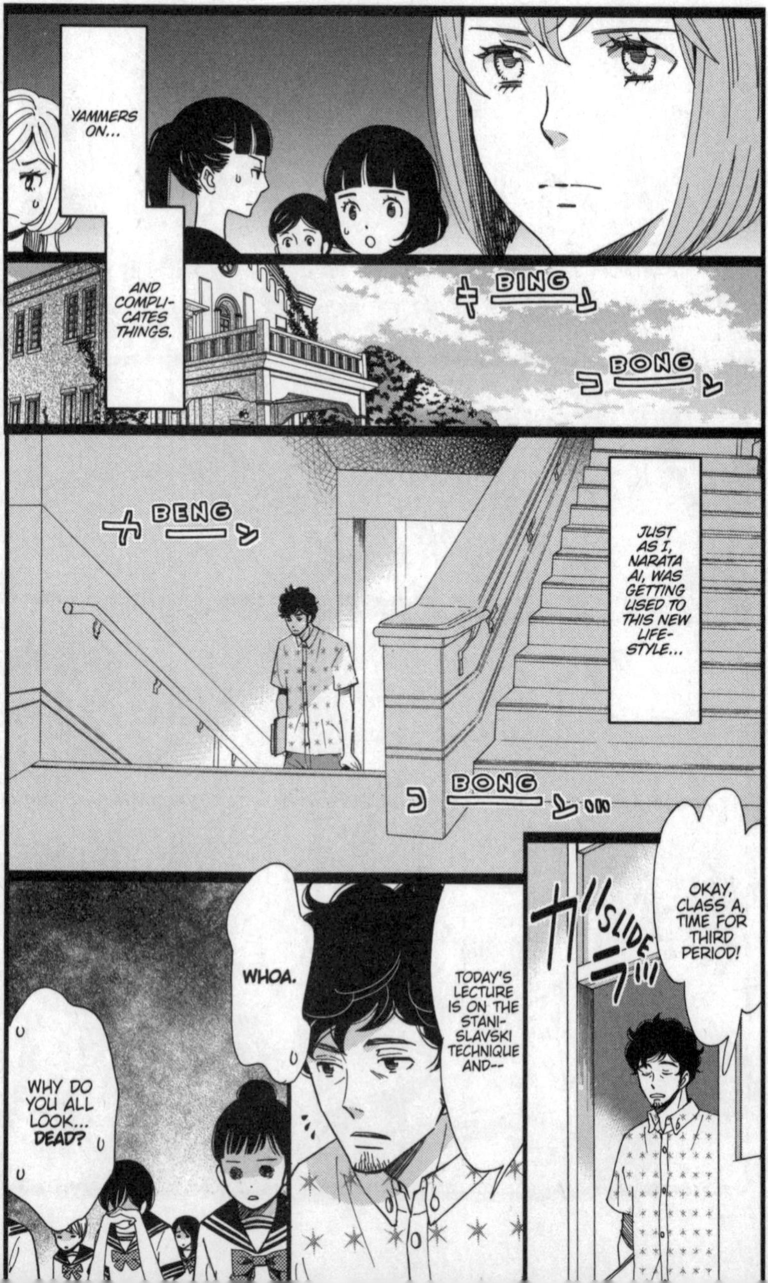
YAMMERS ON...
AND COMPLICATES THINGS.
BING
BONG
JUST AS I, NARATA AI, WAS GETTING USED TO THIS NEW LIFESTYLE...
BENG
BONG
SLIDE
OKAY, CLASS A, TIME FOR THIRD PERIOD!
TODAY'S LECTURE IS ON THE STANISLAVSKI TECHNIQUE AND--
WHOA.
WHY DO YOU ALL LOOK... **DEAD?**

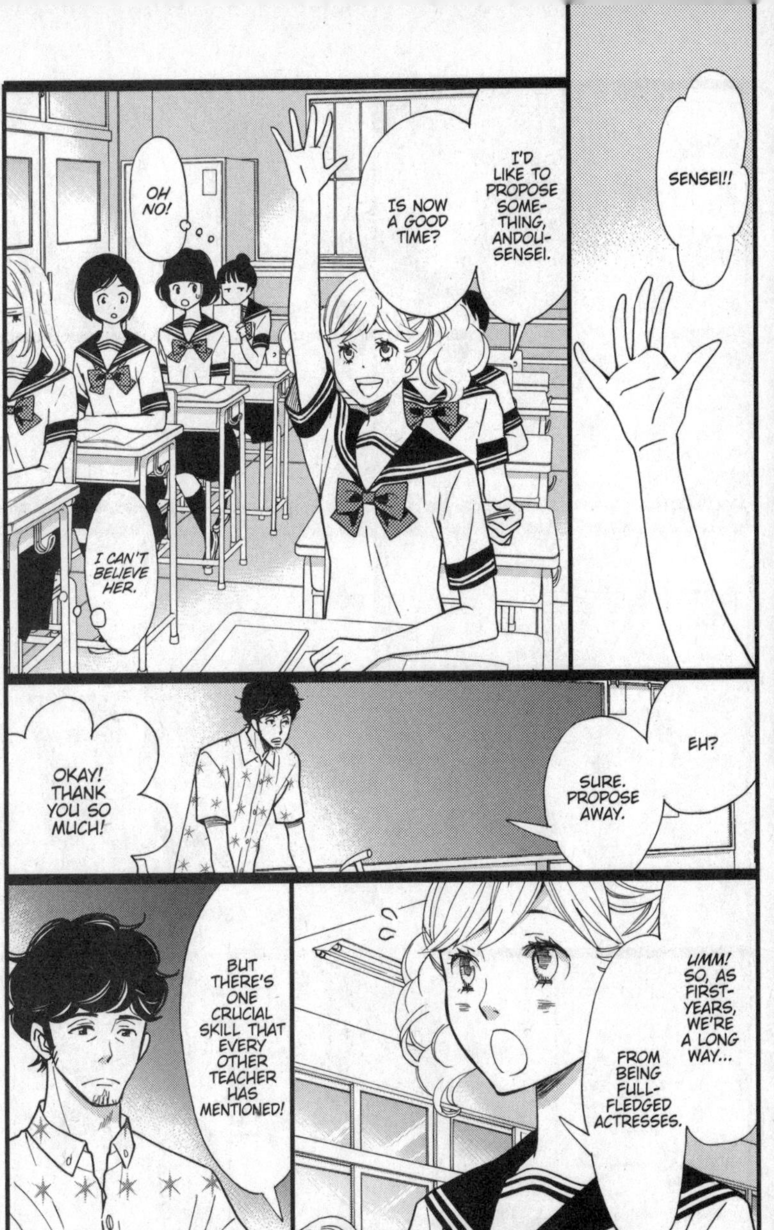
SENSEI!!
I'D LIKE TO PROPOSE SOME-THING, ANDOU-SENSEI.
IS NOW A GOOD TIME?
OH NO!
I CAN'T BELIEVE HER.
EH?
SURE. PROPOSE AWAY.
OKAY! THANK YOU SO MUCH!
UMM! SO, AS FIRST-YEARS, WE'RE A LONG WAY...
FROM BEING FULL-FLEDGED ACTRESSES.
BUT THERE'S ONE CRUCIAL SKILL THAT EVERY OTHER TEACHER HAS MENTIONED!

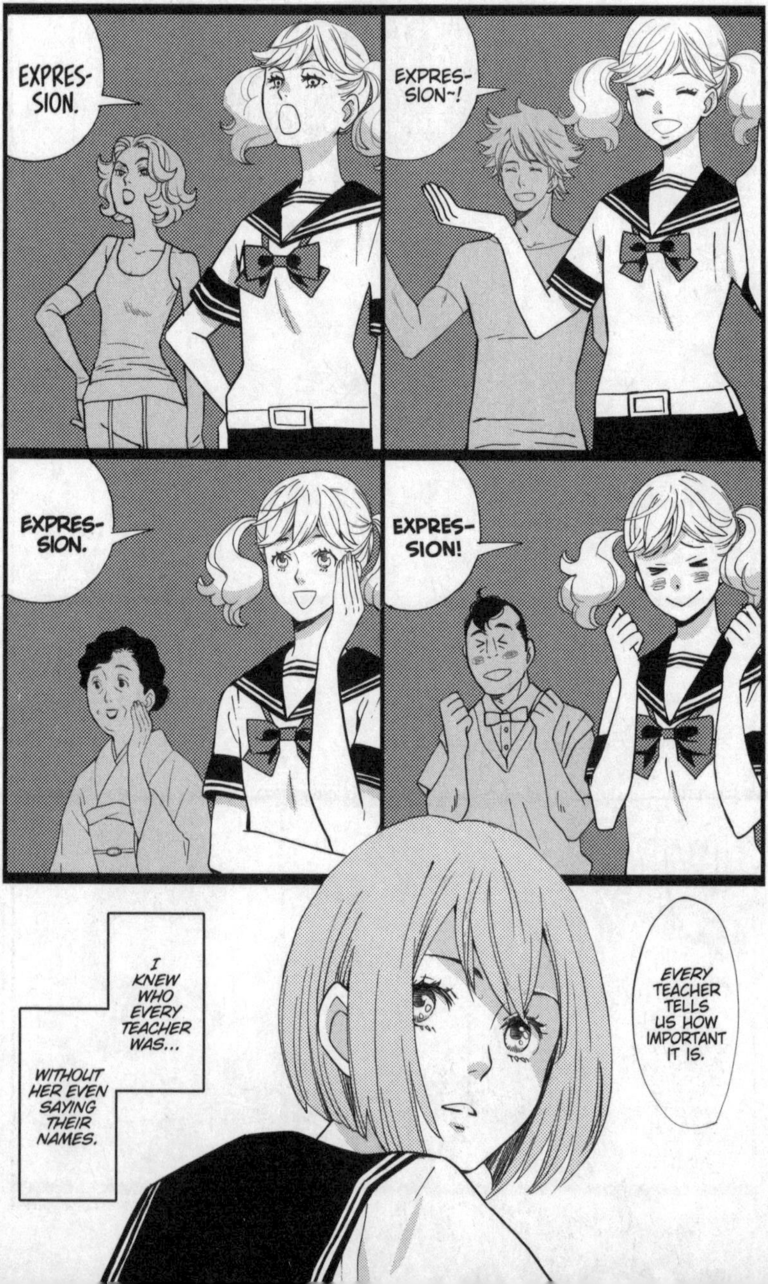
EXPRES-SION~!
EXPRES-SION.
EXPRES-SION!
EXPRES-SION.
EVERY TEACHER TELLS US HOW IMPORTANT IT IS.
I KNEW WHO EVERY TEACHER WAS...
WITHOUT HER EVEN SAYING THEIR NAMES.

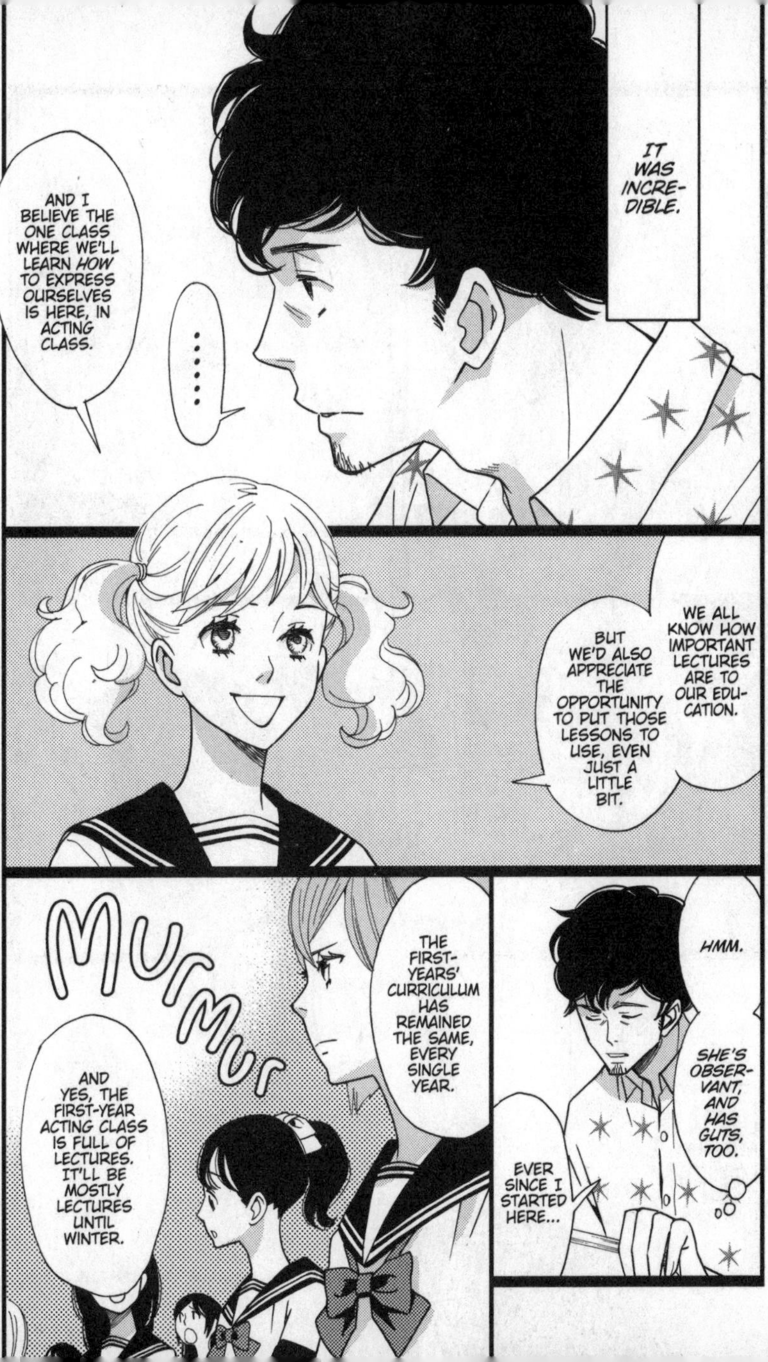
IT WAS INCREDIBLE.
......
AND I BELIEVE THE ONE CLASS WHERE WE'LL LEARN *HOW* TO EXPRESS OURSELVES IS HERE, IN ACTING CLASS.
WE ALL KNOW HOW IMPORTANT LECTURES ARE TO OUR EDUCATION.
BUT WE'D ALSO APPRECIATE THE OPPORTUNITY TO PUT THOSE LESSONS TO USE, EVEN JUST A LITTLE BIT.
HMM.
SHE'S OBSERVANT, AND HAS GUTS, TOO.
EVER SINCE I STARTED HERE...
THE FIRST-YEARS' CURRICULUM HAS REMAINED THE SAME, EVERY SINGLE YEAR.
Murmur
AND YES, THE FIRST-YEAR ACTING CLASS IS FULL OF LECTURES. IT'LL BE MOSTLY LECTURES UNTIL WINTER.

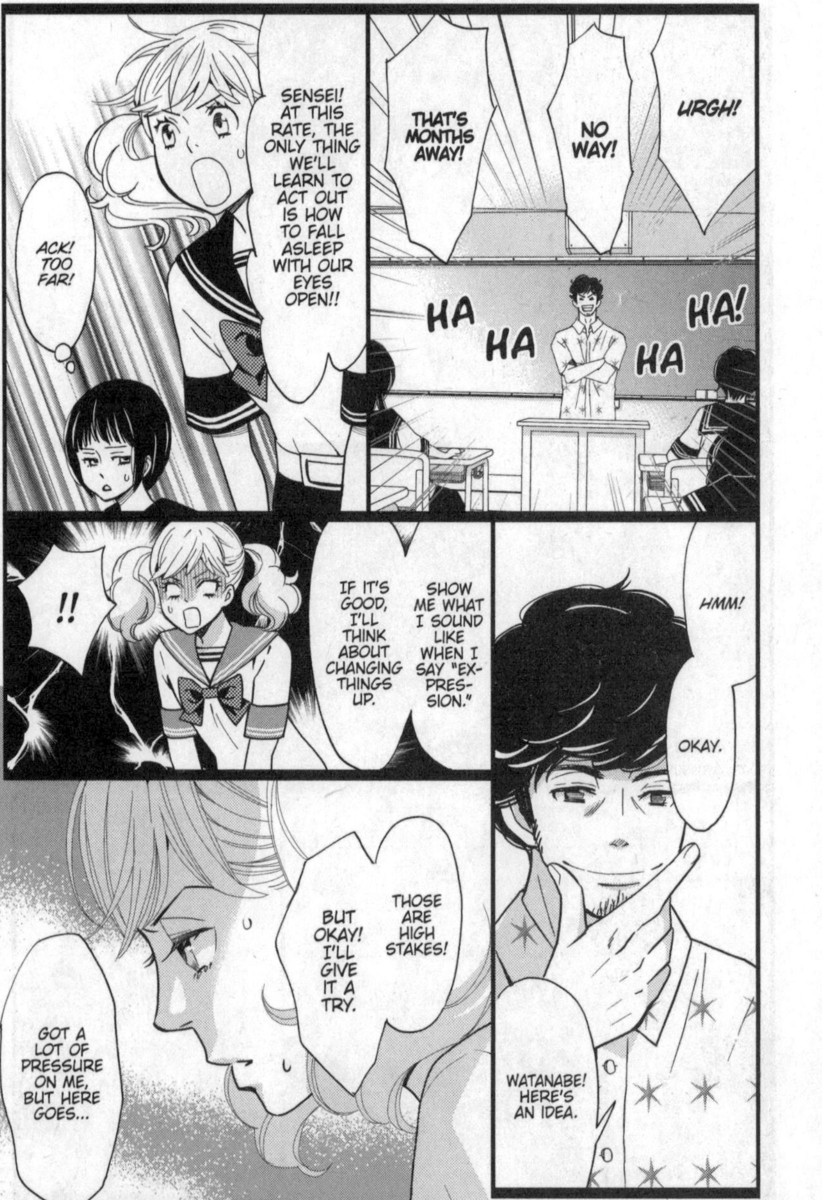
URGH!
NO WAY!
THAT'S MONTHS AWAY!
HA HA HA HA!
SENSEI! AT THIS RATE, THE ONLY THING WE'LL LEARN TO ACT OUT IS HOW TO FALL ASLEEP WITH OUR EYES OPEN!!
ACK! TOO FAR!
HMM!
OKAY.
WATANABE! HERE'S AN IDEA.
SHOW ME WHAT I SOUND LIKE WHEN I SAY "EX-PRES-SION."
IF IT'S GOOD, I'LL THINK ABOUT CHANGING THINGS UP.
!!
THOSE ARE HIGH STAKES!
BUT OKAY! I'LL GIVE IT A TRY.
GOT A LOT OF PRESSURE ON ME, BUT HERE GOES...

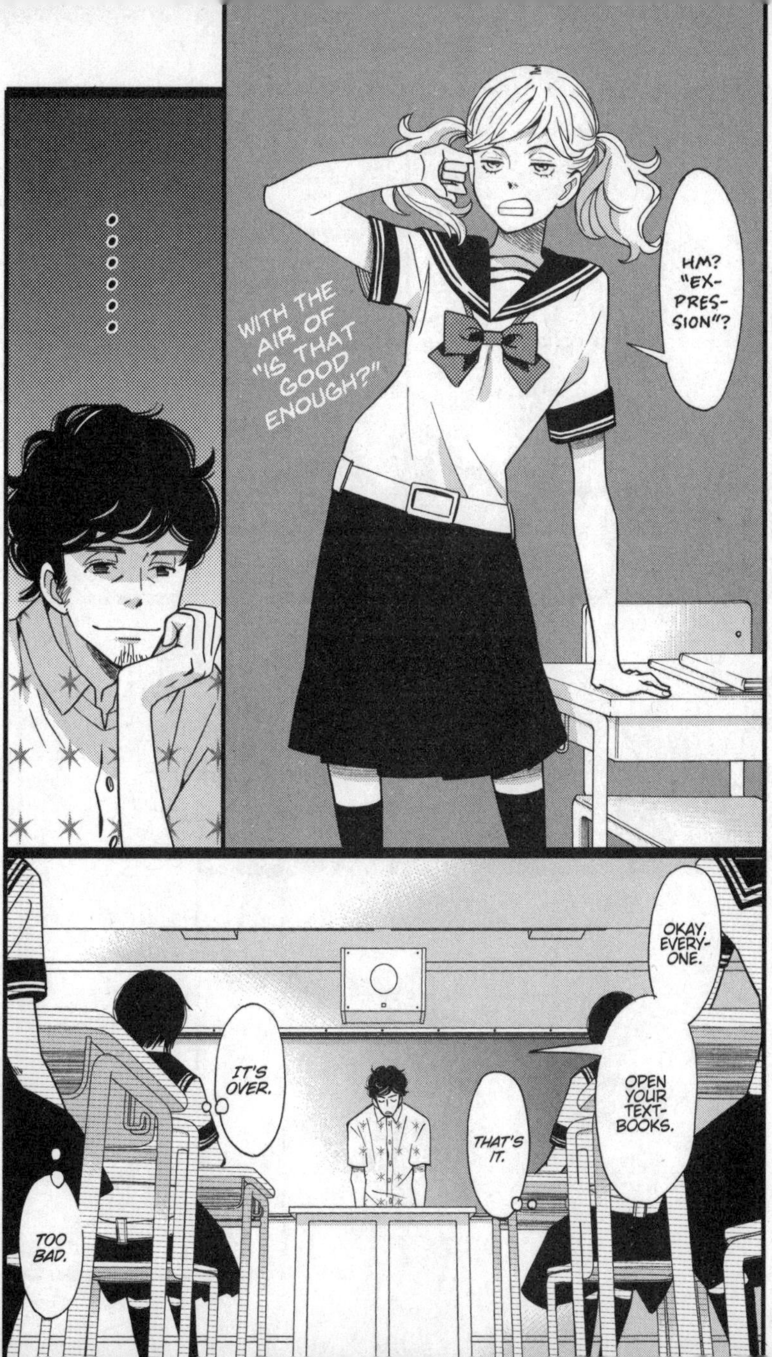
HM? "EX-PRES-SION"?
WITH THE AIR OF "IS THAT GOOD ENOUGH?"
......
OKAY, EVERY-ONE.
OPEN YOUR TEXT-BOOKS.
THAT'S IT.
IT'S OVER.
TOO BAD.

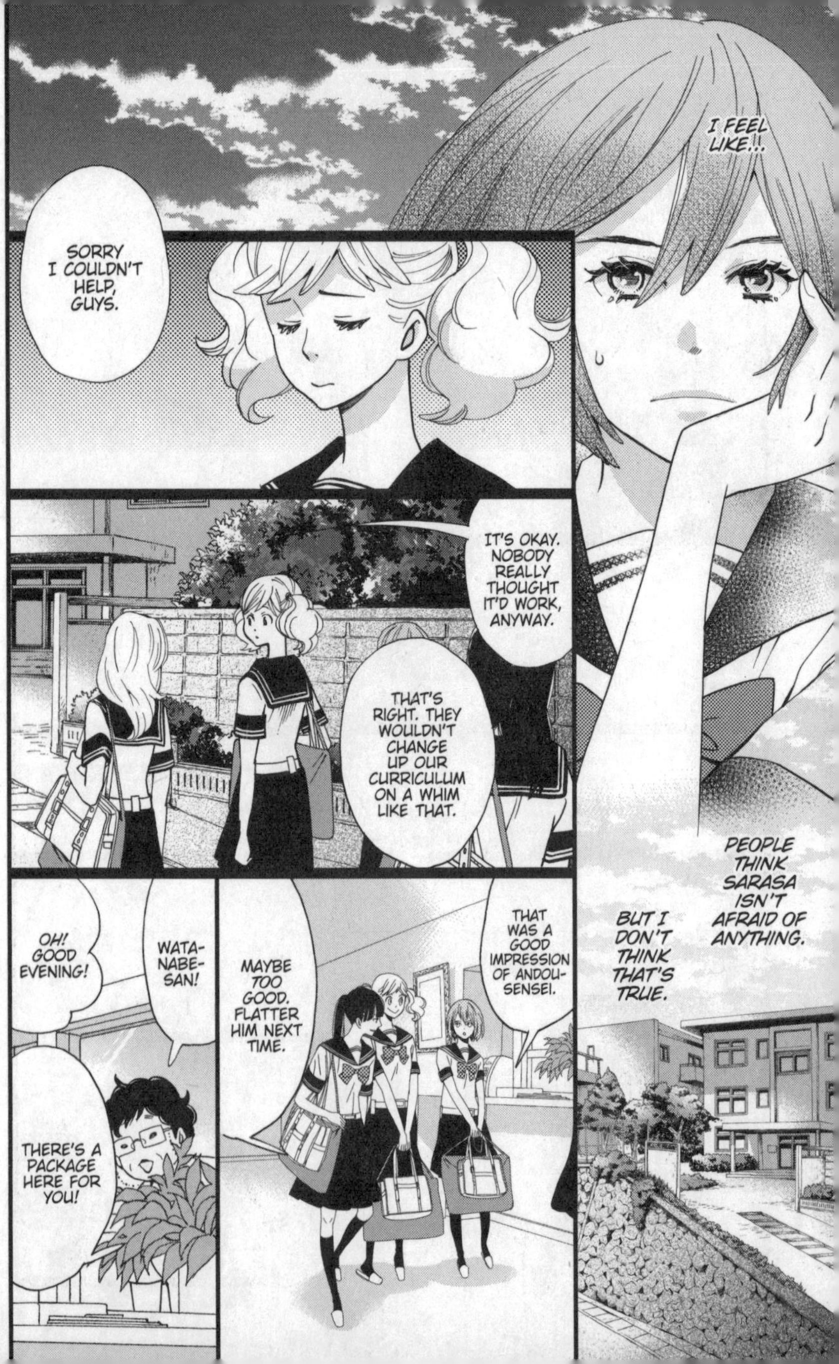
I FEEL LIKE...
SORRY I COULDN'T HELP, GUYS.
IT'S OKAY. NOBODY REALLY THOUGHT IT'D WORK, ANYWAY.
THAT'S RIGHT. THEY WOULDN'T CHANGE UP OUR CURRICULUM ON A WHIM LIKE THAT.
PEOPLE THINK SARASA ISN'T AFRAID OF ANYTHING.
BUT I DON'T THINK THAT'S TRUE.
THAT WAS A GOOD IMPRESSION OF ANDOU-SENSEI.
MAYBE TOO GOOD. FLATTER HIM NEXT TIME.
WATA-NABE-SAN!
OH! GOOD EVENING!
THERE'S A PACKAGE HERE FOR YOU!

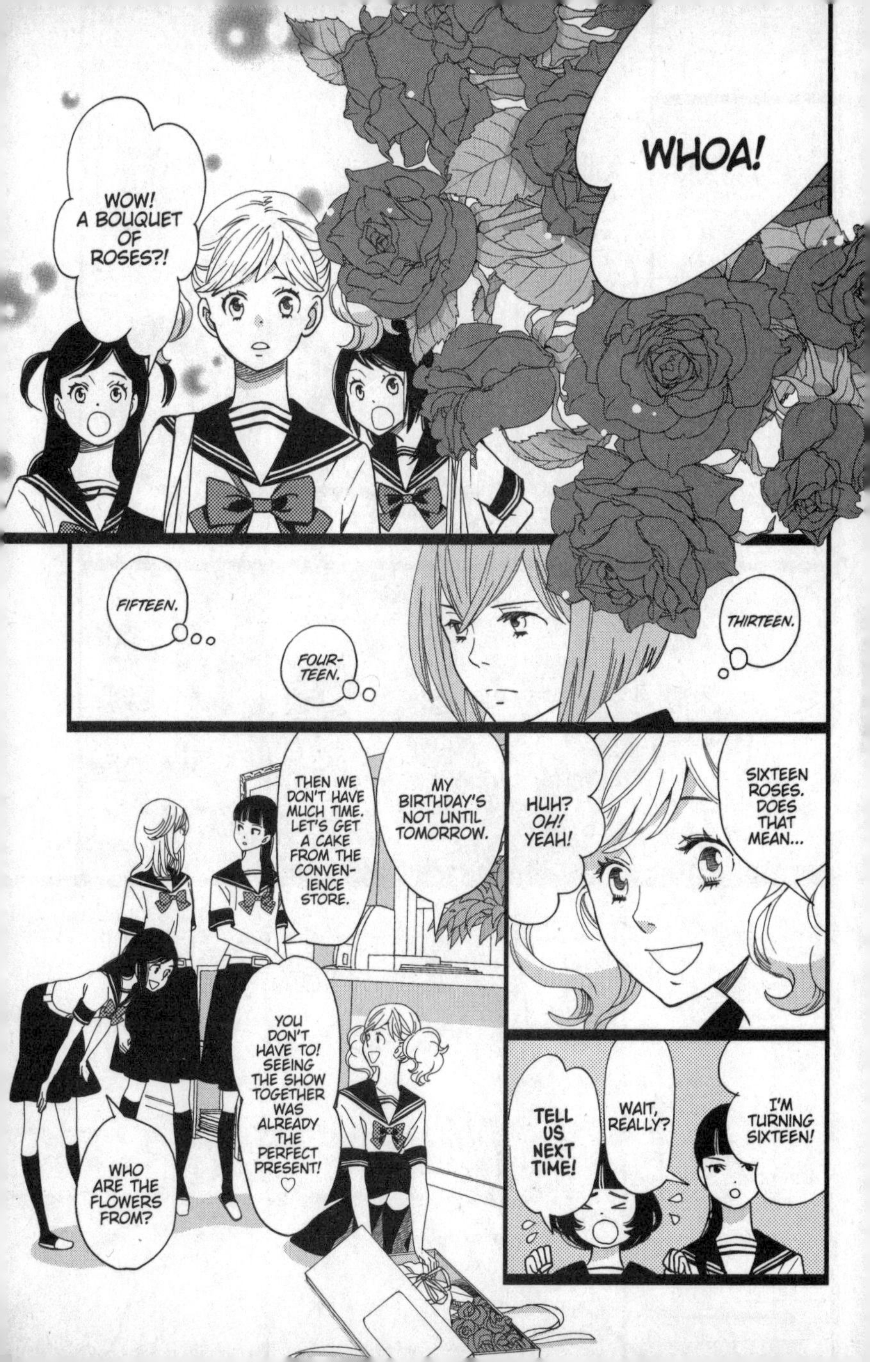
WHOA!
WOW! A BOUQUET OF ROSES?!
THIRTEEN.
FOUR-TEEN.
FIFTEEN.
SIXTEEN ROSES. DOES THAT MEAN...
HUH? OH! YEAH!
I'M TURNING SIXTEEN!
WAIT, REALLY?
TELL US NEXT TIME!
MY BIRTHDAY'S NOT UNTIL TOMORROW.
THEN WE DON'T HAVE MUCH TIME. LET'S GET A CAKE FROM THE CONVEN-IENCE STORE.
YOU DON'T HAVE TO! SEEING THE SHOW TOGETHER WAS ALREADY THE PERFECT PRESENT! ♡
WHO ARE THE FLOWERS FROM?

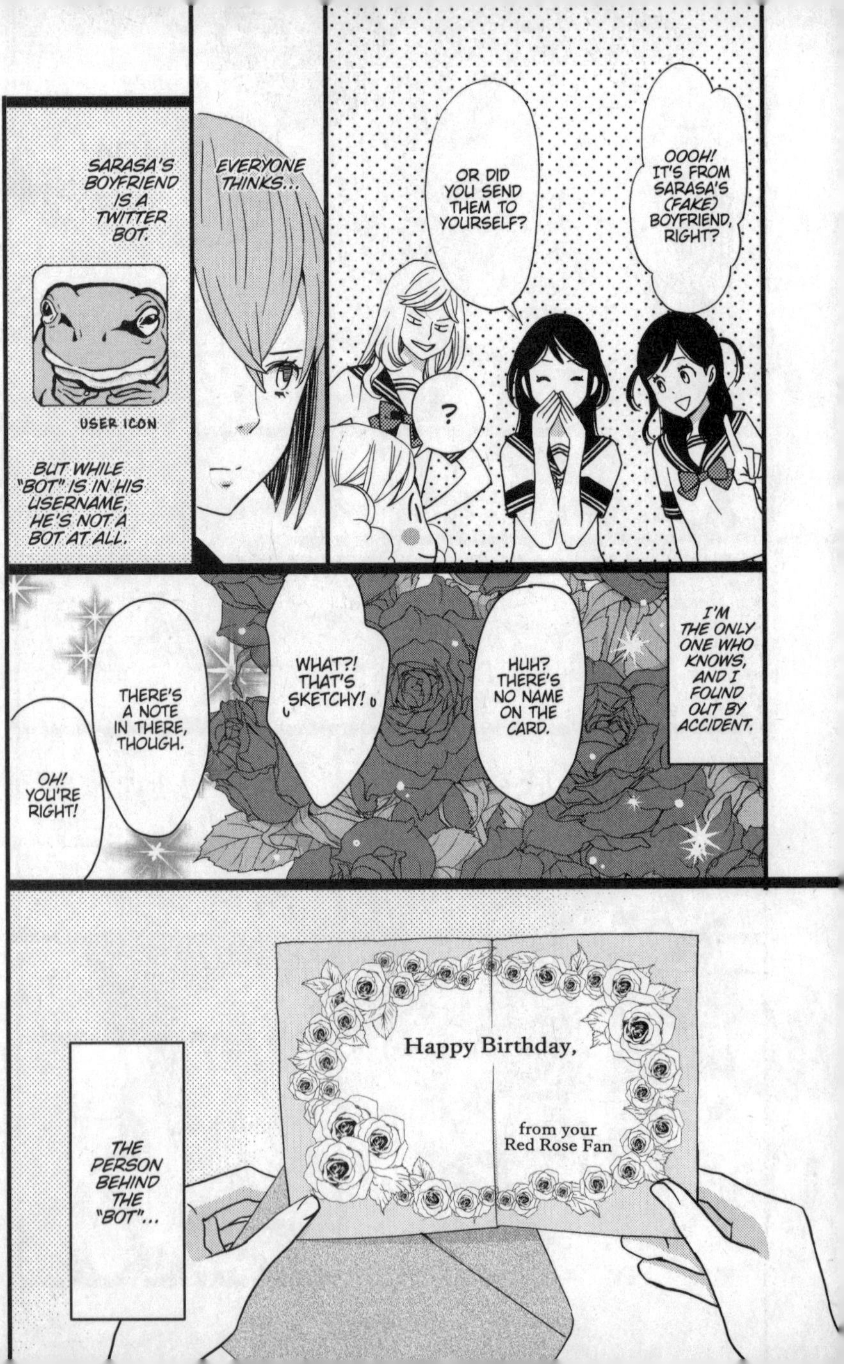
OOOH! IT'S FROM SARASA'S (FAKE) BOYFRIEND, RIGHT?
OR DID YOU SEND THEM TO YOURSELF?
?
EVERYONE THINKS...
SARASA'S BOYFRIEND IS A TWITTER BOT.
USER ICON
BUT WHILE "BOT" IS IN HIS USERNAME, HE'S NOT A BOT AT ALL.
I'M THE ONLY ONE WHO KNOWS, AND I FOUND OUT BY ACCIDENT.
HUH? THERE'S NO NAME ON THE CARD.
WHAT?! THAT'S SKETCHY!
THERE'S A NOTE IN THERE, THOUGH.
OH! YOU'RE RIGHT!
Happy Birthday,
from your Red Rose Fan
THE PERSON BEHIND THE "BOT"...

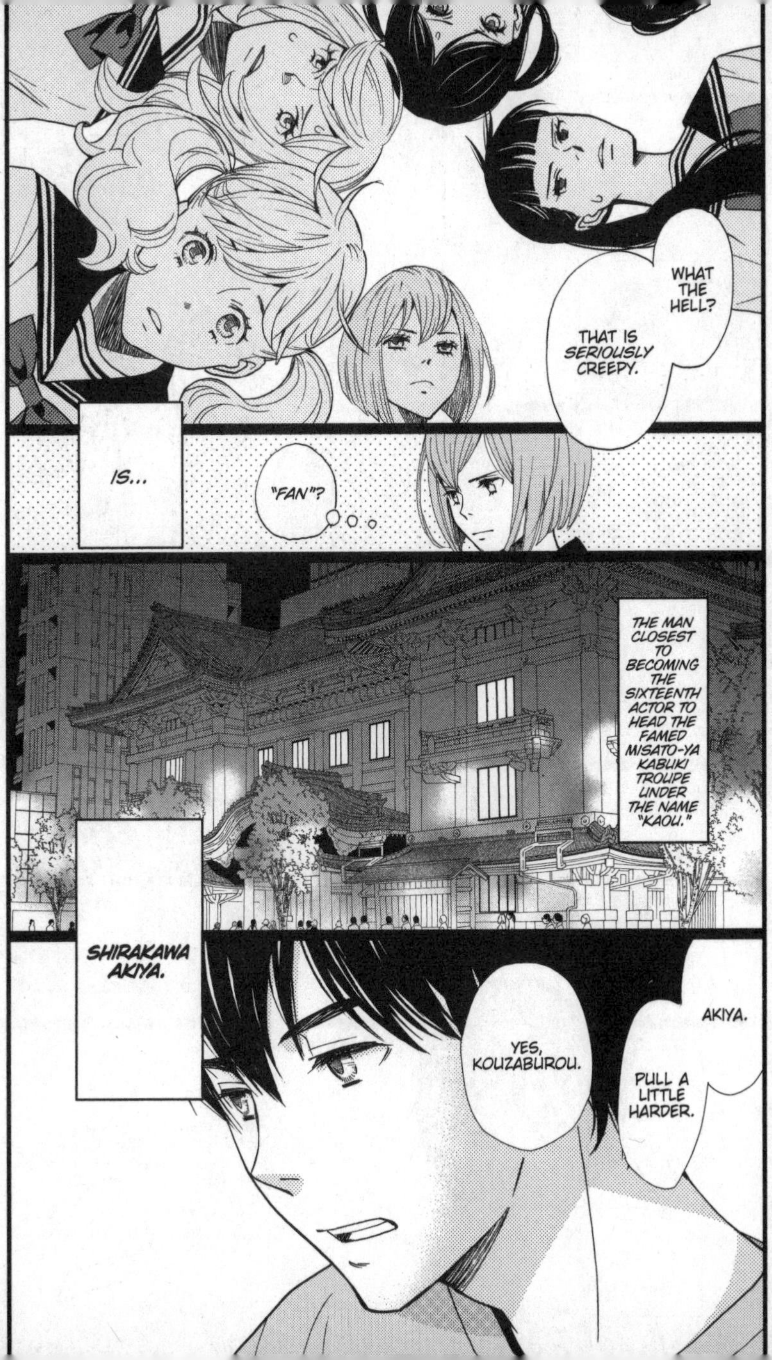
WHAT THE HELL?
THAT IS SERIOUSLY CREEPY.
"FAN"?
IS...
THE MAN CLOSEST TO BECOMING THE SIXTEENTH ACTOR TO HEAD THE FAMED MISATO-YA KABUKI TROUPE UNDER THE NAME "KAOU."
SHIRAKAWA AKIYA.
AKIYA.
PULL A LITTLE HARDER.
YES, KOUZABUROU.

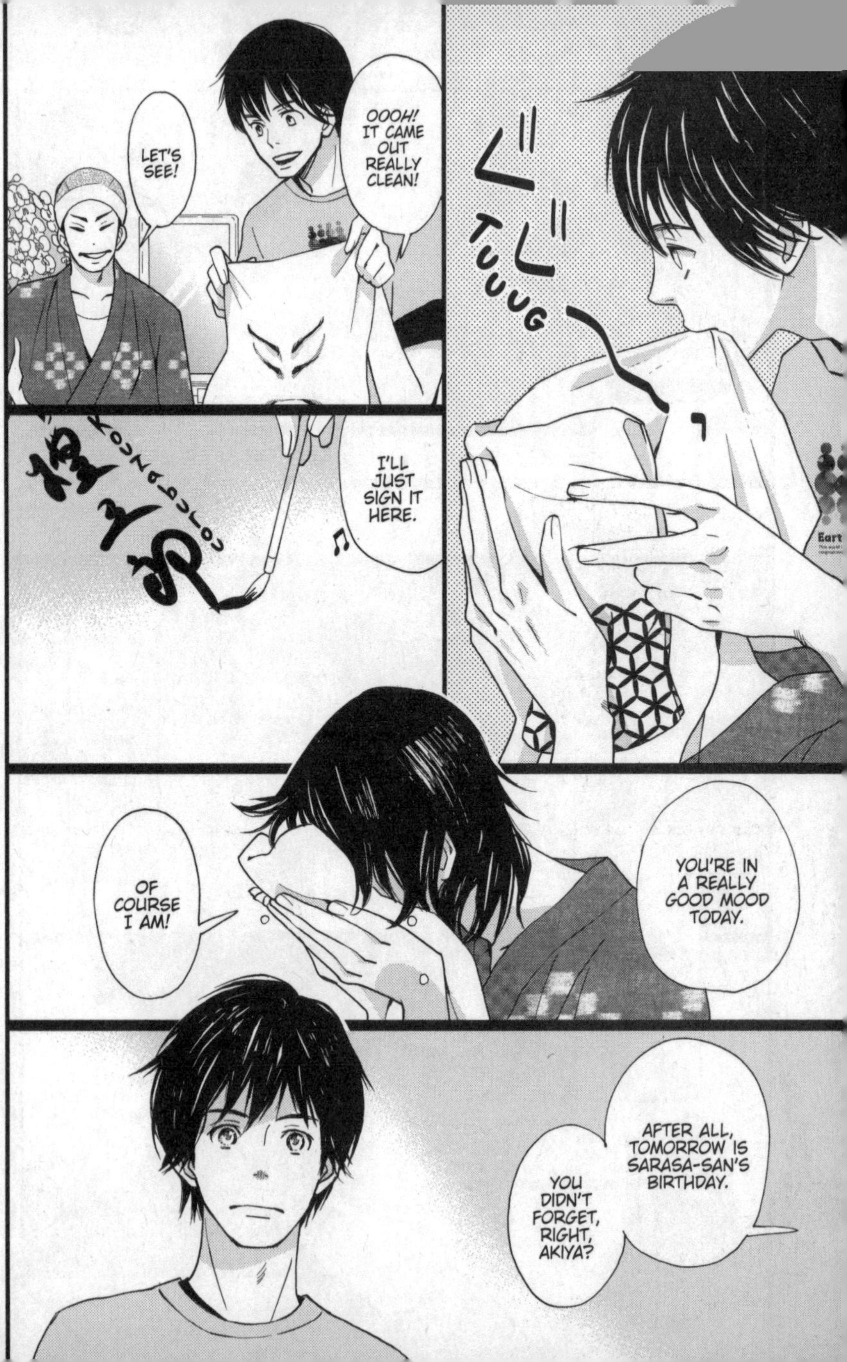
TUUUG
OOOH! IT CAME OUT REALLY CLEAN!
LET'S SEE!
I'LL JUST SIGN IT HERE.
YOU'RE IN A REALLY GOOD MOOD TODAY.
OF COURSE I AM!
AFTER ALL, TOMORROW IS SARASA-SAN'S BIRTHDAY.
YOU DIDN'T FORGET, RIGHT, AKIYA?

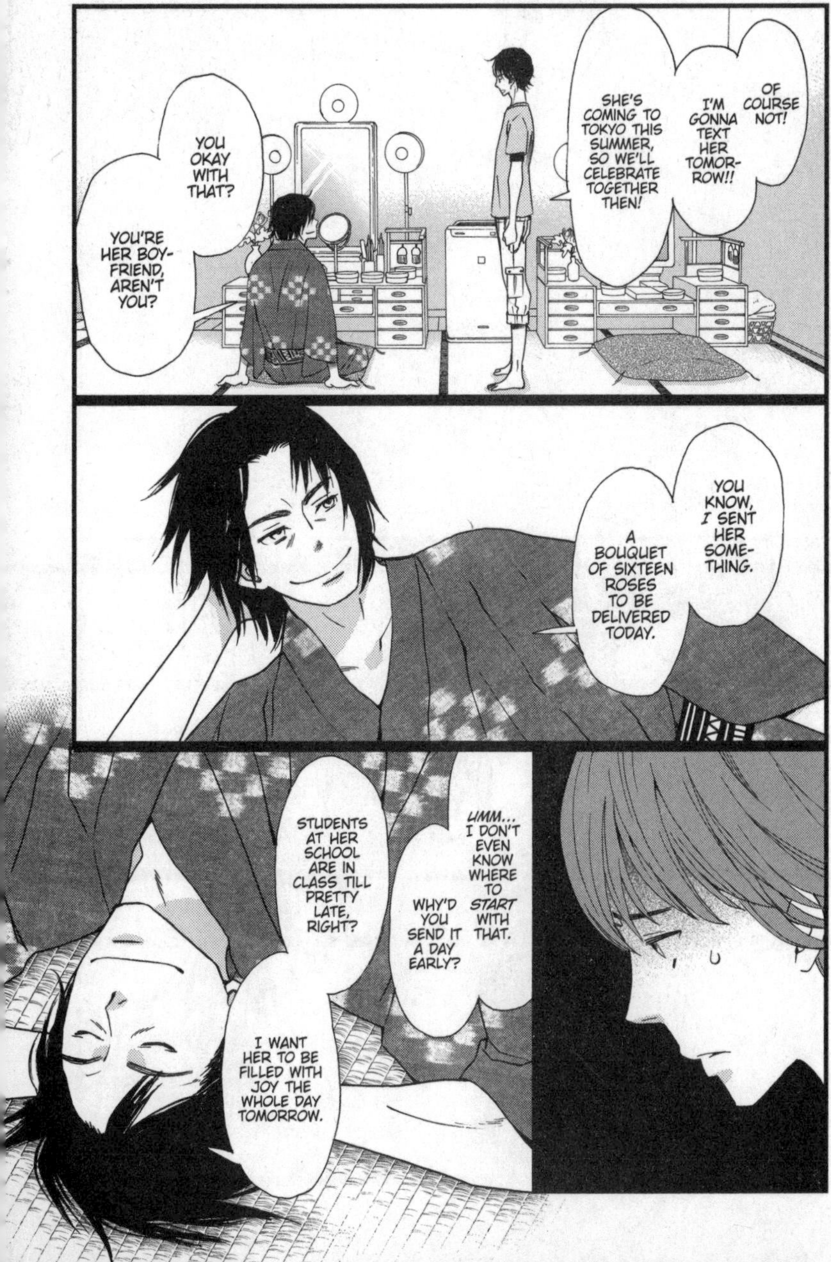
OF COURSE NOT!
I'M GONNA TEXT HER TOMOR-ROW!!
SHE'S COMING TO TOKYO THIS SUMMER, SO WE'LL CELEBRATE TOGETHER THEN!
YOU OKAY WITH THAT?
YOU'RE HER BOY-FRIEND, AREN'T YOU?
YOU KNOW, *I* SENT HER SOME-THING.
A BOUQUET OF SIXTEEN ROSES TO BE DELIVERED TODAY.
UMM... I DON'T EVEN KNOW WHERE TO *START* WITH THAT.
WHY'D YOU SEND IT A DAY EARLY?
STUDENTS AT HER SCHOOL ARE IN CLASS TILL PRETTY LATE, RIGHT?
I WANT HER TO BE FILLED WITH JOY THE WHOLE DAY TOMORROW.

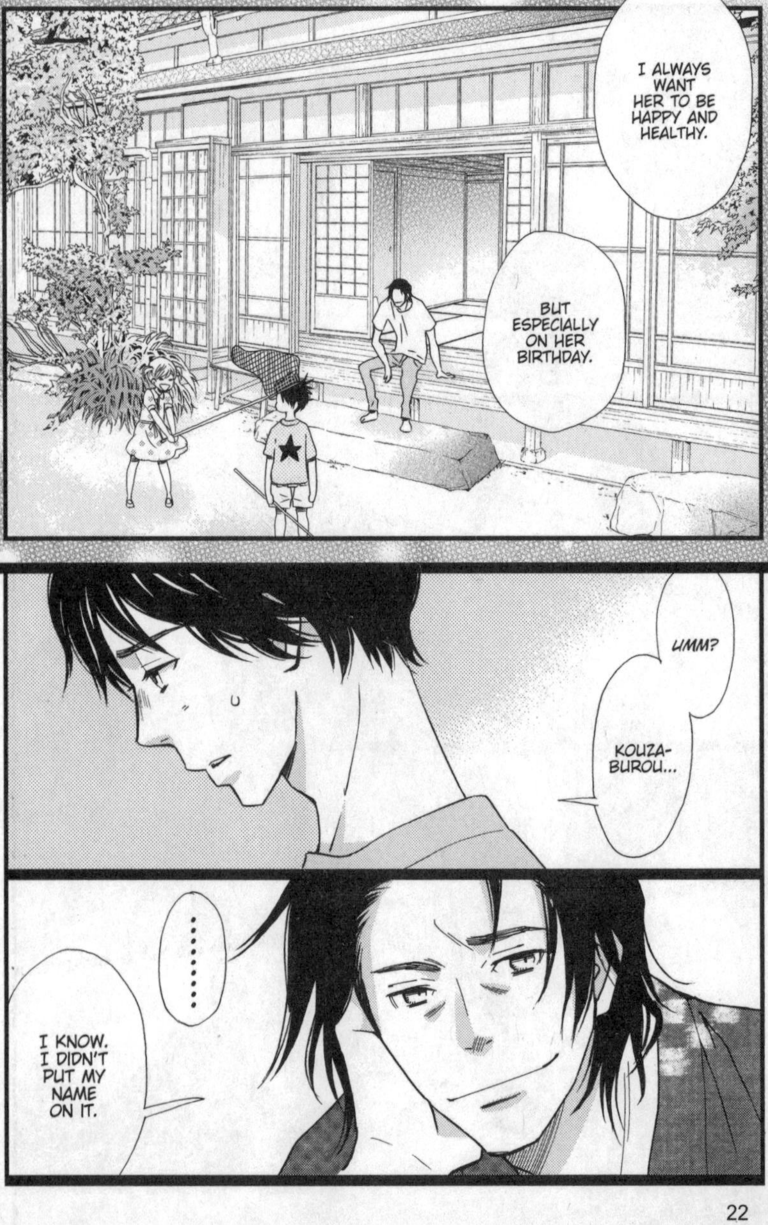
I ALWAYS WANT HER TO BE HAPPY AND HEALTHY.
BUT ESPECIALLY ON HER BIRTHDAY.
UMM?
KOUZA-BUROU...
......
I KNOW. I DIDN'T PUT MY NAME ON IT.

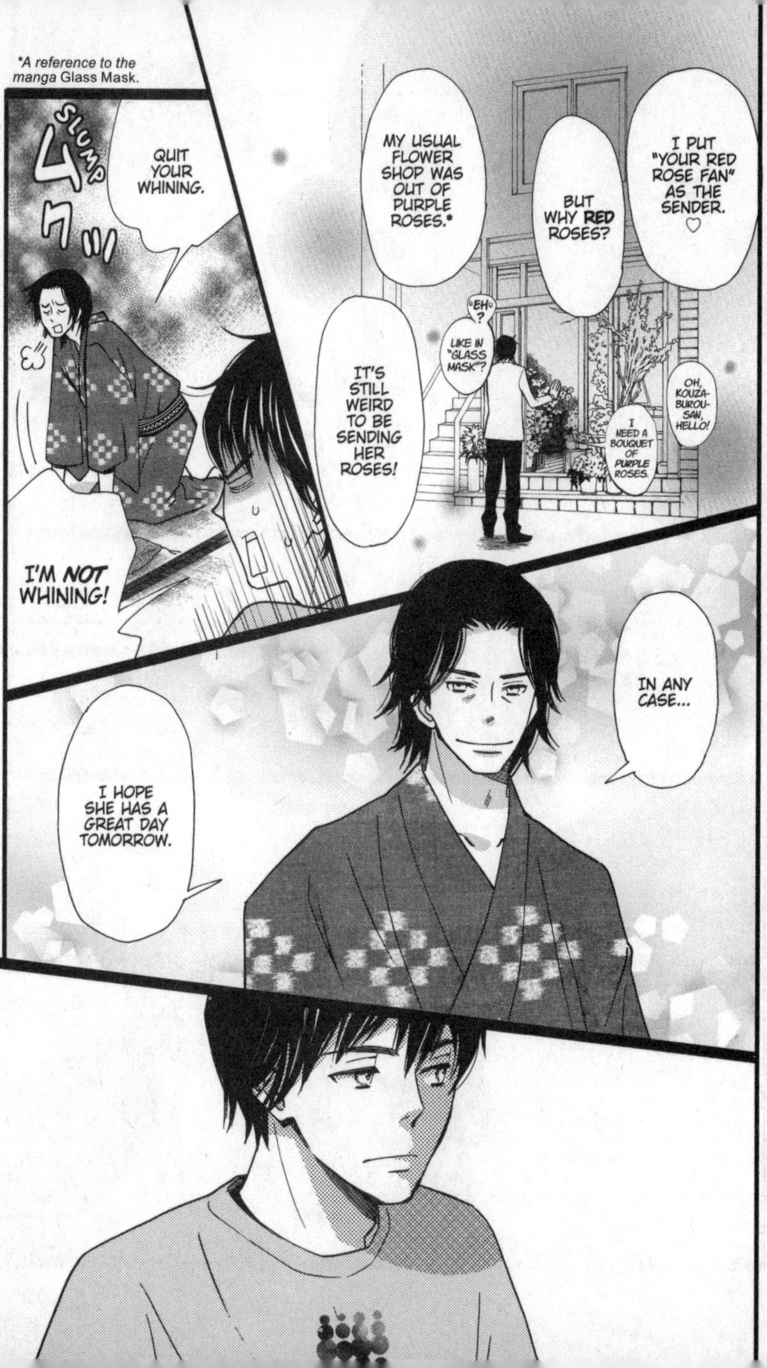
I PUT "YOUR RED ROSE FAN" AS THE SENDER. ♡
BUT WHY **RED** ROSES?
MY USUAL FLOWER SHOP WAS OUT OF PURPLE ROSES.*
OH, KOUZABUROU-SAN, HELLO!
I NEED A BOUQUET OF PURPLE ROSES.
EH?
LIKE IN "GLASS MASK"?
IT'S STILL WEIRD TO BE SENDING HER ROSES!
QUIT YOUR WHINING.
SLUMP
I'M *NOT* WHINING!
IN ANY CASE...
I HOPE SHE HAS A GREAT DAY TOMORROW.

*A reference to the *manga* Glass Mask.

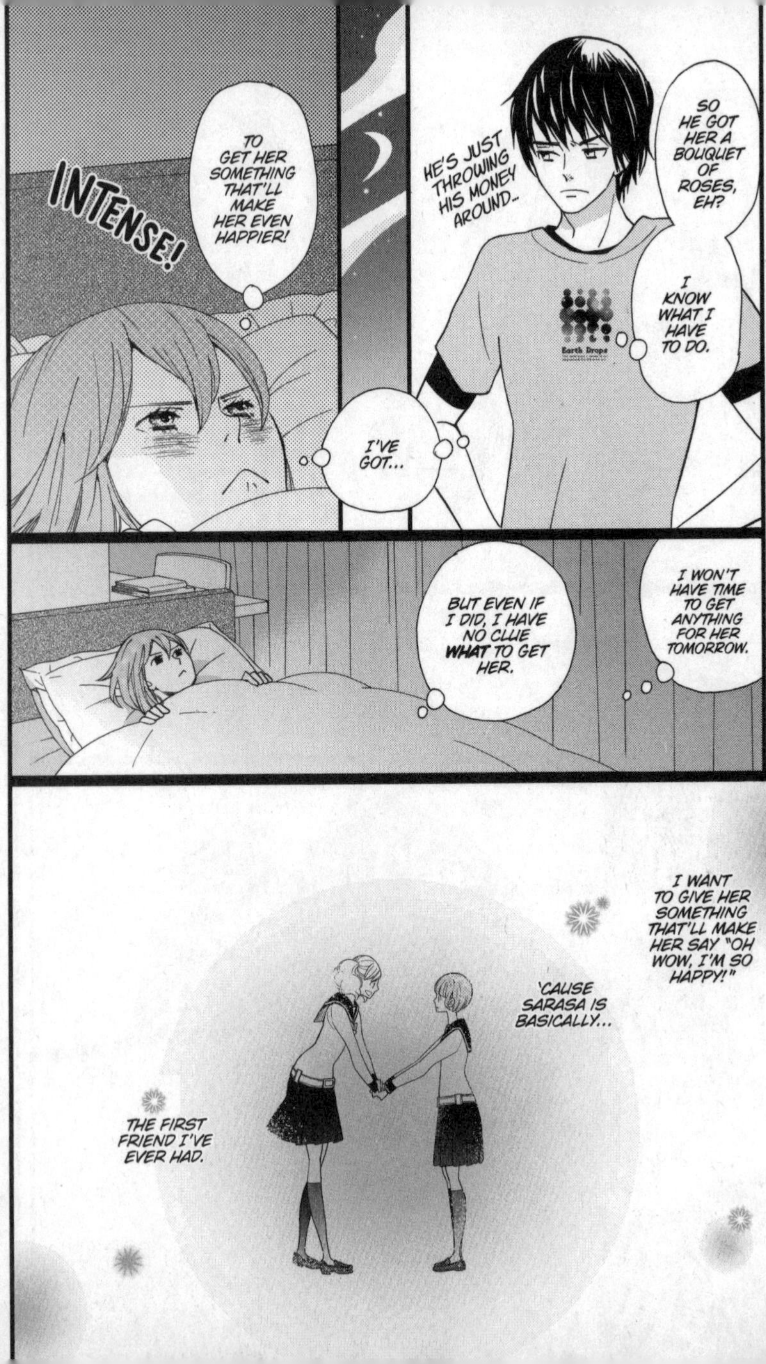
SO HE GOT HER A BOUQUET OF ROSES, EH?
HE'S JUST THROWING HIS MONEY AROUND..
I KNOW WHAT I HAVE TO DO.
I'VE GOT...
TO GET HER SOMETHING THAT'LL MAKE HER EVEN HAPPIER!
INTENSE!
I WON'T HAVE TIME TO GET ANYTHING FOR HER TOMORROW.
BUT EVEN IF I DID, I HAVE NO CLUE **WHAT** TO GET HER.
I WANT TO GIVE HER SOMETHING THAT'LL MAKE HER SAY "OH WOW, I'M SO HAPPY!"
'CAUSE SARASA IS BASICALLY...
THE FIRST FRIEND I'VE EVER HAD.

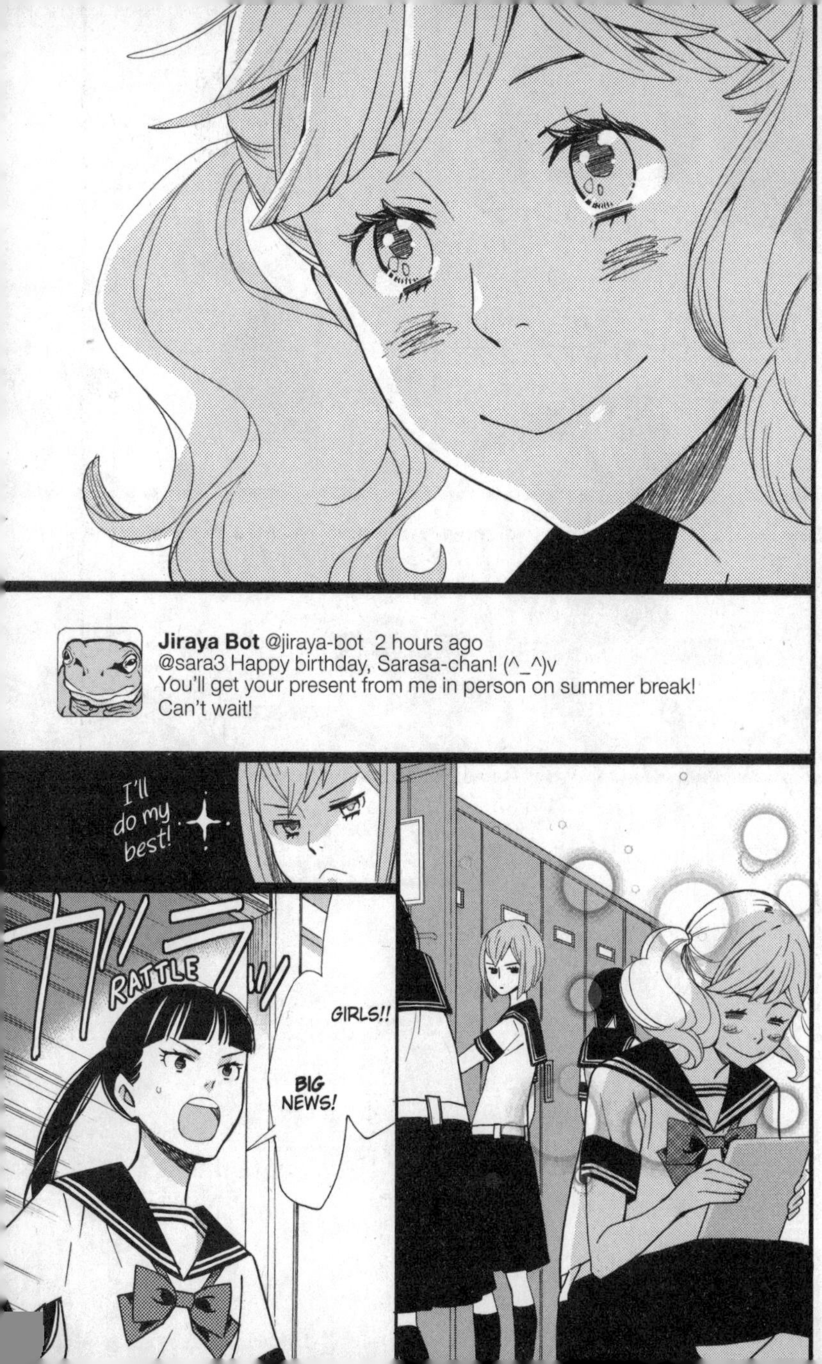
Jiraya Bot @jiraya-bot 2 hours ago
@sara3 Happy birthday, Sarasa-chan! (^_^)v
You'll get your present from me in person on summer break!
Can't wait!
I'll do my best!
RATTLE
GIRLS!!
BIG NEWS!

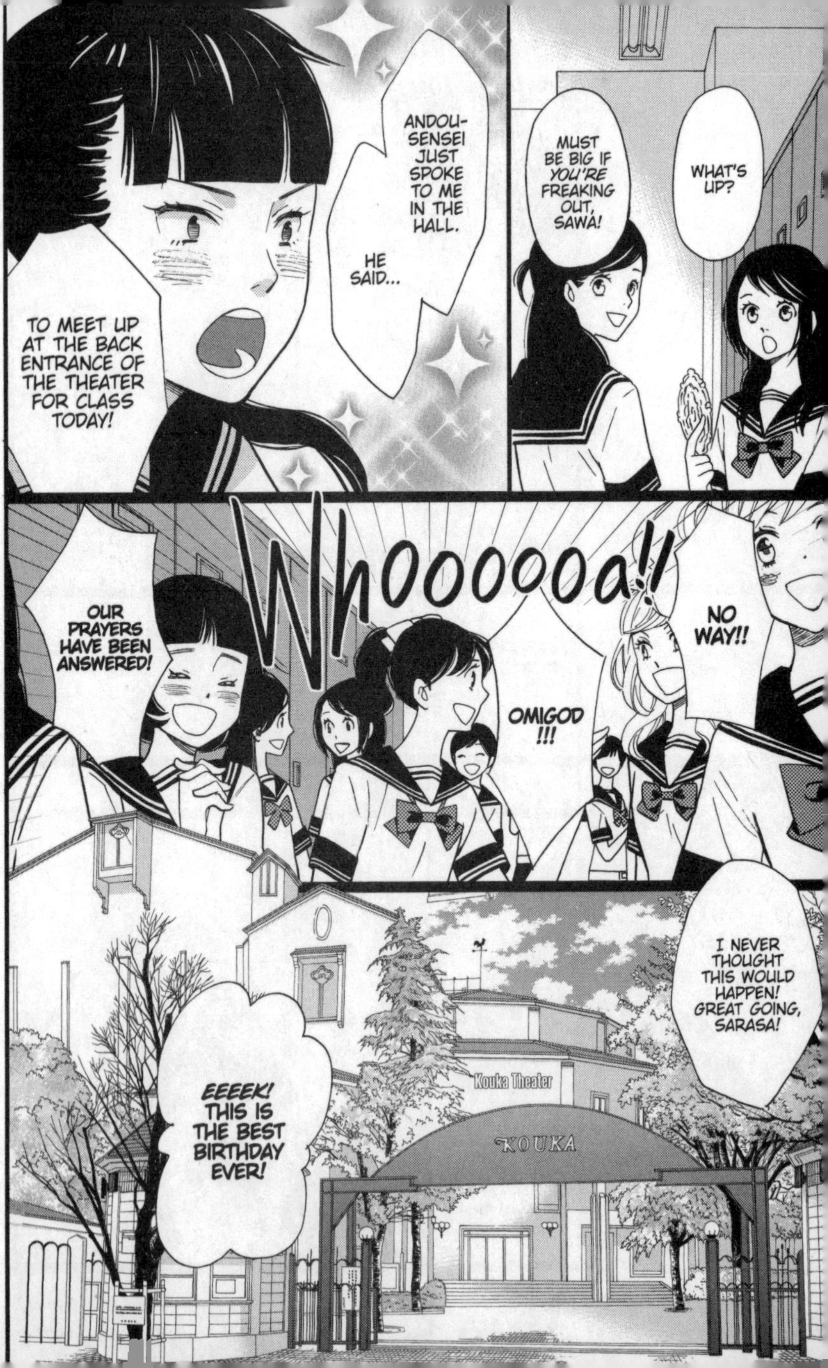
WHAT'S UP?
MUST BE BIG IF *YOU'RE* FREAKING OUT, SAWA!
ANDOU-SENSEI JUST SPOKE TO ME IN THE HALL.
HE SAID...
TO MEET UP AT THE BACK ENTRANCE OF THE THEATER FOR CLASS TODAY!
NO WAY!!
Whoooooa!!
OMIGOD !!!
OUR PRAYERS HAVE BEEN ANSWERED!
I NEVER THOUGHT THIS WOULD HAPPEN! GREAT GOING, SARASA!
Kouka Theater
KOUKA
EEEEK! THIS IS THE BEST BIRTHDAY EVER!

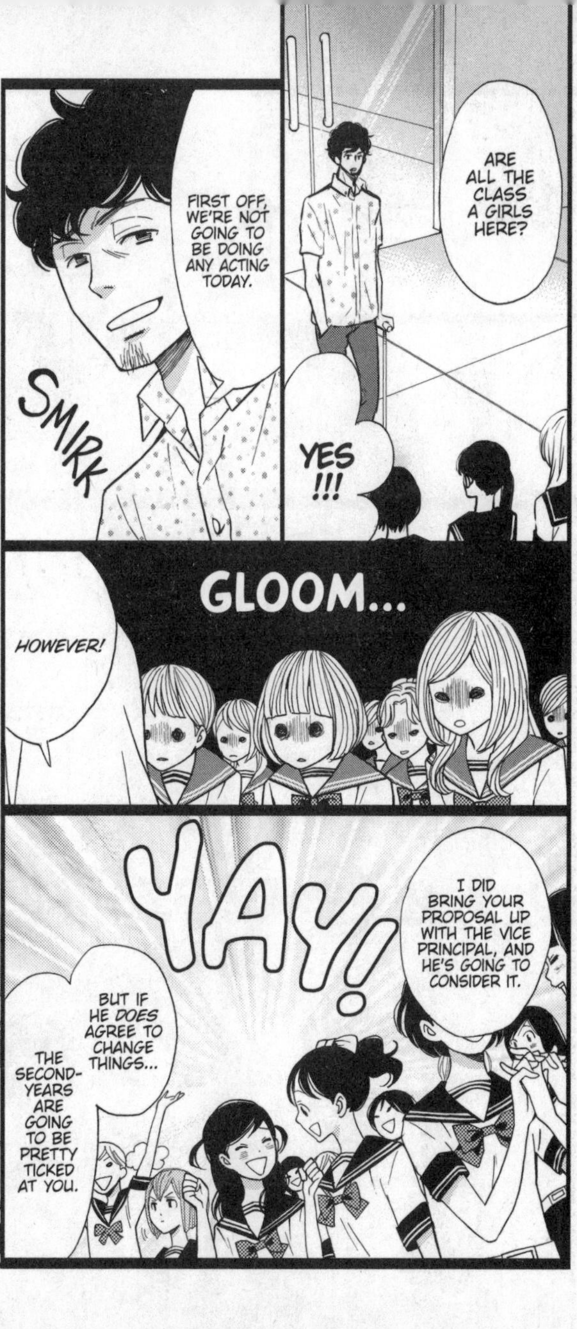
ARE ALL THE CLASS A GIRLS HERE?
YES!!!
FIRST OFF, WE'RE NOT GOING TO BE DOING ANY ACTING TODAY.
SMIRK
GLOOM...
HOWEVER!
I DID BRING YOUR PROPOSAL UP WITH THE VICE PRINCIPAL, AND HE'S GOING TO CONSIDER IT.
YAY!
BUT IF HE *DOES* AGREE TO CHANGE THINGS...
THE SECOND-YEARS ARE GOING TO BE PRETTY TICKED AT YOU.

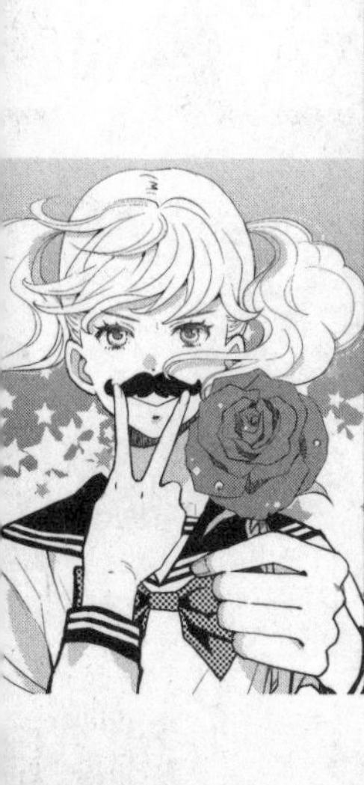

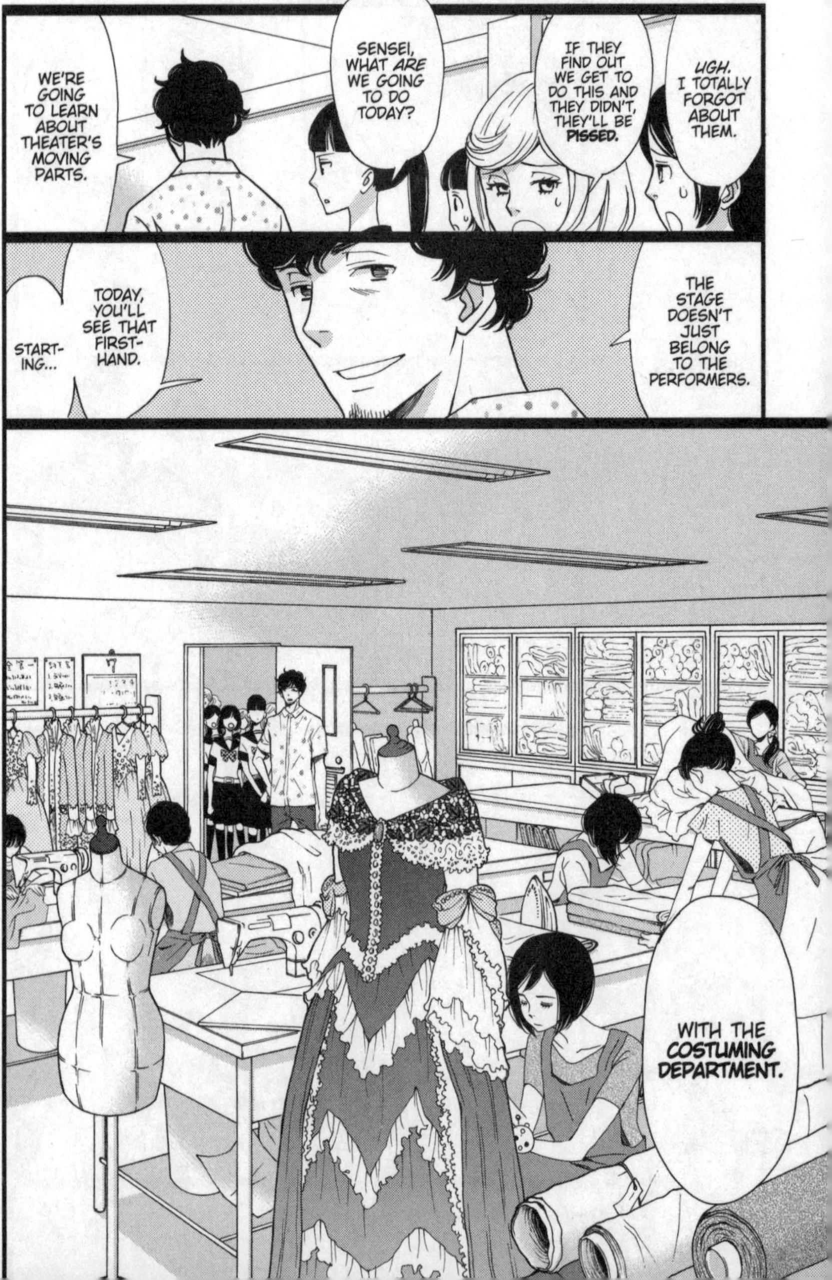
UGH. I TOTALLY FORGOT ABOUT THEM.
IF THEY FIND OUT WE GET TO DO THIS AND THEY DIDN'T, THEY'LL BE **PISSED.**
SENSEI, WHAT *ARE* WE GOING TO DO TODAY?
WE'RE GOING TO LEARN ABOUT THEATER'S MOVING PARTS.
THE STAGE DOESN'T JUST BELONG TO THE PERFORMERS.
TODAY, YOU'LL SEE THAT FIRST-HAND.
STARTING...
WITH THE **COSTUMING DEPARTMENT.**

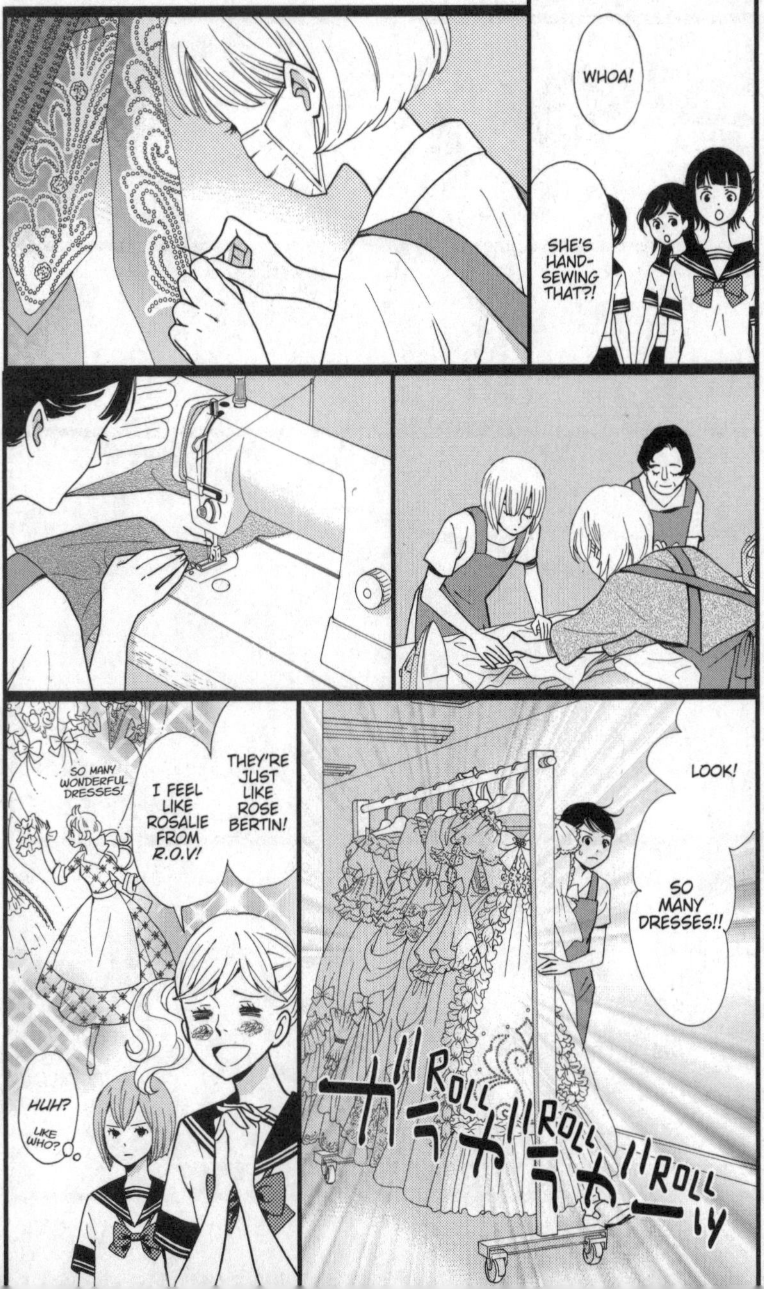
WHOA!
SHE'S HAND-SEWING THAT?!
LOOK!
SO MANY DRESSES!!
ROLL ROLL ROLL
THEY'RE JUST LIKE ROSE BERTIN!
I FEEL LIKE ROSALIE FROM R.O.V!
SO MANY WONDERFUL DRESSES!
HUH?
LIKE WHO?

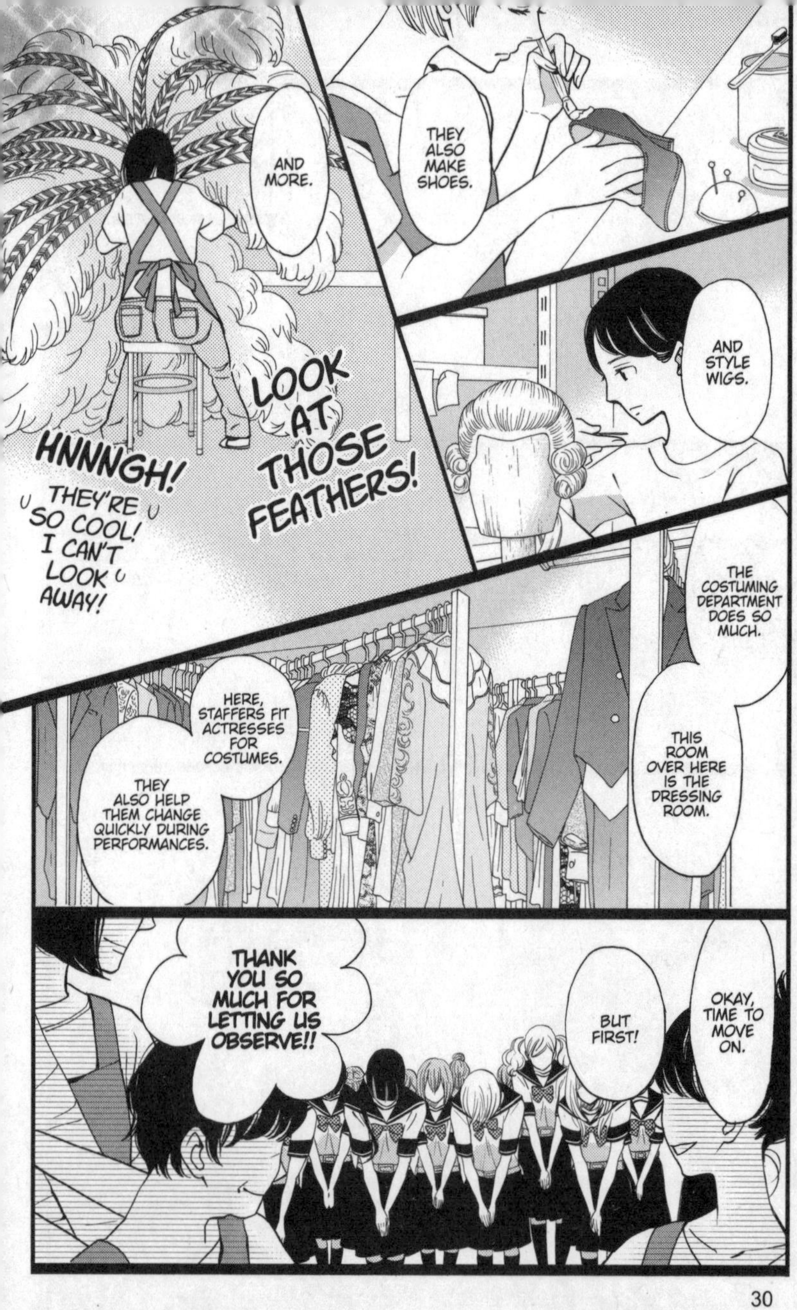
THEY ALSO MAKE SHOES.
AND STYLE WIGS.
AND MORE.
LOOK AT THOSE FEATHERS!
HNNNGH!
THEY'RE SO COOL! I CAN'T LOOK AWAY!
THE COSTUMING DEPARTMENT DOES SO MUCH.
THIS ROOM OVER HERE IS THE DRESSING ROOM.
HERE, STAFFERS FIT ACTRESSES FOR COSTUMES.
THEY ALSO HELP THEM CHANGE QUICKLY DURING PERFORMANCES.
OKAY, TIME TO MOVE ON.
BUT FIRST!
THANK YOU SO MUCH FOR LETTING US OBSERVE!!

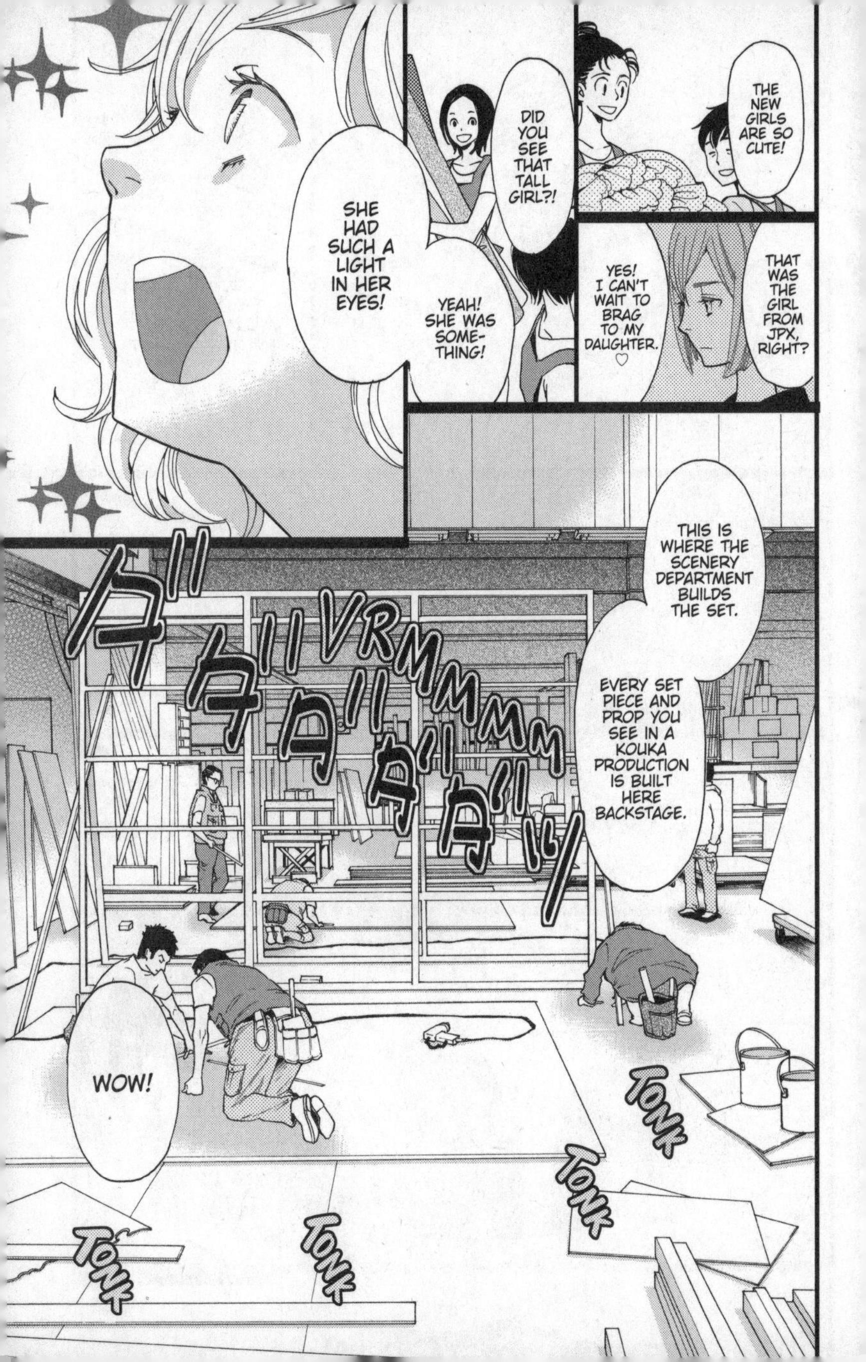
THE NEW GIRLS ARE SO CUTE!
THAT WAS THE GIRL FROM JPX, RIGHT?
YES! I CAN'T WAIT TO BRAG TO MY DAUGHTER. ♡
DID YOU SEE THAT TALL GIRL?!
YEAH! SHE WAS SOME-THING!
SHE HAD SUCH A LIGHT IN HER EYES!
THIS IS WHERE THE SCENERY DEPARTMENT BUILDS THE SET.
EVERY SET PIECE AND PROP YOU SEE IN A KOUKA PRODUCTION IS BUILT HERE BACKSTAGE.
VRMMMMMM
WOW!
TONK
TONK
TONK
TONK

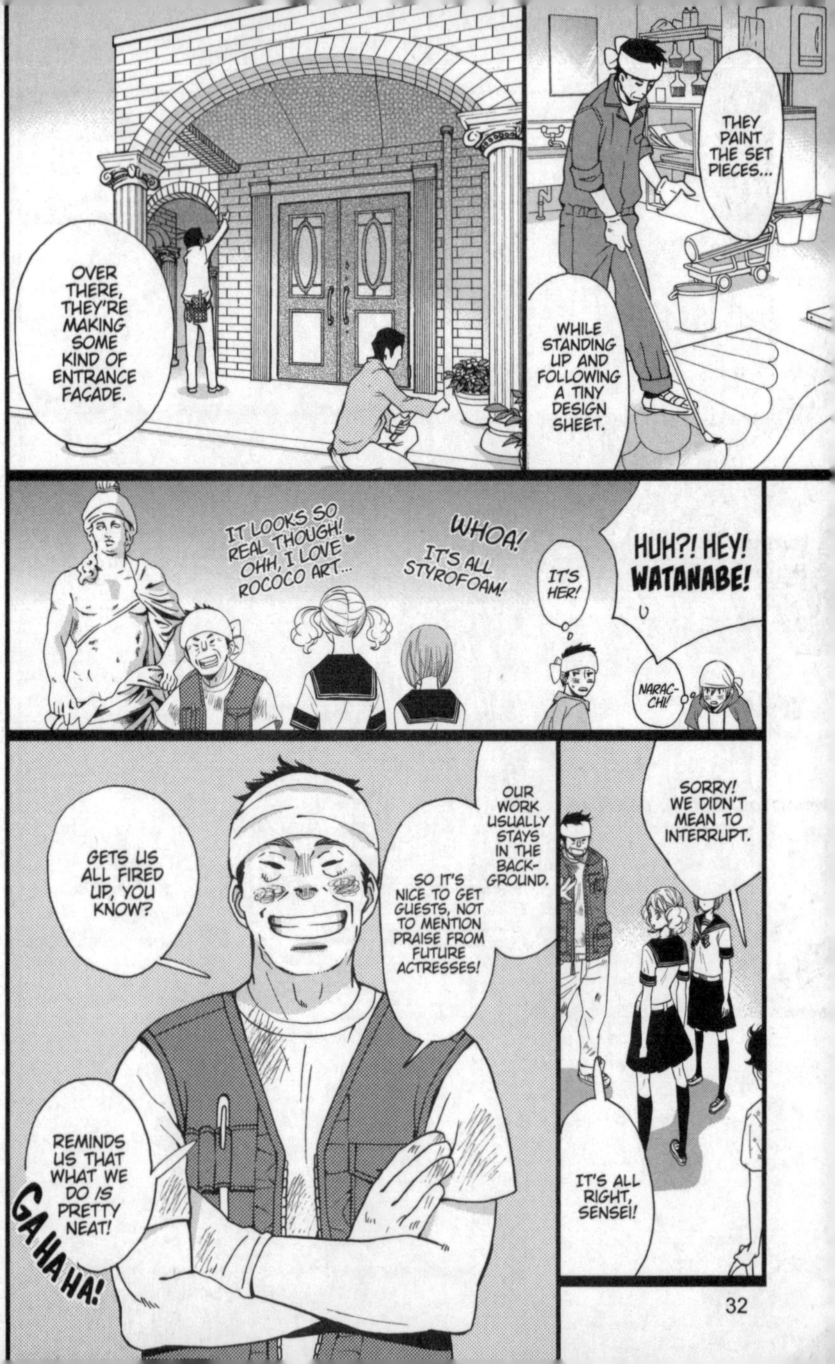
THEY PAINT THE SET PIECES...
WHILE STANDING UP AND FOLLOWING A TINY DESIGN SHEET.
OVER THERE, THEY'RE MAKING SOME KIND OF ENTRANCE FAÇADE.
HUH?! HEY! WATANABE!
NARAC-CHI!
IT'S HER!
WHOA! IT'S ALL STYROFOAM!
IT LOOKS SO REAL THOUGH! OHH, I LOVE ROCOCO ART...
SORRY! WE DIDN'T MEAN TO INTERRUPT.
IT'S ALL RIGHT, SENSEI!
OUR WORK USUALLY STAYS IN THE BACK-GROUND.
SO IT'S NICE TO GET GUESTS, NOT TO MENTION PRAISE FROM FUTURE ACTRESSES!
GETS US ALL FIRED UP, YOU KNOW?
REMINDS US THAT WHAT WE DO IS PRETTY NEAT!
GA HA HA!

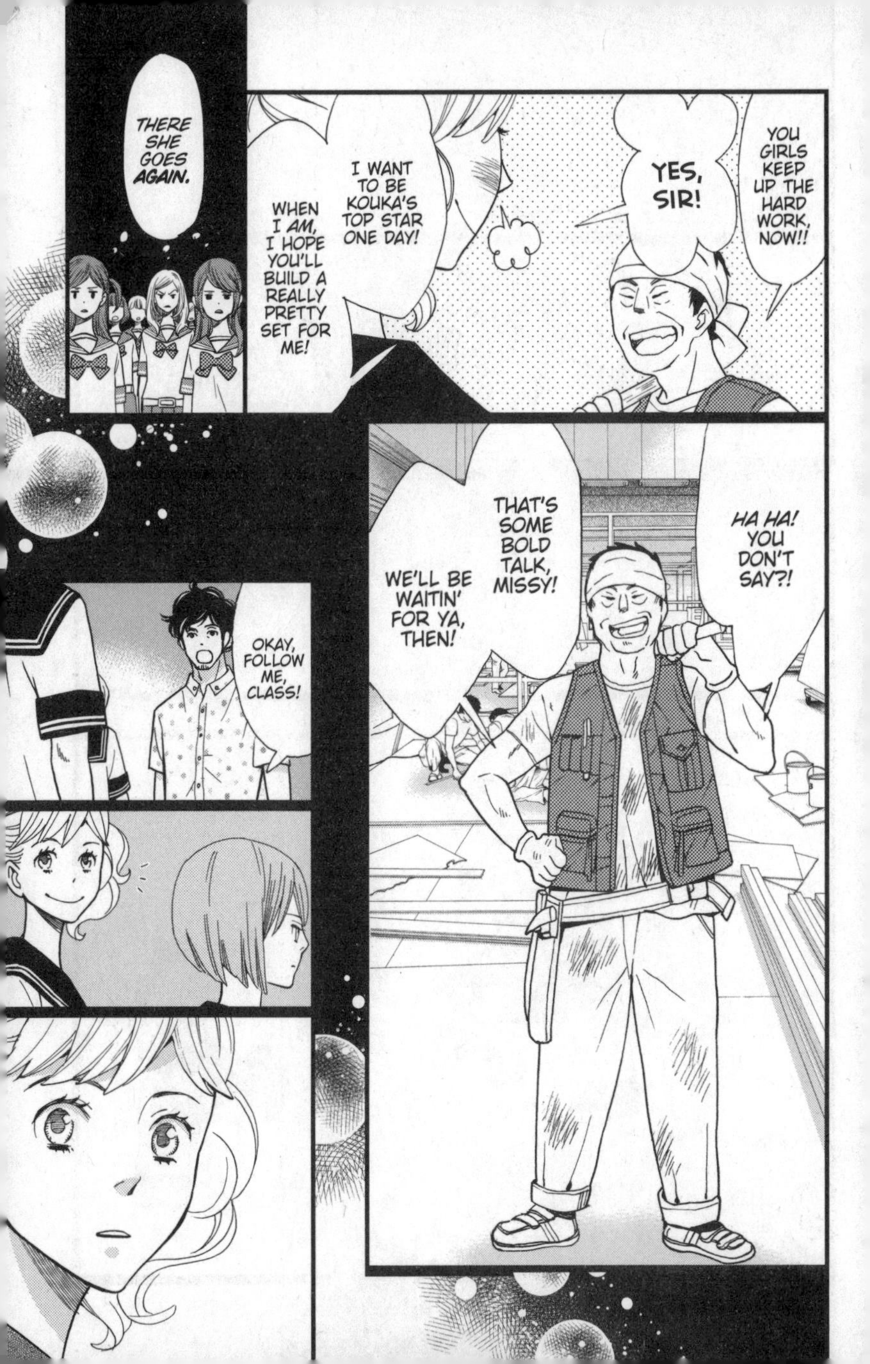
YOU GIRLS KEEP UP THE HARD WORK, NOW!!
YES, SIR!
I WANT TO BE KOUKA'S TOP STAR ONE DAY!
WHEN I *AM*, I HOPE YOU'LL BUILD A REALLY PRETTY SET FOR ME!
THERE SHE GOES *AGAIN*.
HA HA! YOU DON'T SAY?!
THAT'S SOME BOLD TALK, MISSY!
WE'LL BE WAITIN' FOR YA, THEN!
OKAY, FOLLOW ME, CLASS!

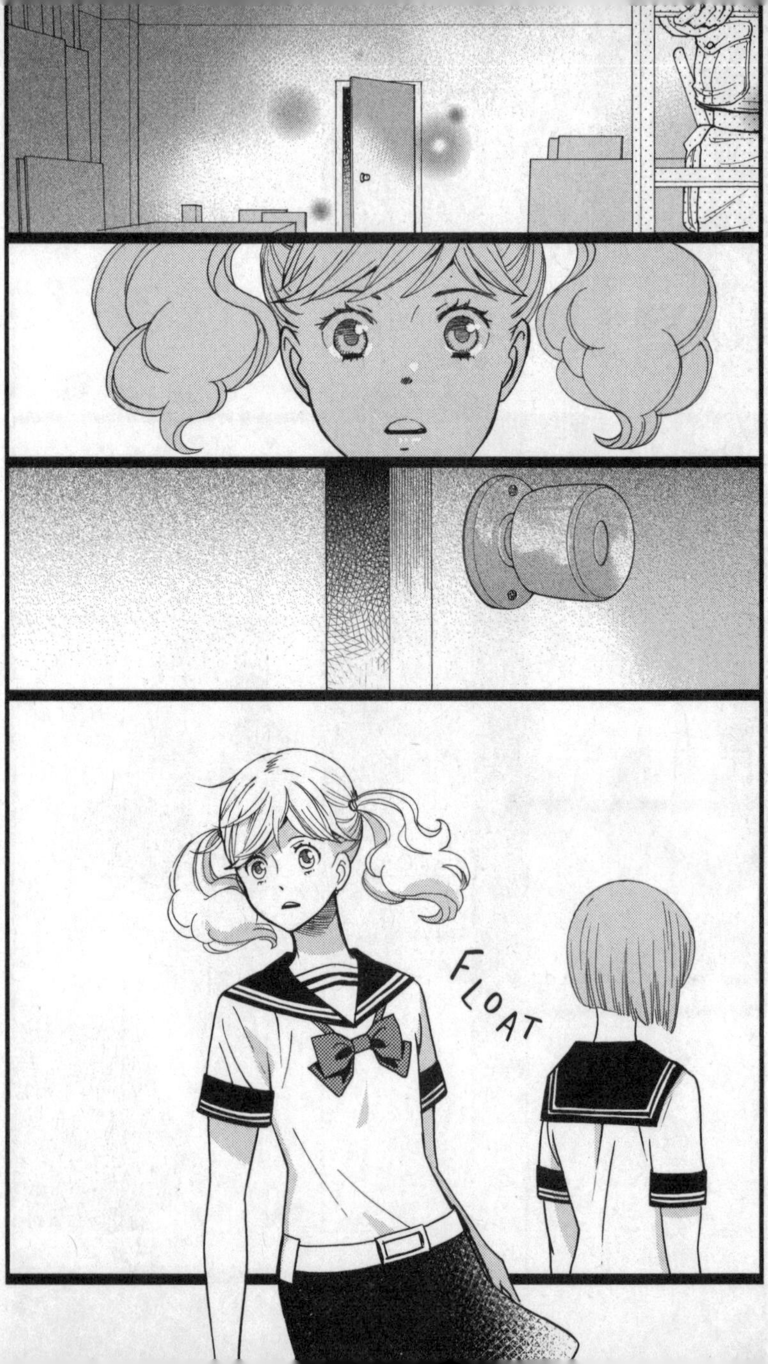
FLOAT

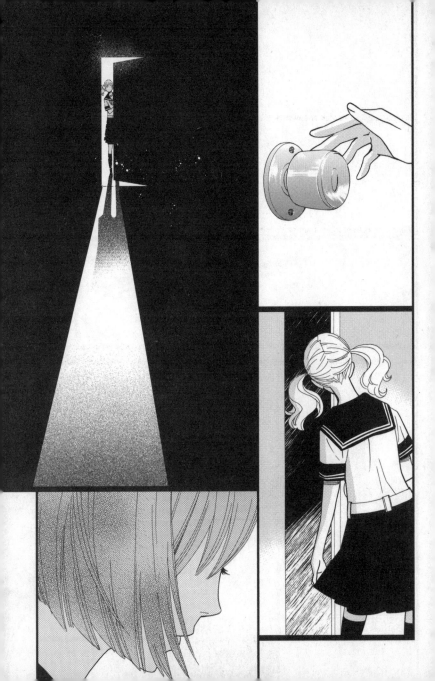

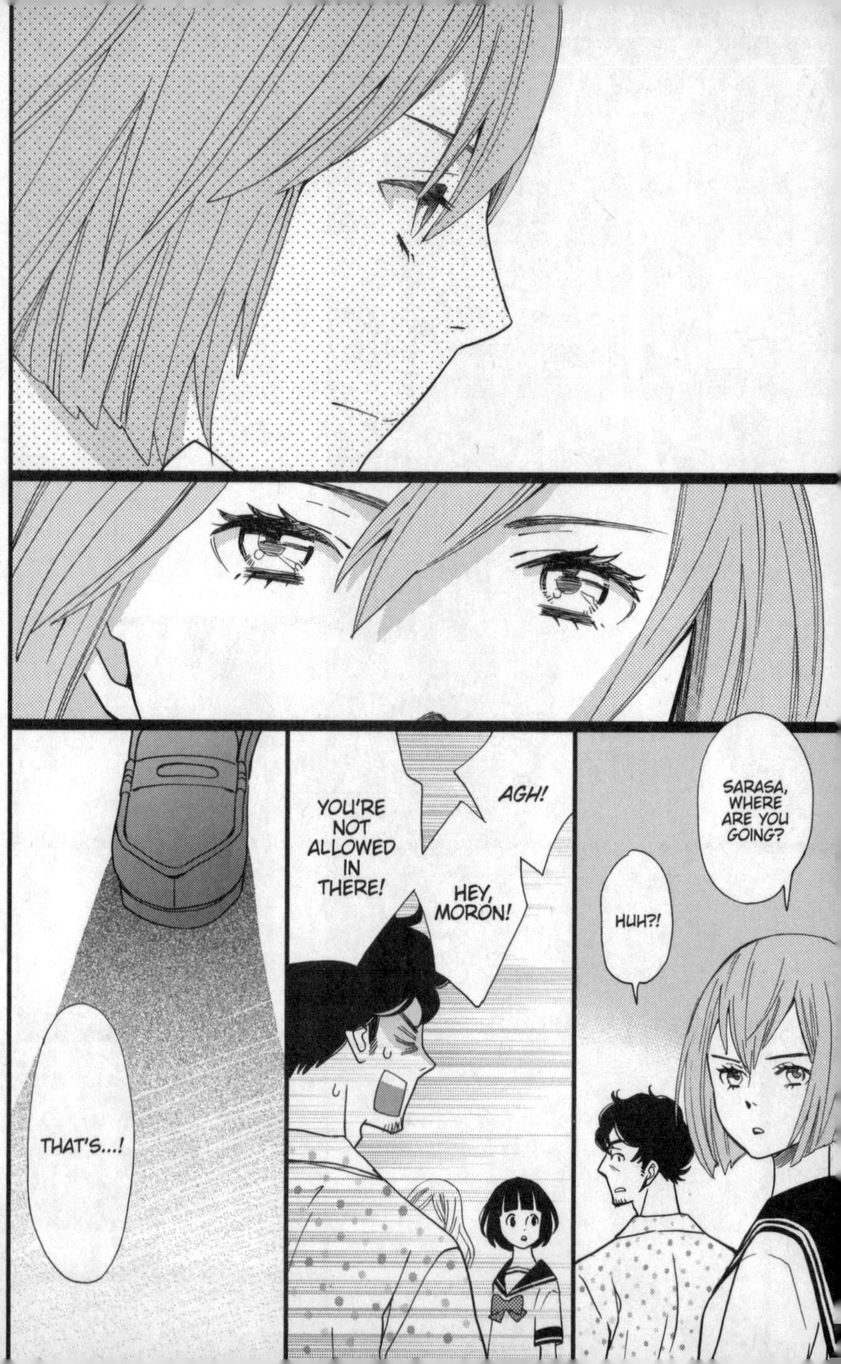
SARASA, WHERE ARE YOU GOING?
HUH?!
AGH!
HEY, MORON!
YOU'RE NOT ALLOWED IN THERE!
THAT'S...!

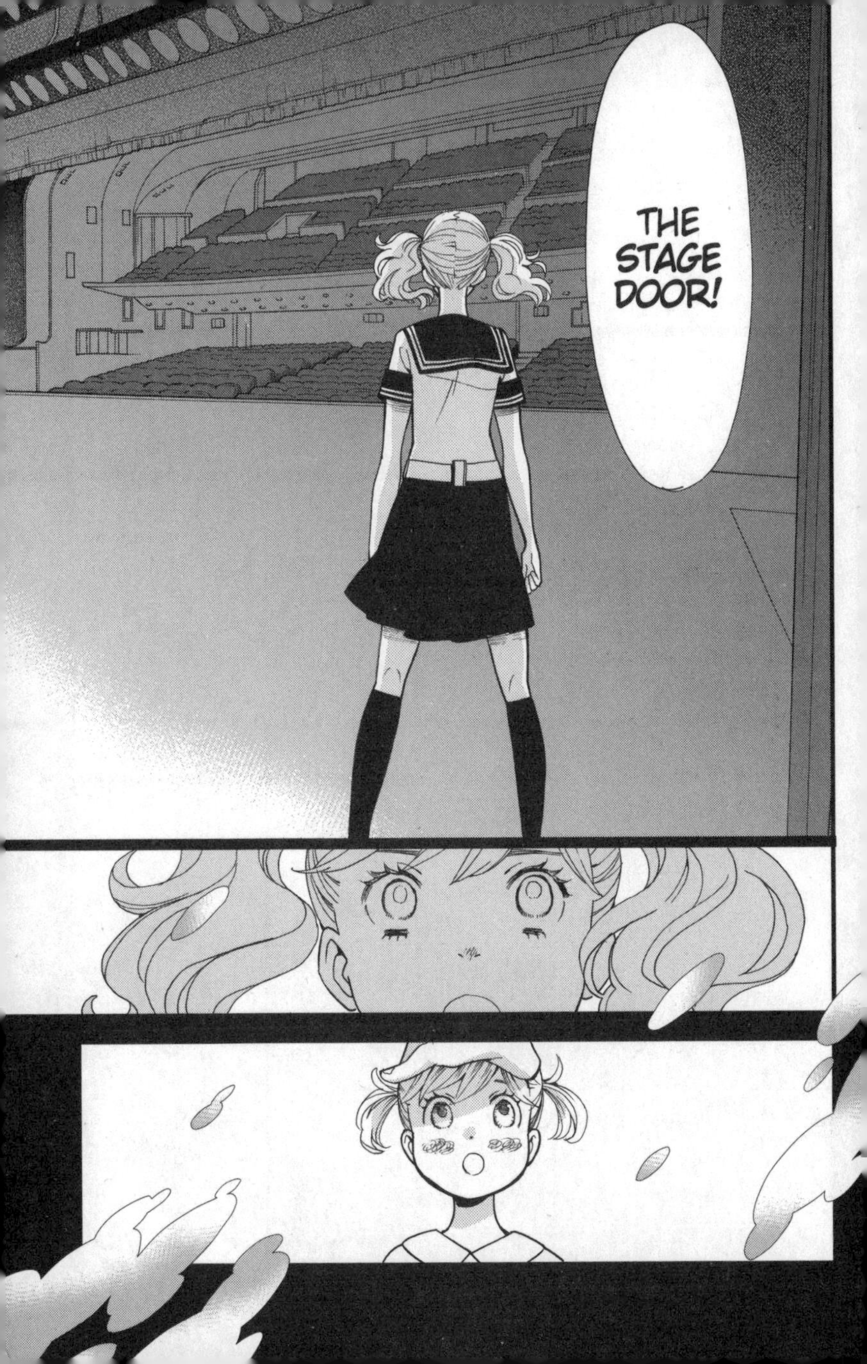
THE STAGE DOOR!

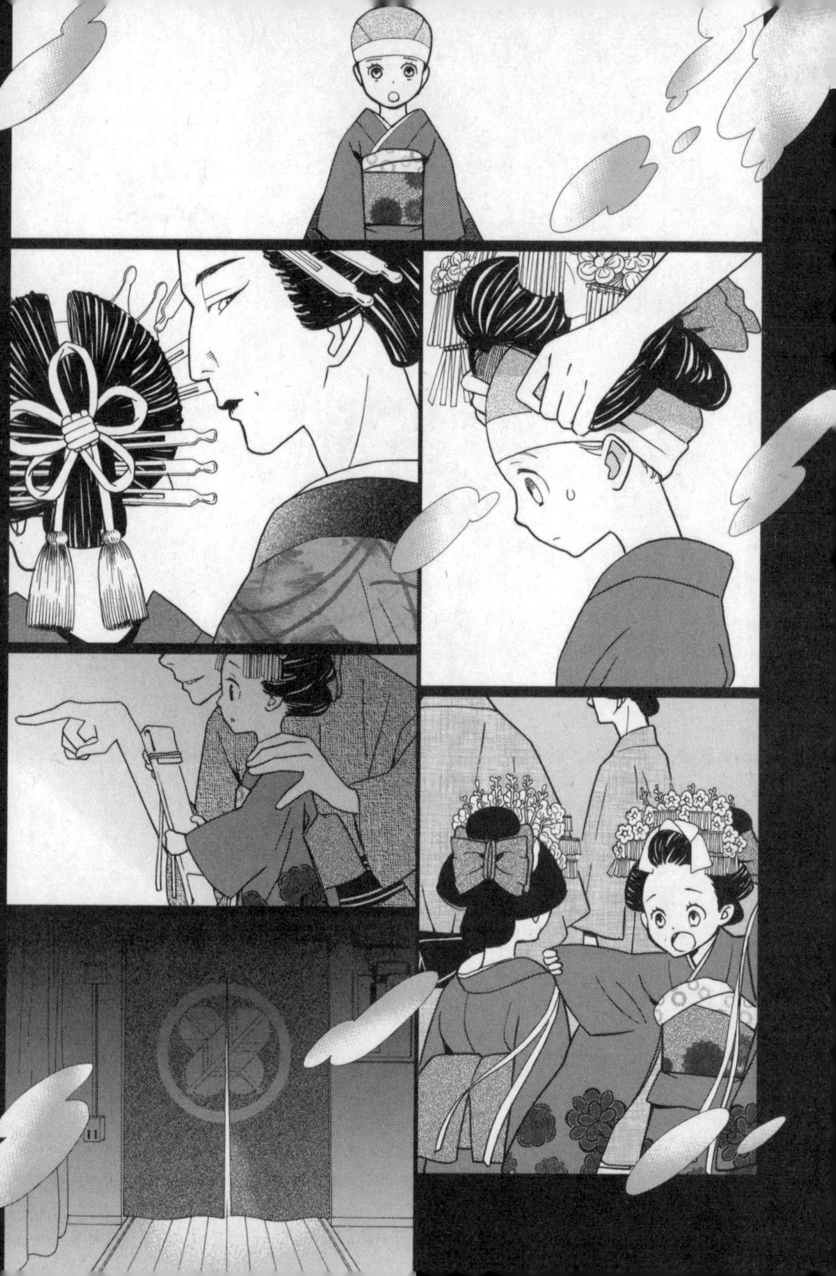

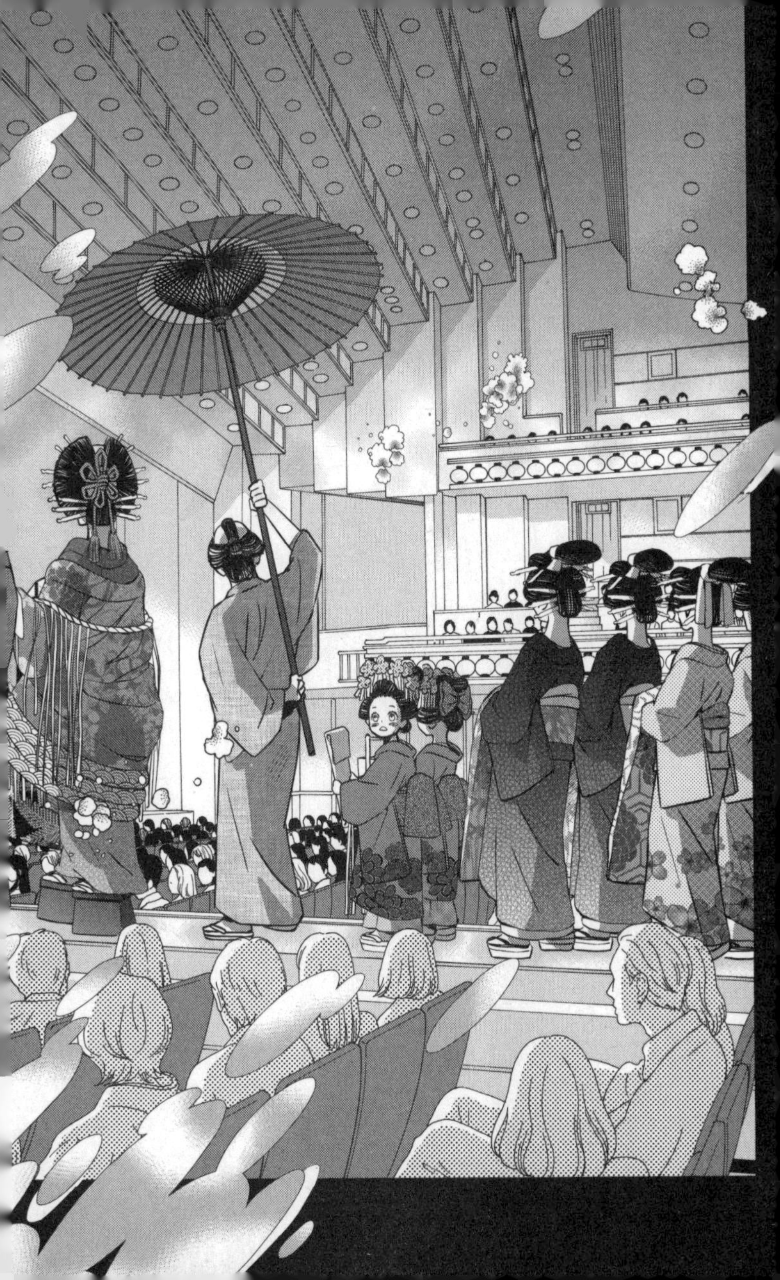

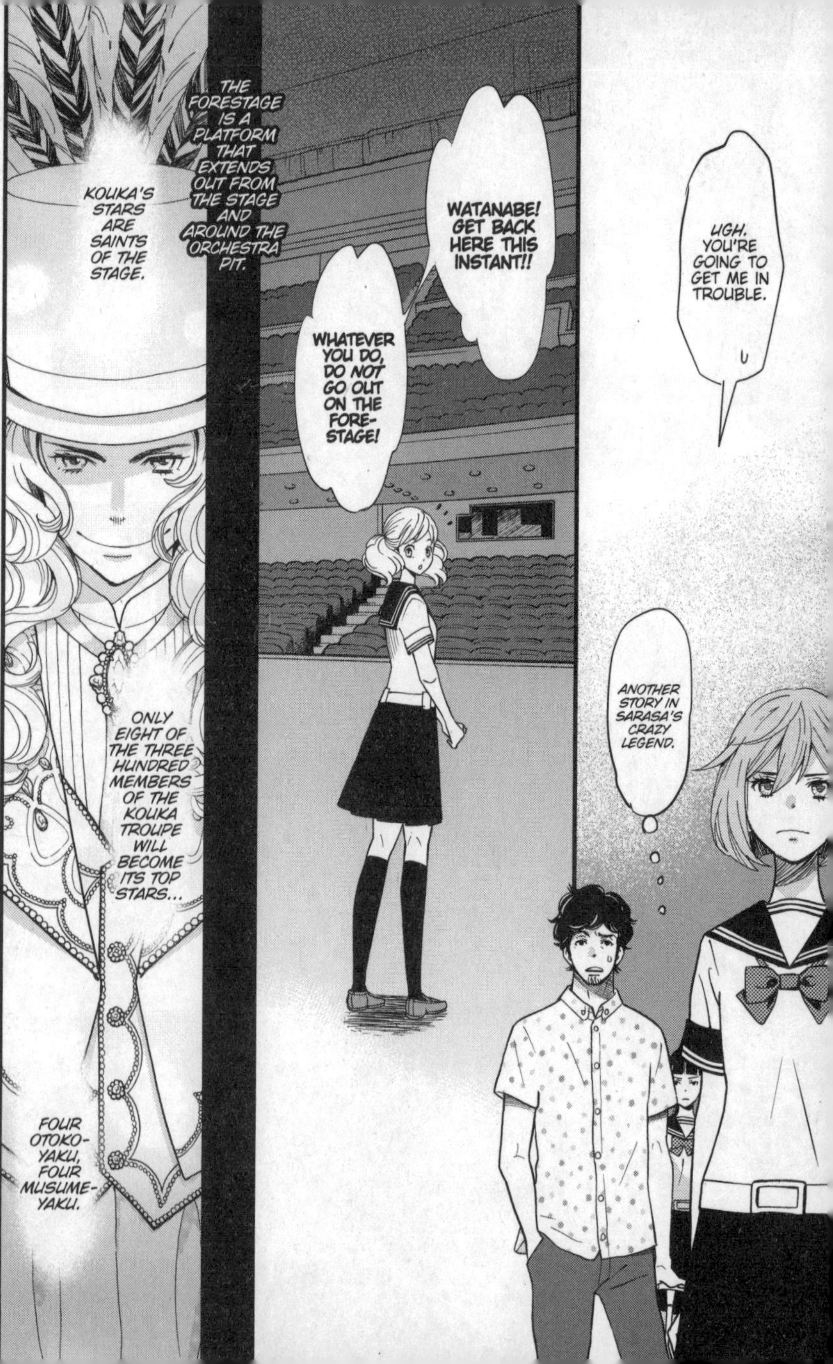

UGH. YOU'RE GOING TO GET ME IN TROUBLE.
ANOTHER STORY IN SARASA'S CRAZY LEGEND.
WATANABE! GET BACK HERE THIS INSTANT!!
THE FORESTAGE IS A PLATFORM THAT EXTENDS OUT FROM THE STAGE AND AROUND THE ORCHESTRA PIT.
WHATEVER YOU DO, DO NOT GO OUT ON THE FORE-STAGE!
KOUKA'S STARS ARE SAINTS OF THE STAGE.
ONLY EIGHT OF THE THREE HUNDRED MEMBERS OF THE KOUKA TROUPE WILL BECOME ITS TOP STARS...
FOUR OTOKO-YAKU, FOUR MUSUME-YAKU.

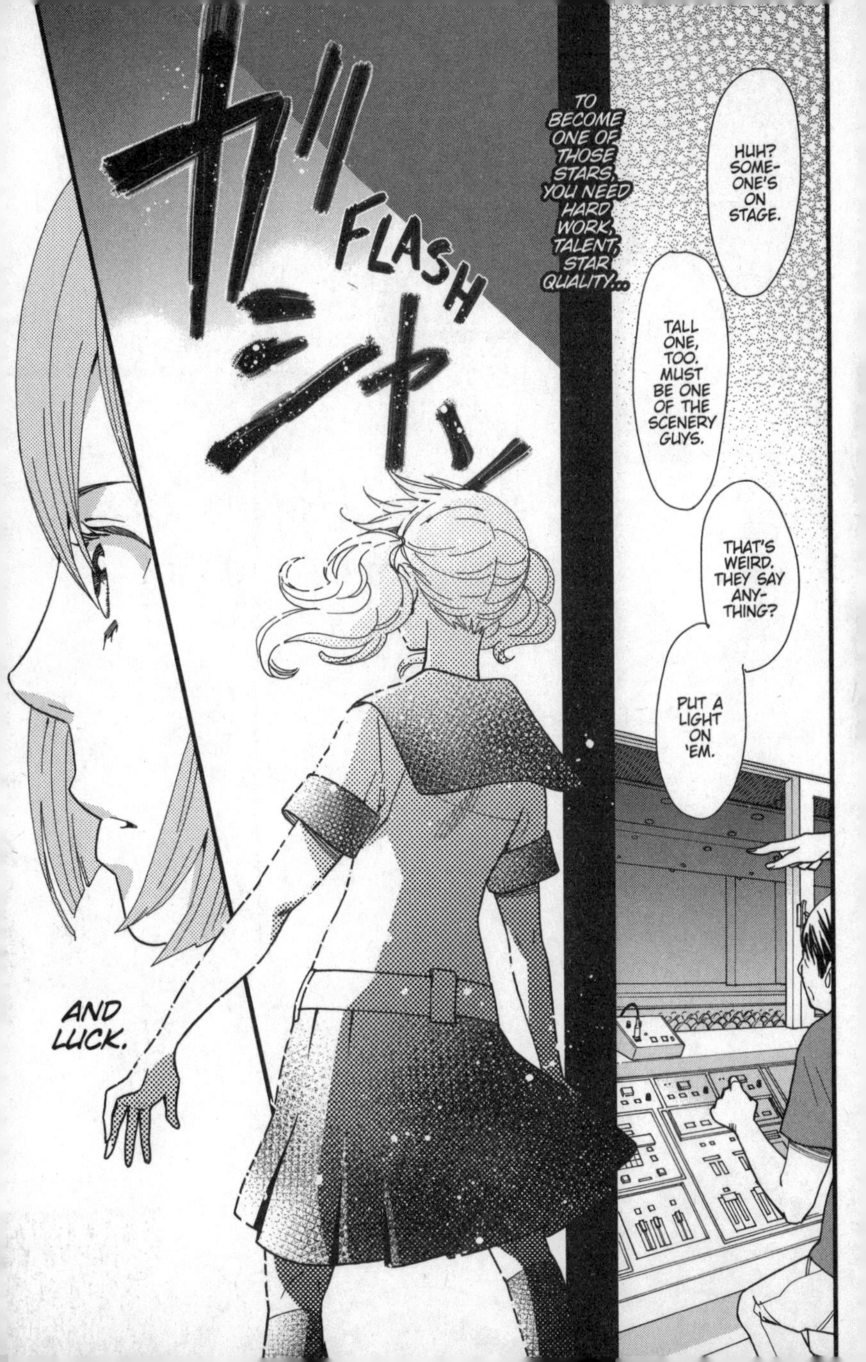
HUH? SOME-ONE'S ON STAGE.
TALL ONE, TOO. MUST BE ONE OF THE SCENERY GUYS.
THAT'S WEIRD. THEY SAY ANY-THING?
PUT A LIGHT ON 'EM.
TO BECOME ONE OF THOSE STARS, YOU NEED HARD WORK, TALENT, STAR QUALITY...
FLASH
AND LUCK.

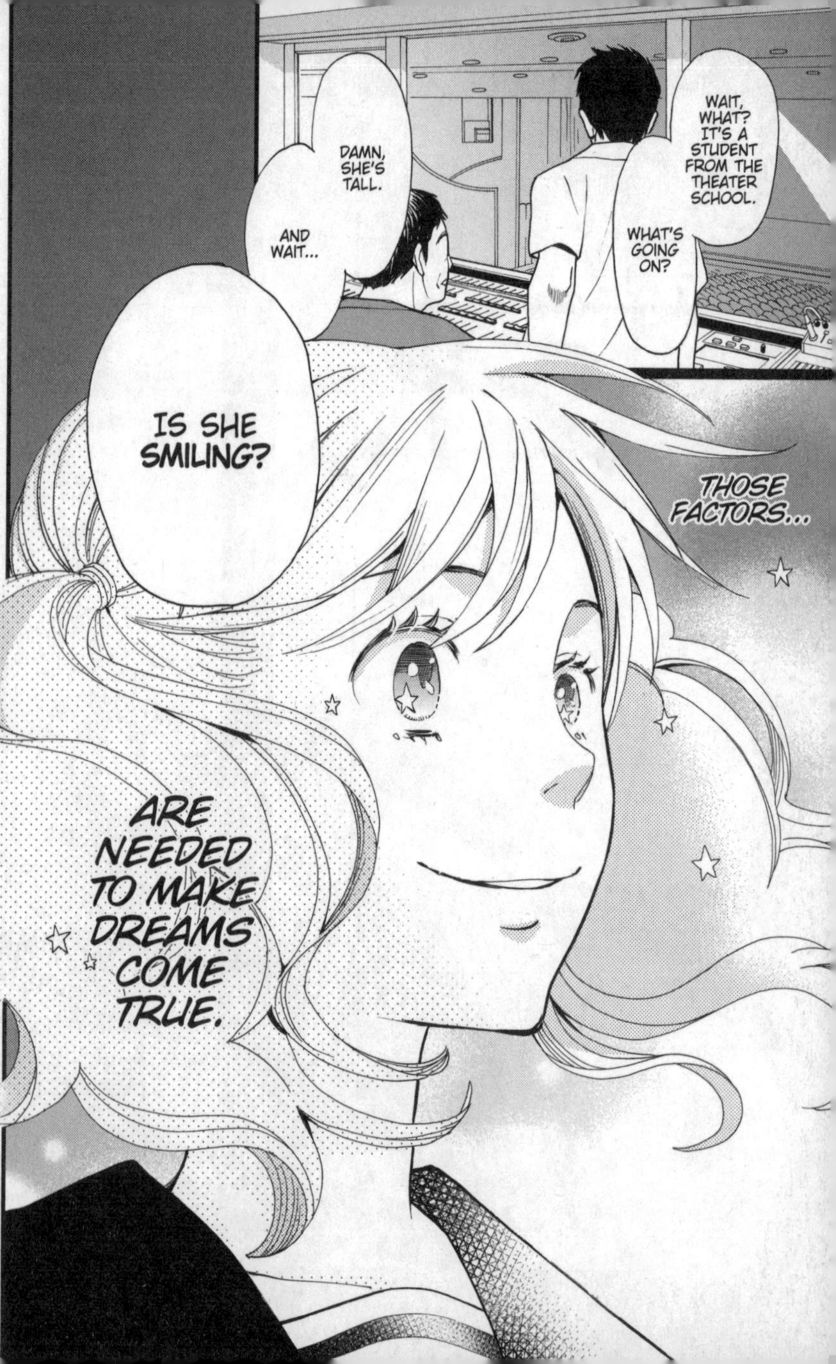
WAIT, WHAT? IT'S A STUDENT FROM THE THEATER SCHOOL.
WHAT'S GOING ON?
DAMN, SHE'S TALL.
AND WAIT...
IS SHE SMILING?
THOSE FACTORS...
ARE NEEDED TO MAKE DREAMS COME TRUE.

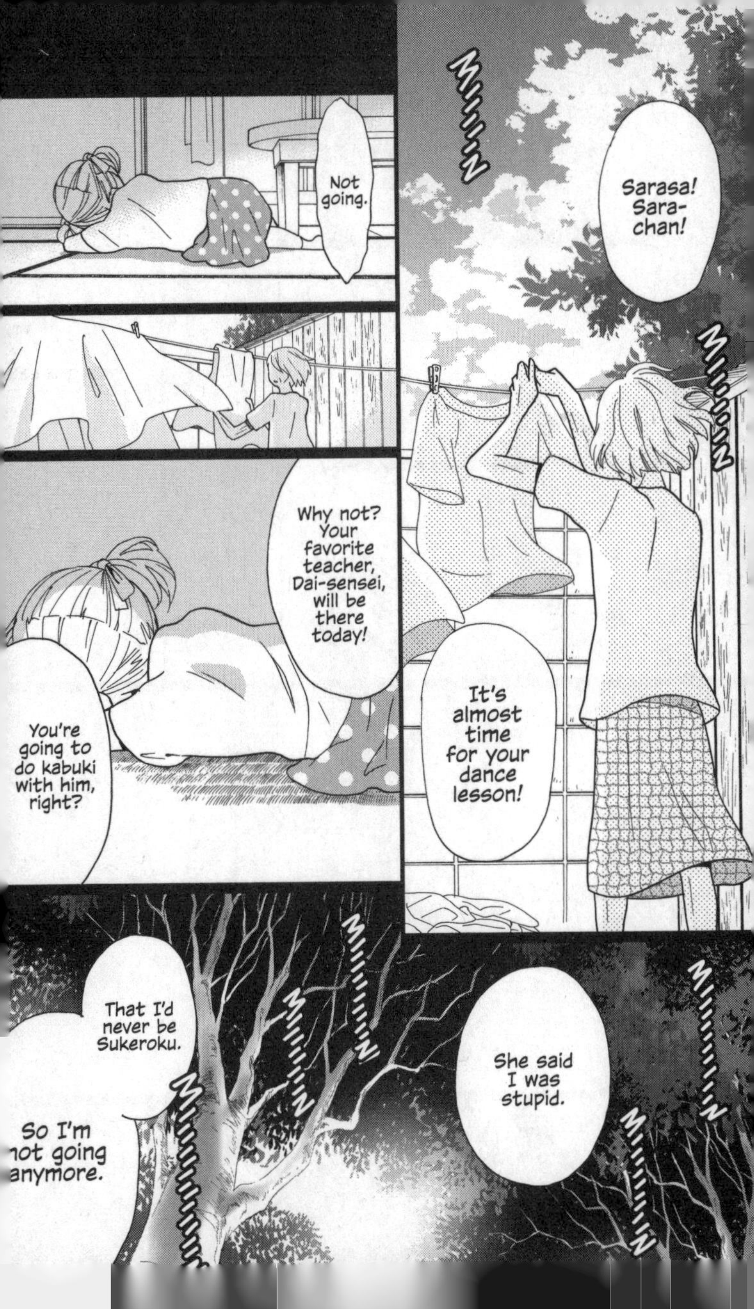
Sarasa! Sara-chan!
MIIIIN
MIIIIIIN
It's almost time for your dance lesson!
Not going.
Why not? Your favorite teacher, Dai-sensei, will be there today!
You're going to do kabuki with him, right?
MIIIIIIN
She said I was stupid.
MIIIIIIN
MIIIIIIN
That I'd never be Sukeroku.
MIIIIIIIN
So I'm not going anymore.

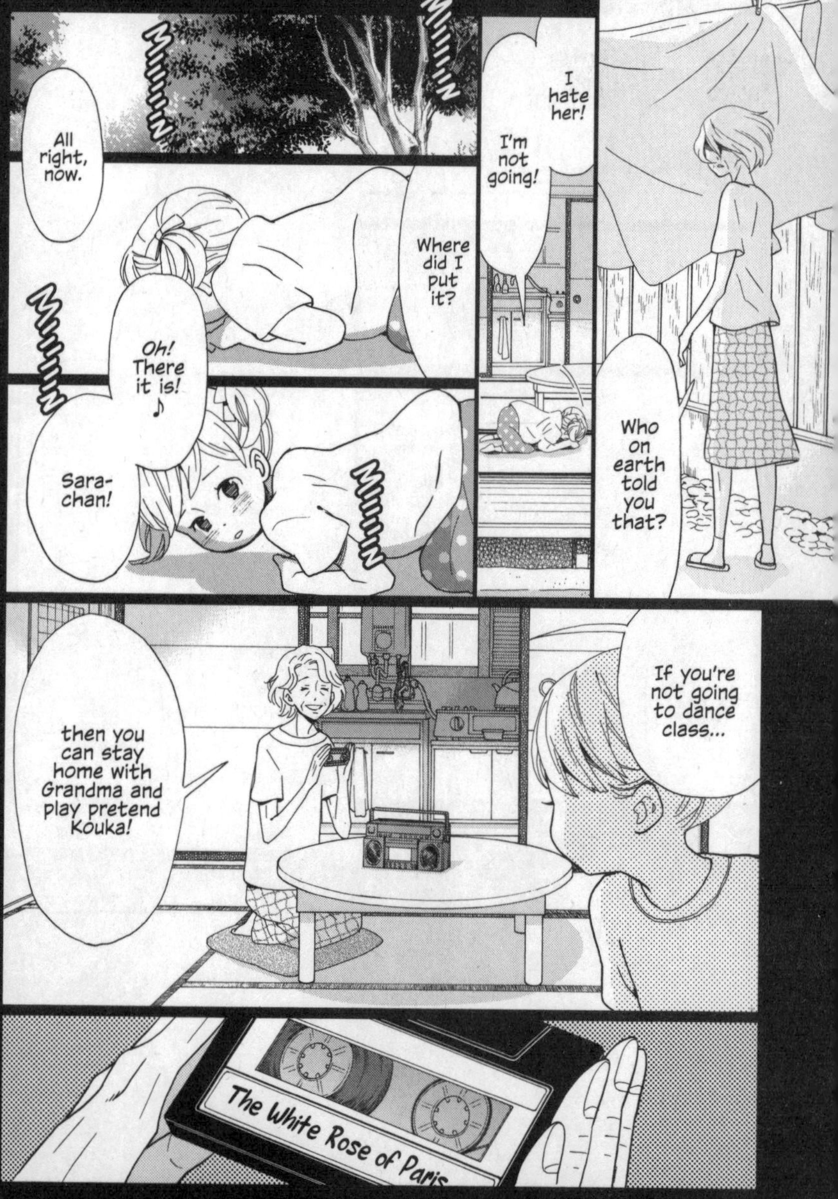
Who on earth told you that?
I hate her!
I'm not going!
MIIIIN
MIIIIN
All right, now.
Where did I put it?
MIIIIN
Oh! There it is! ♪
Sara-chan!
MIIIIN
If you're not going to dance class...
then you can stay home with Grandma and play pretend Kouka!
The White Rose of Paris

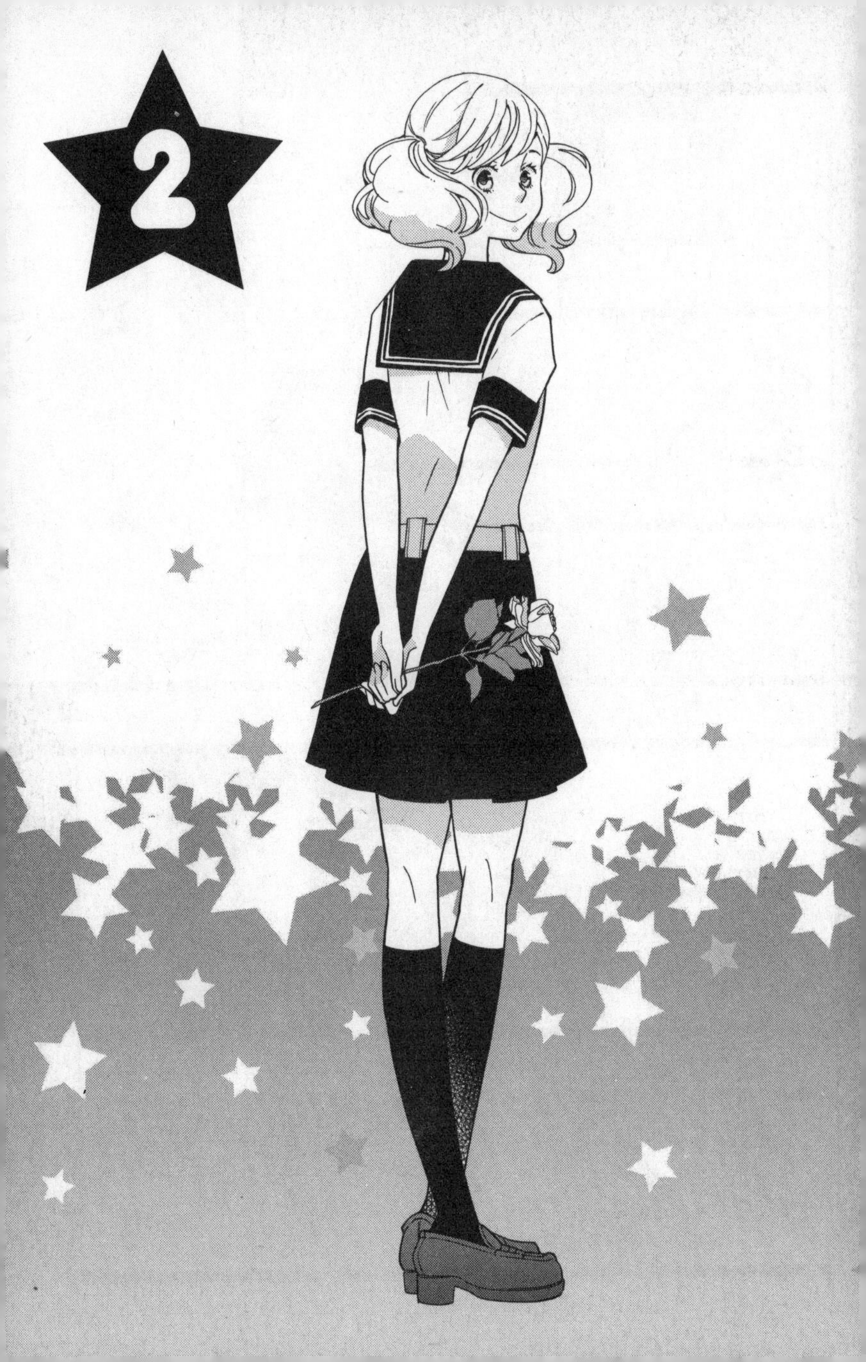
2

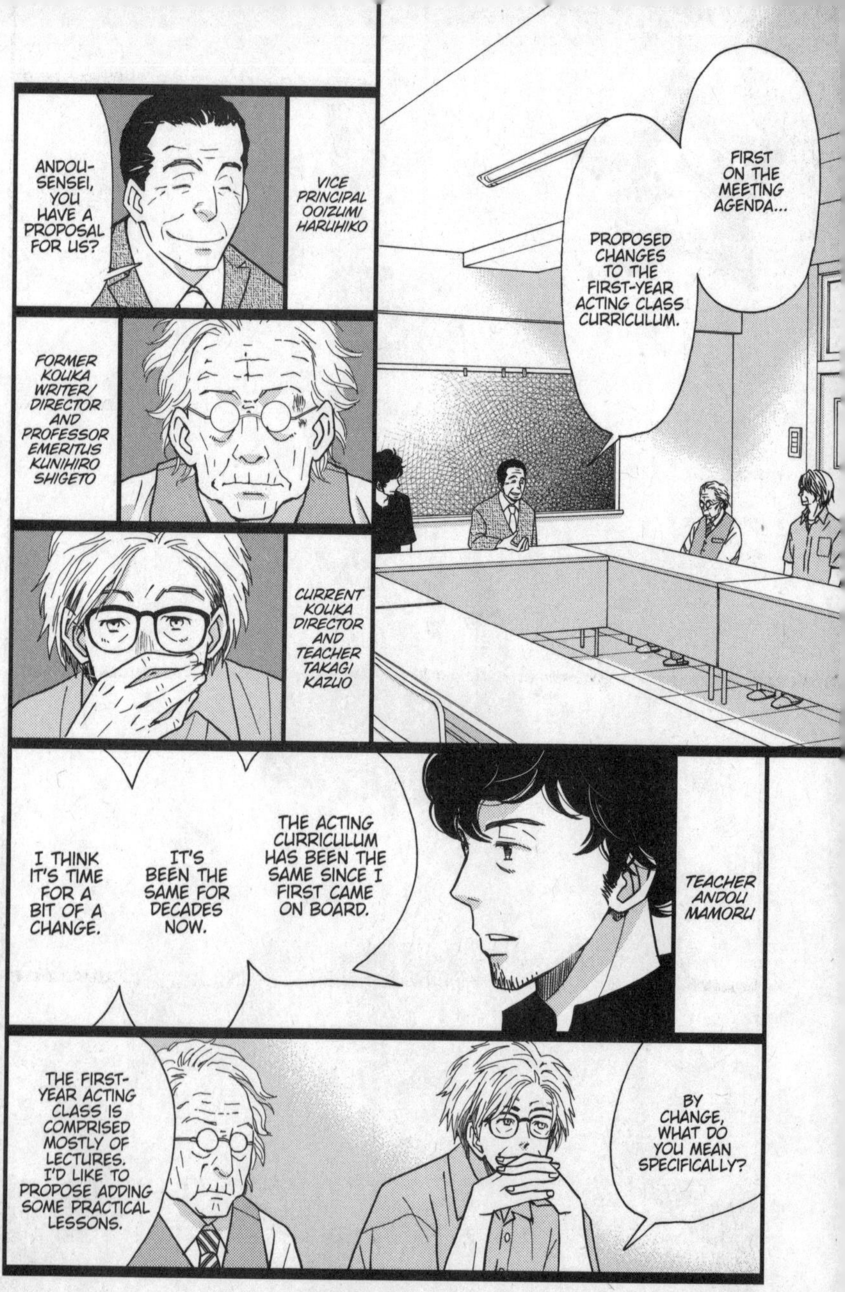
FIRST ON THE MEETING AGENDA...
PROPOSED CHANGES TO THE FIRST-YEAR ACTING CLASS CURRICULUM.
VICE PRINCIPAL OOIZUMI HARUHIKO
ANDOU-SENSEI, YOU HAVE A PROPOSAL FOR US?
FORMER KOUKA WRITER/ DIRECTOR AND PROFESSOR EMERITUS KUNIHIRO SHIGETO
CURRENT KOUKA DIRECTOR AND TEACHER TAKAGI KAZUO
TEACHER ANDOU MAMORU
THE ACTING CURRICULUM HAS BEEN THE SAME SINCE I FIRST CAME ON BOARD.
IT'S BEEN THE SAME FOR DECADES NOW.
I THINK IT'S TIME FOR A BIT OF A CHANGE.
BY CHANGE, WHAT DO YOU MEAN SPECIFICALLY?
THE FIRST-YEAR ACTING CLASS IS COMPRISED MOSTLY OF LECTURES. I'D LIKE TO PROPOSE ADDING SOME PRACTICAL LESSONS.

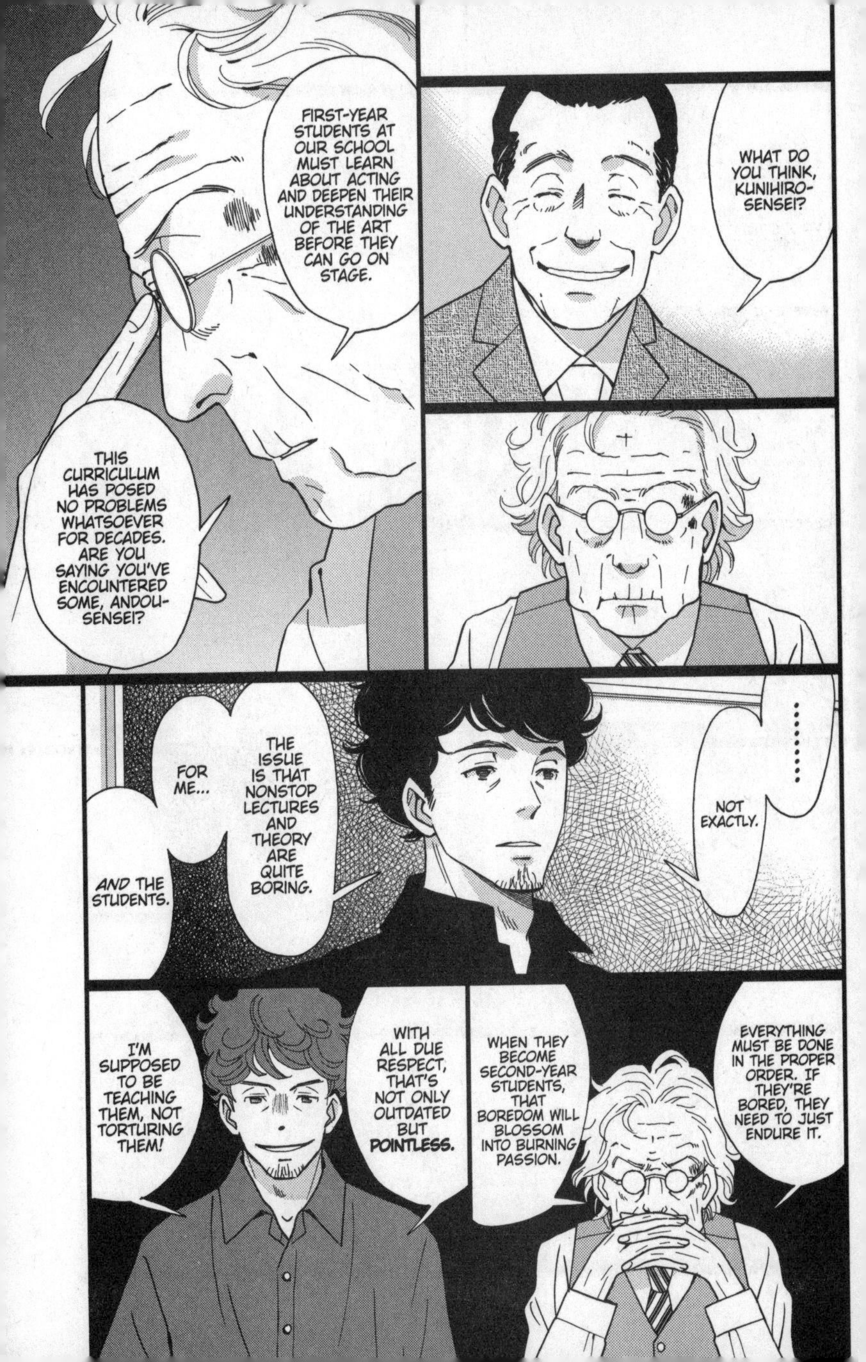
WHAT DO YOU THINK, KUNIHIRO-SENSEI?
FIRST-YEAR STUDENTS AT OUR SCHOOL MUST LEARN ABOUT ACTING AND DEEPEN THEIR UNDERSTANDING OF THE ART BEFORE THEY CAN GO ON STAGE.
THIS CURRICULUM HAS POSED NO PROBLEMS WHATSOEVER FOR DECADES. ARE YOU SAYING YOU'VE ENCOUNTERED SOME, ANDOU-SENSEI?
......
NOT EXACTLY.
THE ISSUE IS THAT NONSTOP LECTURES AND THEORY ARE QUITE BORING.
FOR ME...
AND THE STUDENTS.
EVERYTHING MUST BE DONE IN THE PROPER ORDER. IF THEY'RE BORED, THEY NEED TO JUST ENDURE IT.
WHEN THEY BECOME SECOND-YEAR STUDENTS, THAT BOREDOM WILL BLOSSOM INTO BURNING PASSION.
WITH ALL DUE RESPECT, THAT'S NOT ONLY OUTDATED BUT **POINTLESS.**
I'M SUPPOSED TO BE TEACHING THEM, NOT TORTURING THEM!

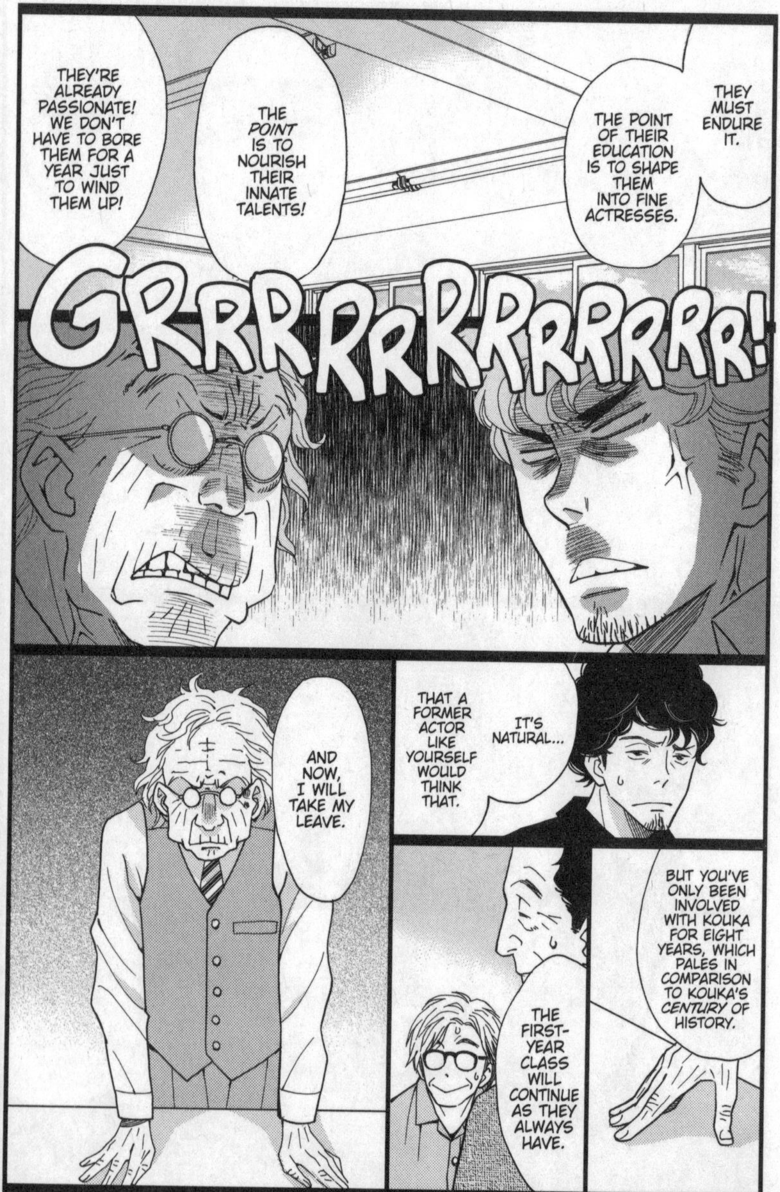
THE POINT OF THEIR EDUCATION IS TO SHAPE THEM INTO FINE ACTRESSES.
THEY MUST ENDURE IT.
THE *POINT* IS TO NOURISH THEIR INNATE TALENTS!
THEY'RE ALREADY PASSIONATE! WE DON'T HAVE TO BORE THEM FOR A YEAR JUST TO WIND THEM UP!
GRRRRRRRRRRRR!
IT'S NATURAL...
THAT A FORMER ACTOR LIKE YOURSELF WOULD THINK THAT.
BUT YOU'VE ONLY BEEN INVOLVED WITH KOUKA FOR EIGHT YEARS, WHICH PALES IN COMPARISON TO KOUKA'S *CENTURY* OF HISTORY.
THE FIRST-YEAR CLASS WILL CONTINUE AS THEY ALWAYS HAVE.
AND NOW, I WILL TAKE MY LEAVE.

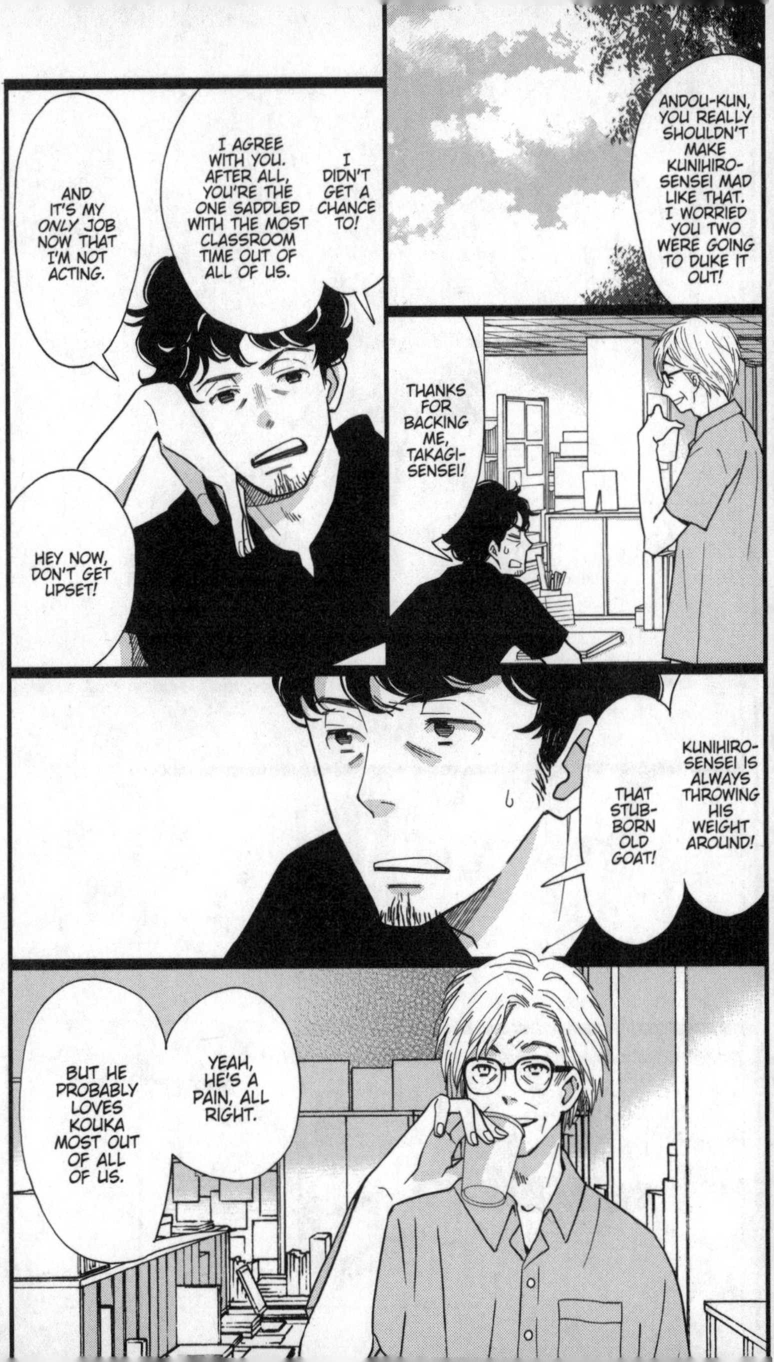

ANDOU-KUN, YOU REALLY SHOULDN'T MAKE KUNIHIRO-SENSEI MAD LIKE THAT. I WORRIED YOU TWO WERE GOING TO DUKE IT OUT!
THANKS FOR BACKING ME, TAKAGI-SENSEI!
I DIDN'T GET A CHANCE TO!
I AGREE WITH YOU. AFTER ALL, YOU'RE THE ONE SADDLED WITH THE MOST CLASSROOM TIME OUT OF ALL OF US.
AND IT'S MY *ONLY* JOB NOW THAT I'M NOT ACTING.
HEY NOW, DON'T GET UPSET!
KUNIHIRO-SENSEI IS ALWAYS THROWING HIS WEIGHT AROUND!
THAT STUBBORN OLD GOAT!
YEAH, HE'S A PAIN, ALL RIGHT.
BUT HE PROBABLY LOVES KOUKA MOST OUT OF ALL OF US.

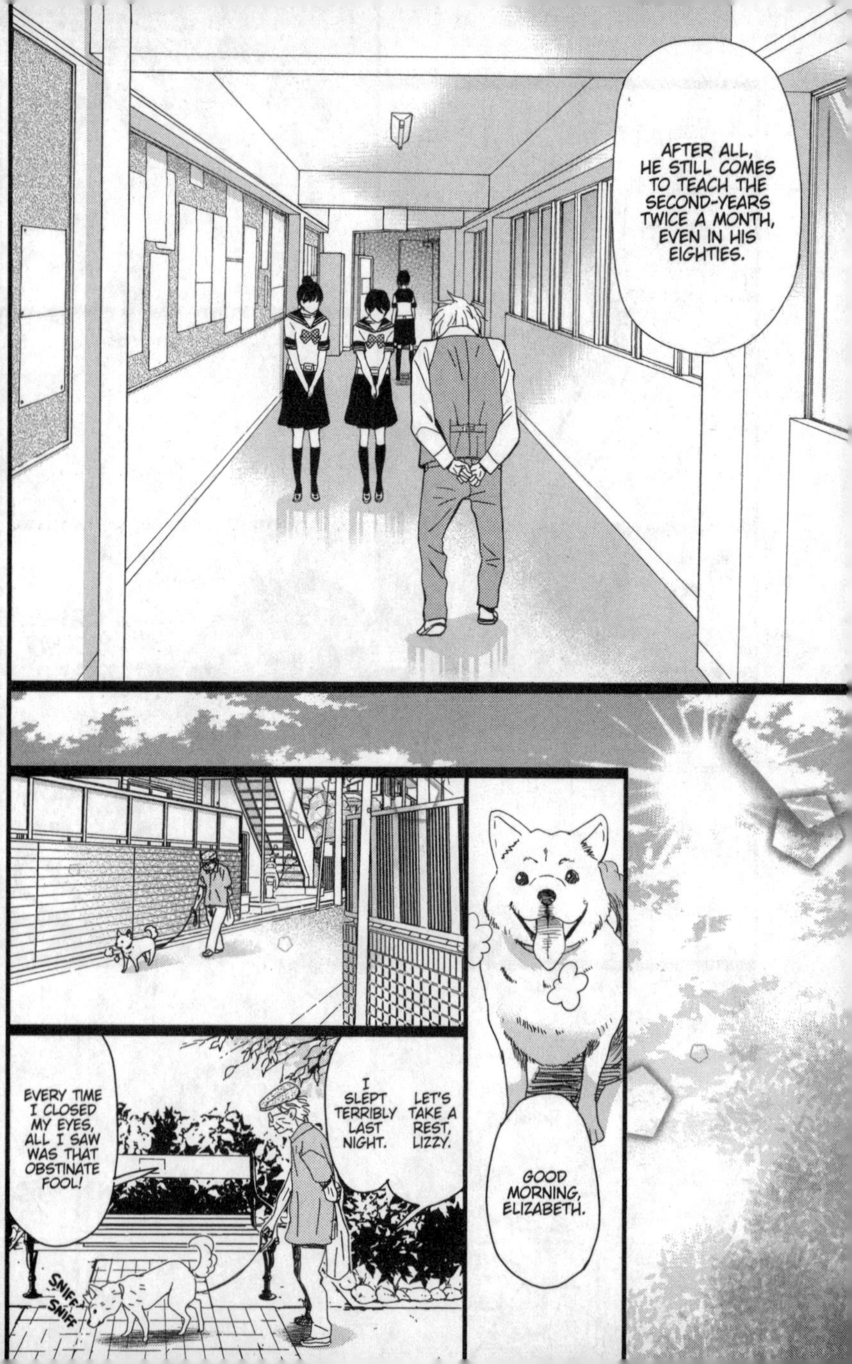
AFTER ALL, HE STILL COMES TO TEACH THE SECOND-YEARS TWICE A MONTH, EVEN IN HIS EIGHTIES.
GOOD MORNING, ELIZABETH.
LET'S TAKE A REST, LIZZY.
I SLEPT TERRIBLY LAST NIGHT.
EVERY TIME I CLOSED MY EYES, ALL I SAW WAS THAT OBSTINATE FOOL!
SNIFF SNIFF

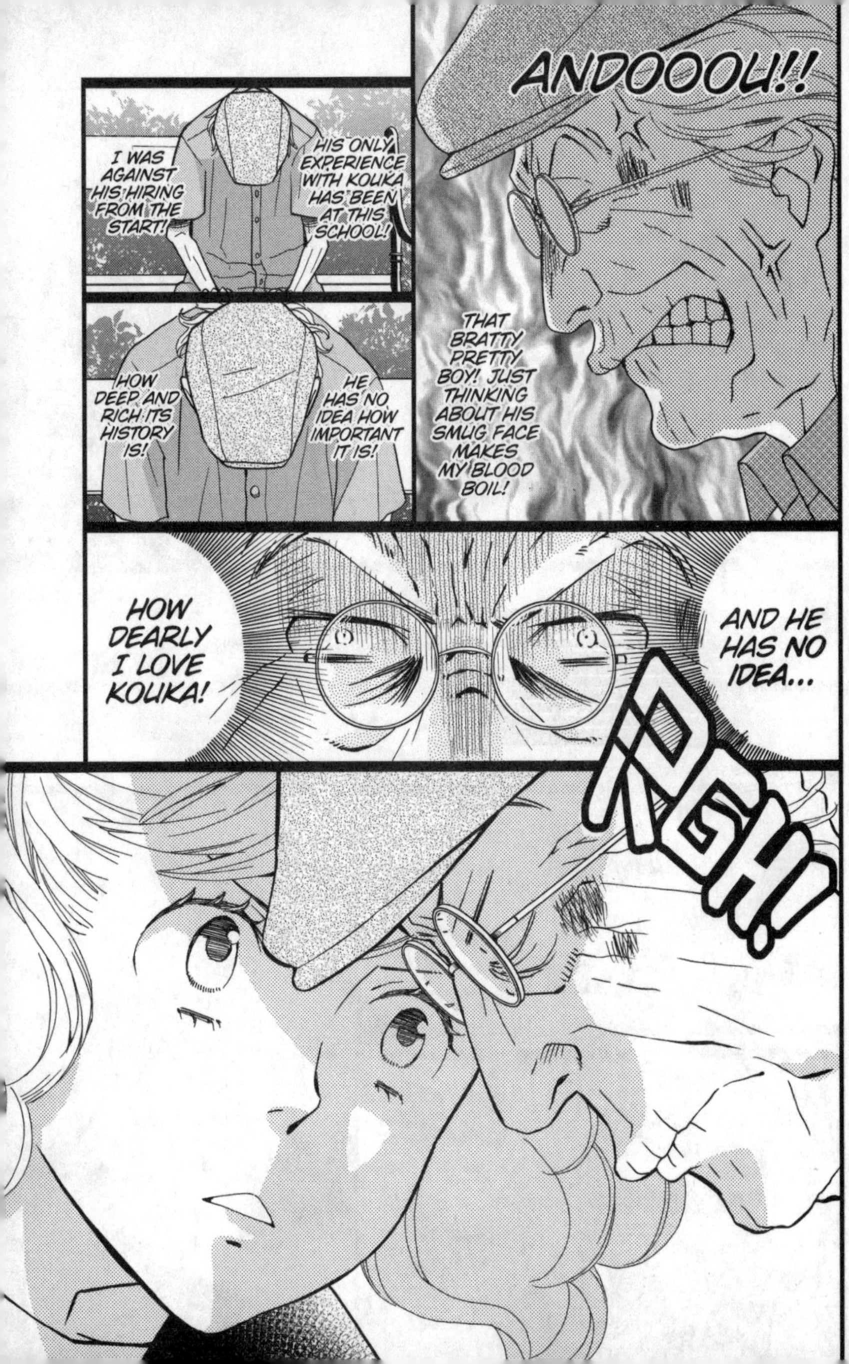

ANDOOOU!!
THAT BRATTY PRETTY BOY! JUST THINKING ABOUT HIS SMUG FACE MAKES MY BLOOD BOIL!
HIS ONLY EXPERIENCE WITH KOUKA HAS BEEN AT THIS SCHOOL!
I WAS AGAINST HIS HIRING FROM THE START!
HE HAS NO IDEA HOW IMPORTANT IT IS!
HOW DEEP AND RICH ITS HISTORY IS!
AND HE HAS NO IDEA...
HOW DEARLY I LOVE KOUKA!
RGH!

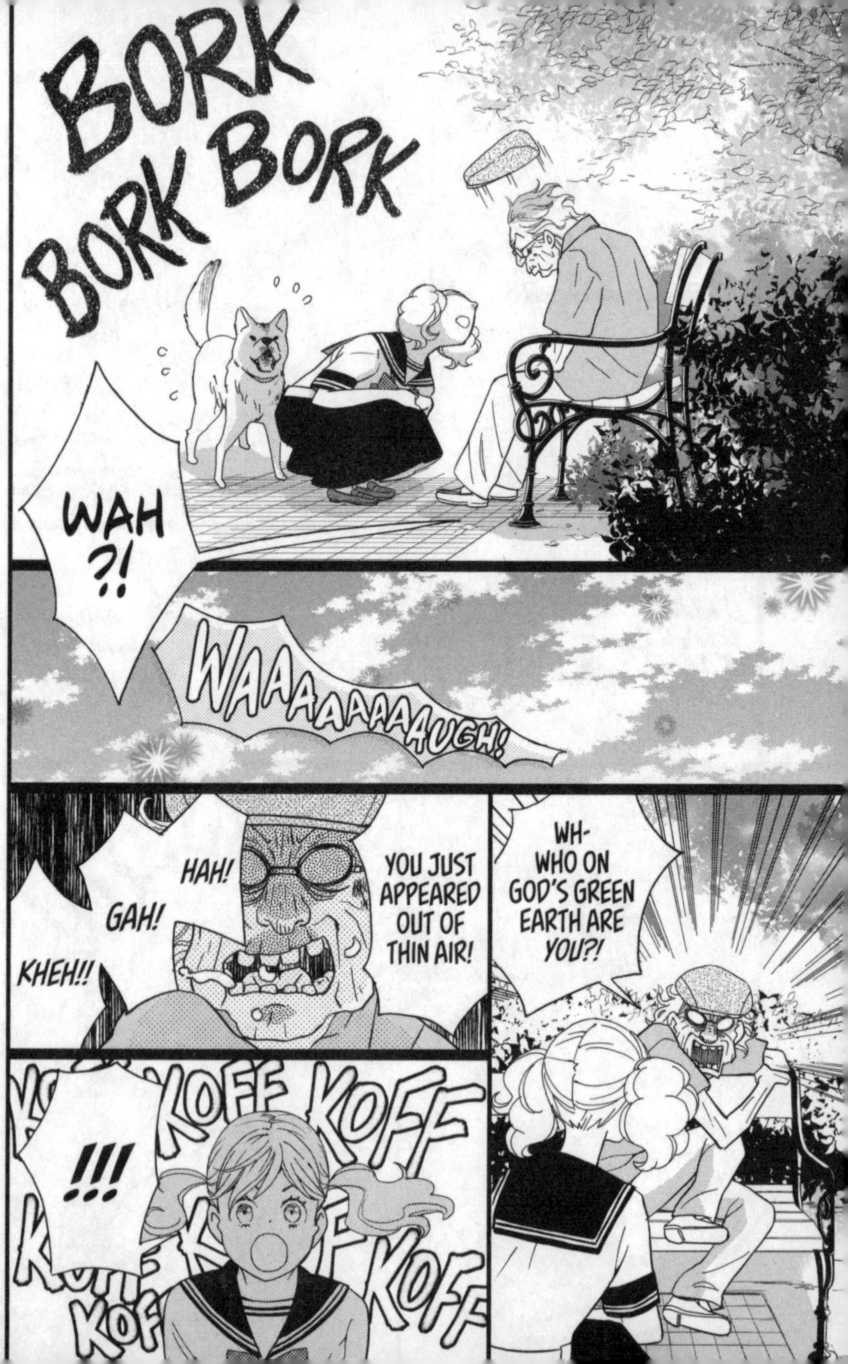
BORK BORK BORK
WAH ?!
WAAAAAAAAAUGH!
WH- WHO ON GOD'S GREEN EARTH ARE YOU?!
YOU JUST APPEARED OUT OF THIN AIR!
HAH!
GAH!
KHEH!!
KOFF KOFF
!!!
KOFF KOFF KOFF KOFF

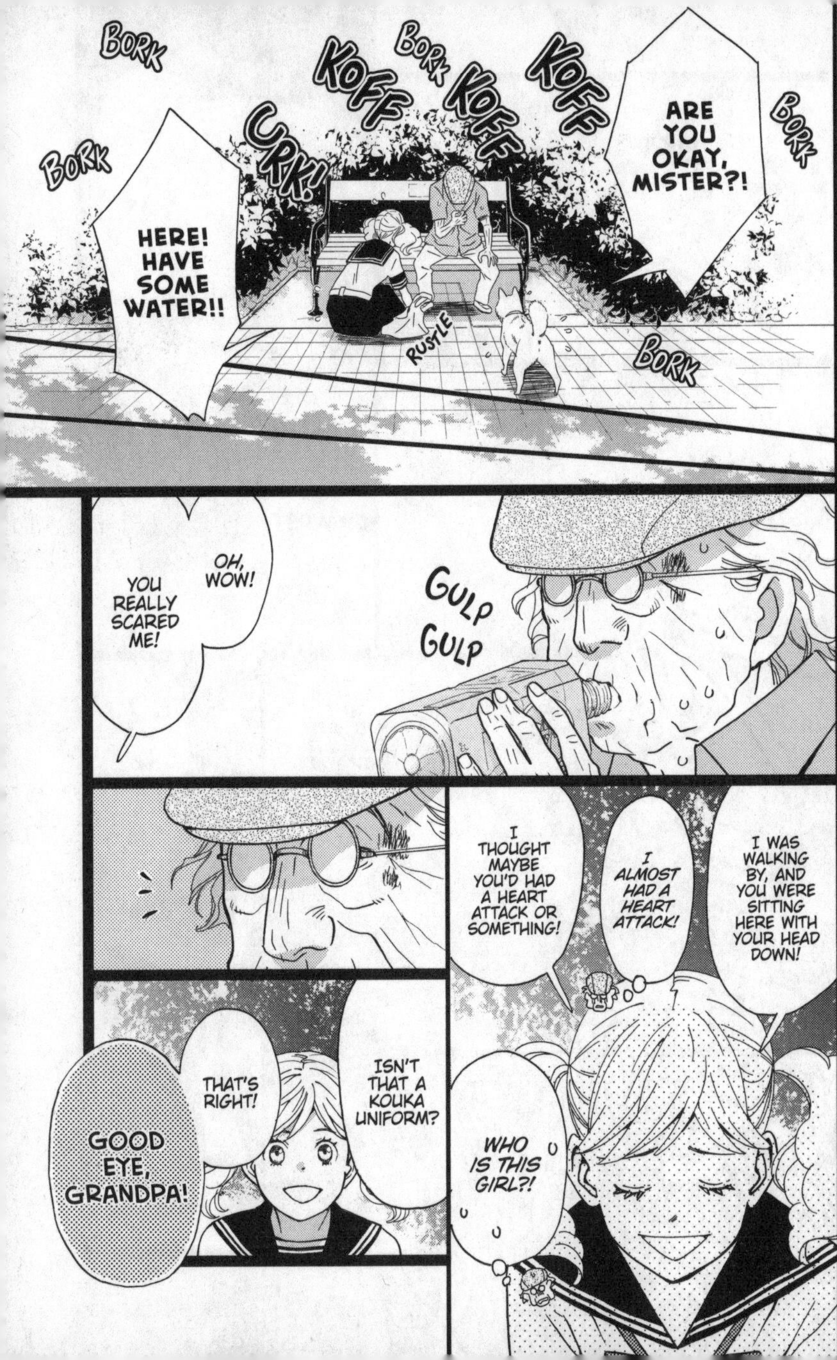
BORK
ARE YOU OKAY, MISTER?!
KOFF
KOFF
BORK
KOFF
URK!
BORK
HERE! HAVE SOME WATER!!
BORK
RUSTLE
BORK
GULP GULP
OH, WOW!
YOU REALLY SCARED ME!
I WAS WALKING BY, AND YOU WERE SITTING HERE WITH YOUR HEAD DOWN!
I ALMOST HAD A HEART ATTACK!
I THOUGHT MAYBE YOU'D HAD A HEART ATTACK OR SOMETHING!
WHO IS THIS GIRL?!
ISN'T THAT A KOUKA UNIFORM?
THAT'S RIGHT!
GOOD EYE, GRANDPA!

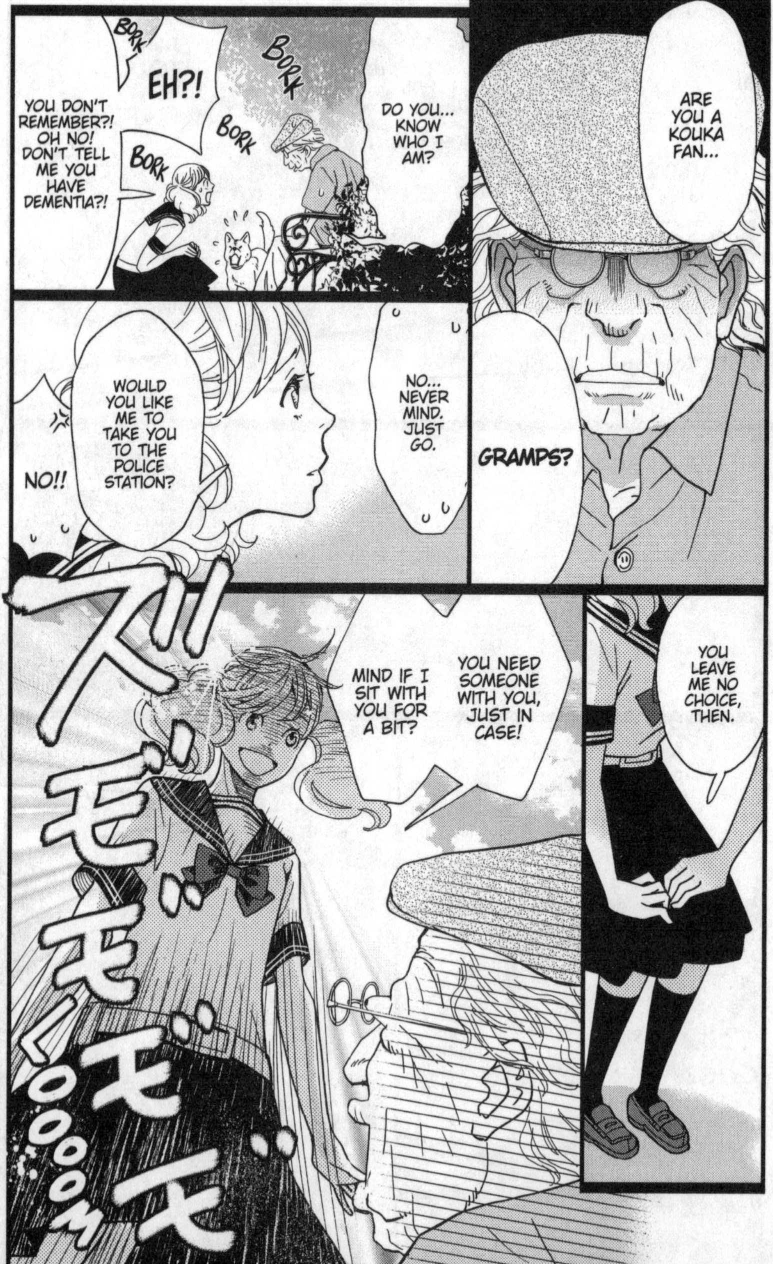
ARE YOU A KOUKA FAN...
GRAMPS?
DO YOU... KNOW WHO I AM?
BORK
BORK
EH?!
BORK
YOU DON'T REMEMBER?! OH NO! DON'T TELL ME YOU HAVE DEMENTIA?!
BORK
NO... NEVER MIND. JUST GO.
WOULD YOU LIKE ME TO TAKE YOU TO THE POLICE STATION?
NO!!
YOU LEAVE ME NO CHOICE, THEN.
YOU NEED SOMEONE WITH YOU, JUST IN CASE!
MIND IF I SIT WITH YOU FOR A BIT?
OOOOM

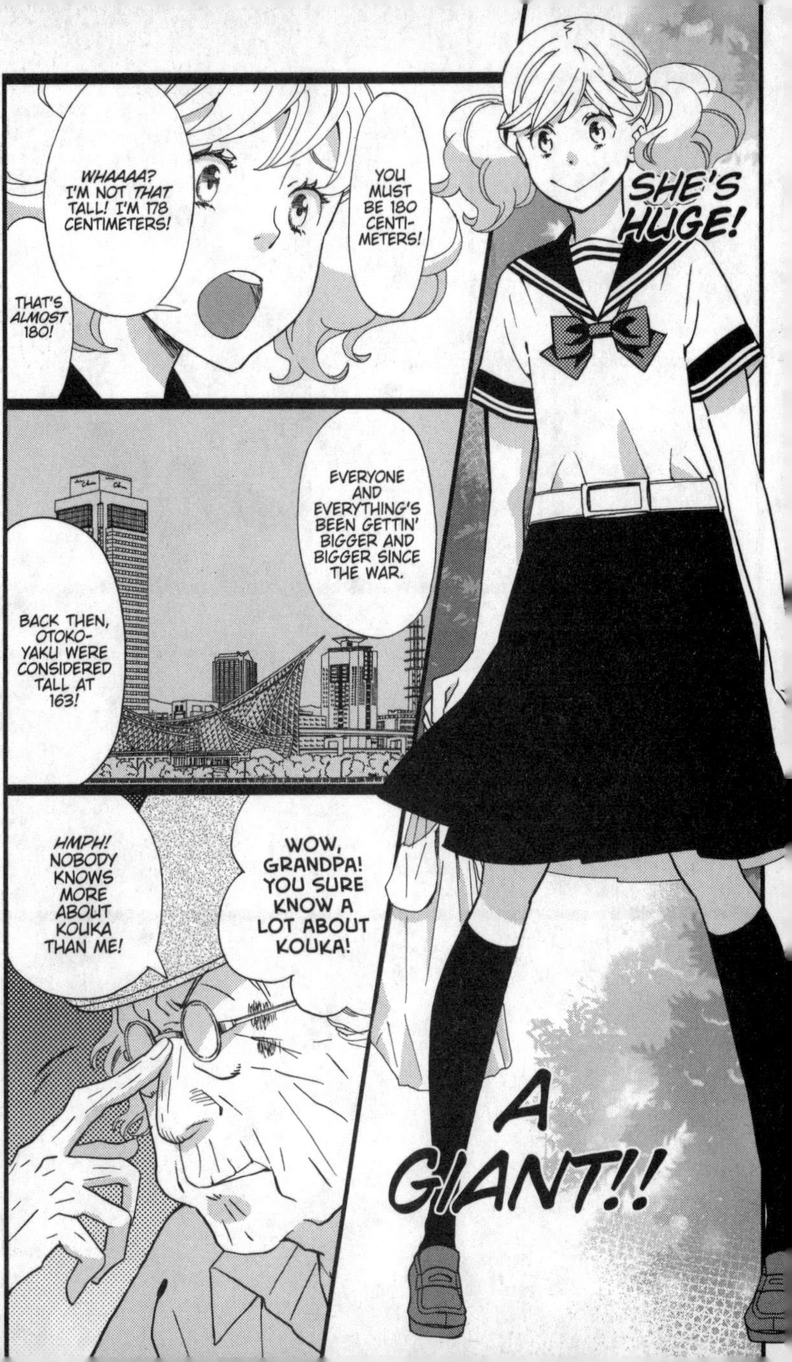
SHE'S HUGE!
A GIANT!!
YOU MUST BE 180 CENTIMETERS!
WHAAAA? I'M NOT *THAT* TALL! I'M 178 CENTIMETERS!
THAT'S *ALMOST* 180!
EVERYONE AND EVERYTHING'S BEEN GETTIN' BIGGER AND BIGGER SINCE THE WAR.
BACK THEN, OTOKO-YAKU WERE CONSIDERED TALL AT 163!
WOW, GRANDPA! YOU SURE KNOW A LOT ABOUT KOUKA!
HMPH! NOBODY KNOWS MORE ABOUT KOUKA THAN ME!

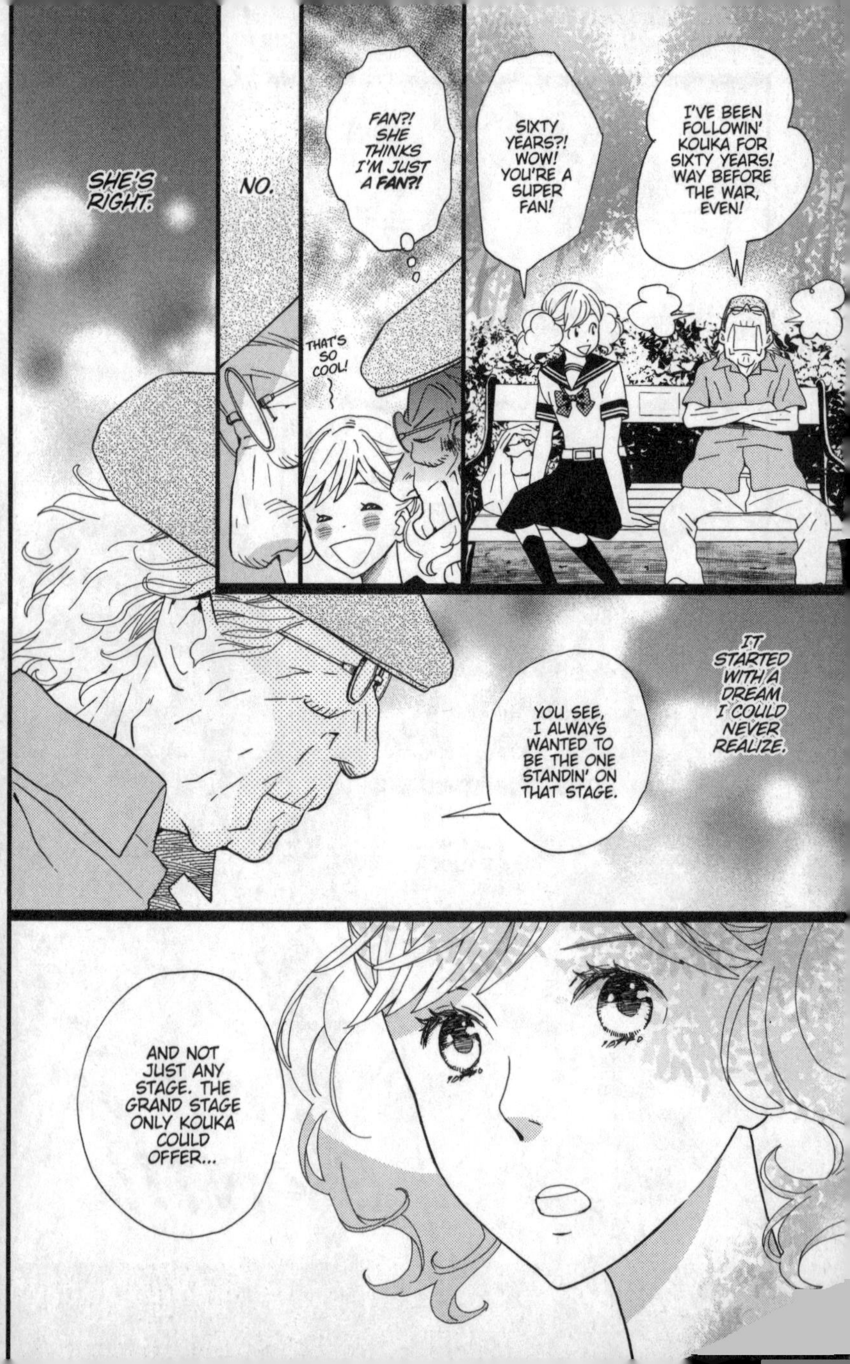
I'VE BEEN FOLLOWIN' KOUKA FOR SIXTY YEARS! WAY BEFORE THE WAR, EVEN!
SIXTY YEARS?! WOW! YOU'RE A SUPER FAN!
FAN?! SHE THINKS I'M JUST A FAN?!
THAT'S SO COOL!
NO.
SHE'S RIGHT.
IT STARTED WITH A DREAM I COULD NEVER REALIZE.
YOU SEE, I ALWAYS WANTED TO BE THE ONE STANDIN' ON THAT STAGE.
AND NOT JUST ANY STAGE. THE GRAND STAGE ONLY KOUKA COULD OFFER...

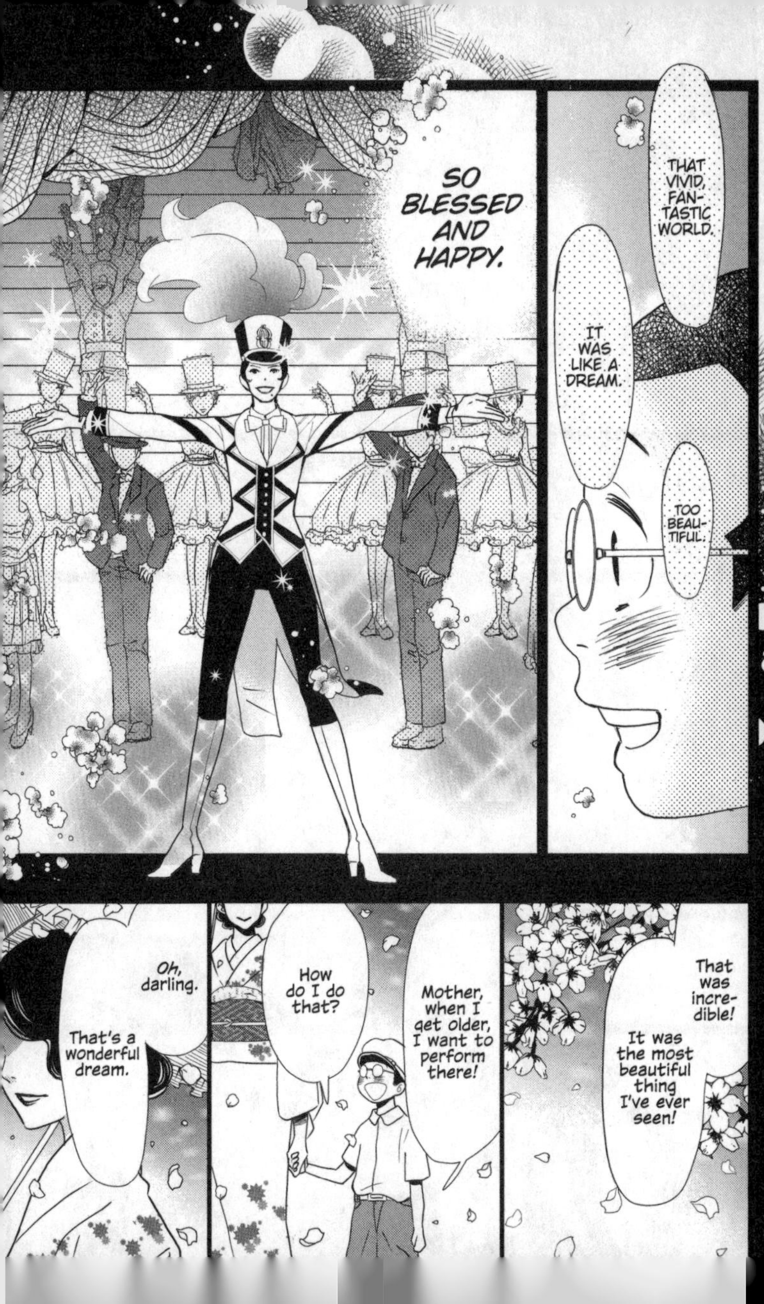
THAT VIVID, FAN-TASTIC WORLD.
IT WAS LIKE A DREAM.
TOO BEAU-TIFUL.
SO BLESSED AND HAPPY.
That was incre-dible!
It was the most beautiful thing I've ever seen!
Mother, when I get older, I want to perform there!
How do I do that?
Oh, darling.
That's a wonderful dream.

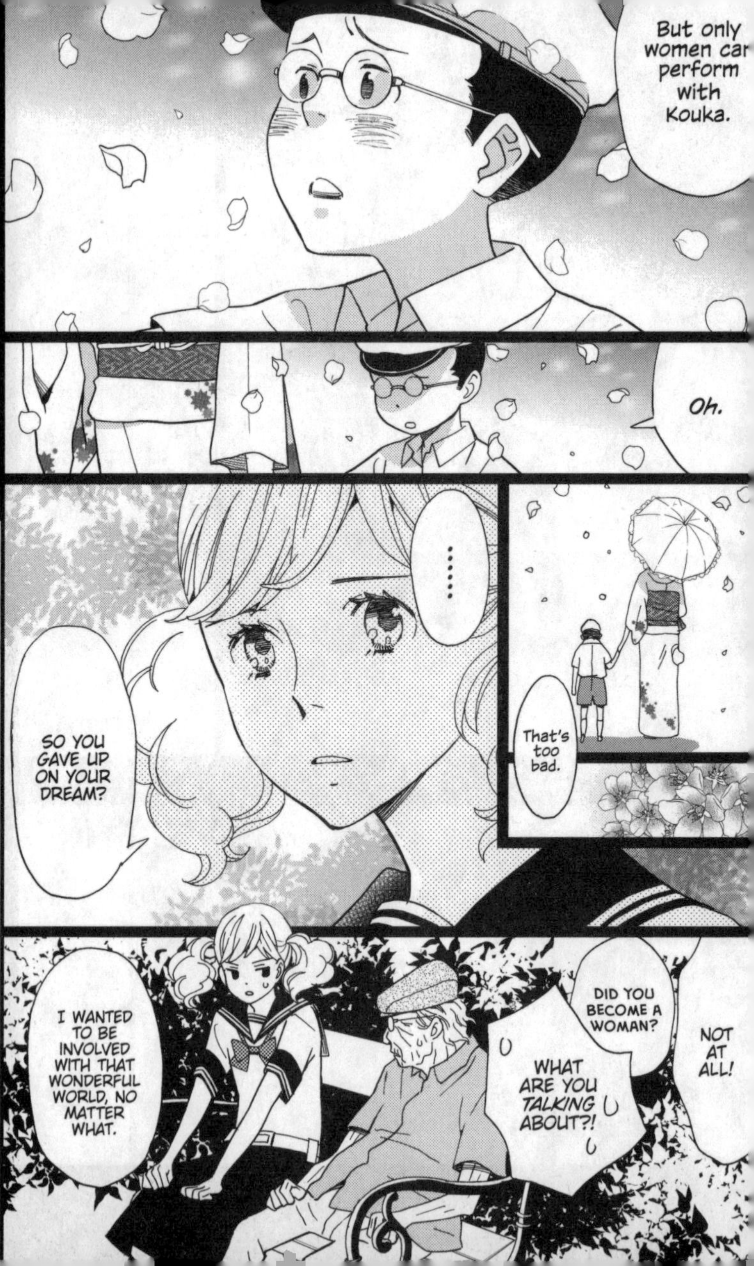
But only women ca perform with Kouka.
Oh.
That's too bad.
……
SO YOU GAVE UP ON YOUR DREAM?
NOT AT ALL!
DID YOU BECOME A WOMAN?
WHAT ARE YOU TALKING ABOUT?!
I WANTED TO BE INVOLVED WITH THAT WONDERFUL WORLD, NO MATTER WHAT.

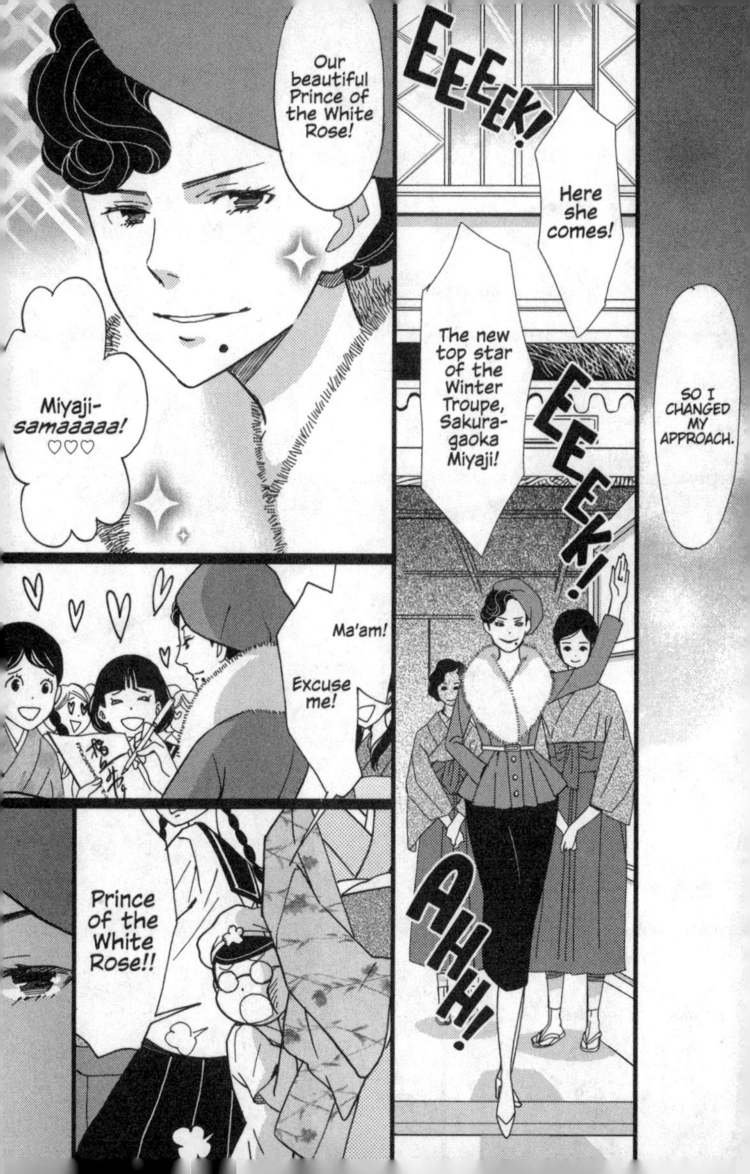
SO I CHANGED MY APPROACH.
EEEEK!
Here she comes!
The new top star of the Winter Troupe, Sakura-gaoka Miyaji!
EEEEK!
AHH!
Our beautiful Prince of the White Rose!
Miyaji-samaaaaa! ♡♡♡
Ma'am!
Excuse me!
Prince of the White Rose!!

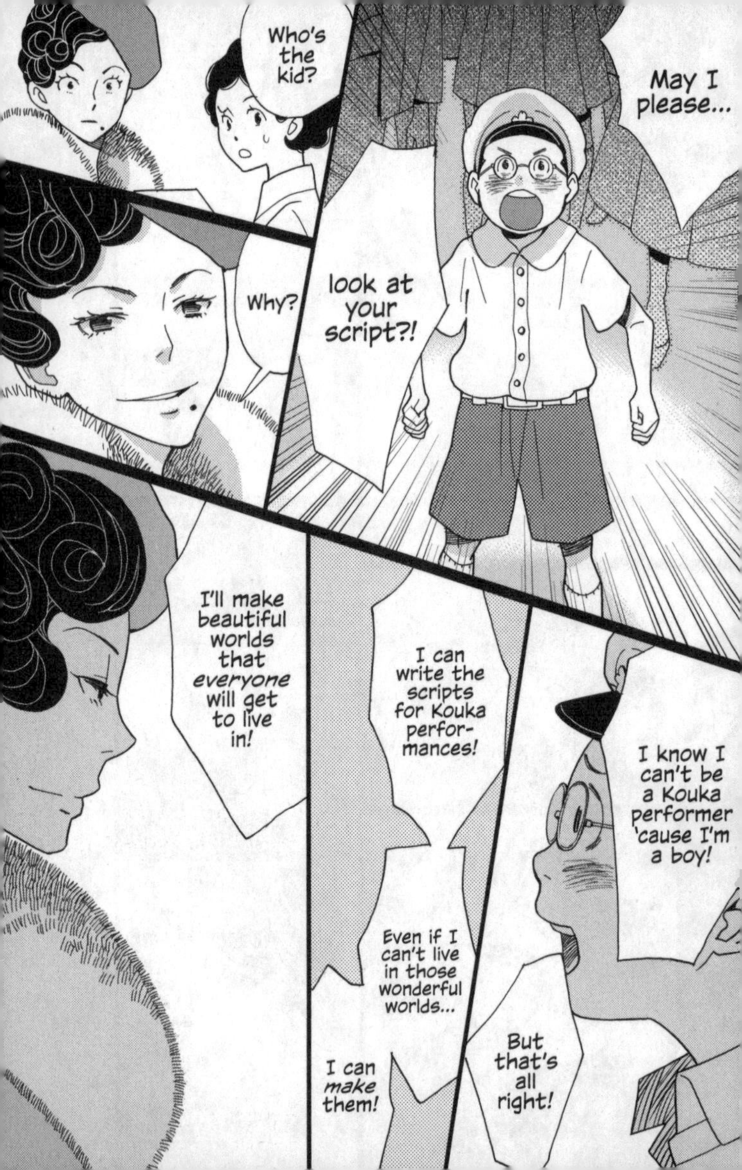
May I please...
look at your script?!
Who's the kid?
Why?
I know I can't be a Kouka performer 'cause I'm a boy!
But that's all right!
I can write the scripts for Kouka performances!
Even if I can't live in those wonderful worlds...
I can *make* them!
I'll make beautiful worlds that *everyone* will get to live in!

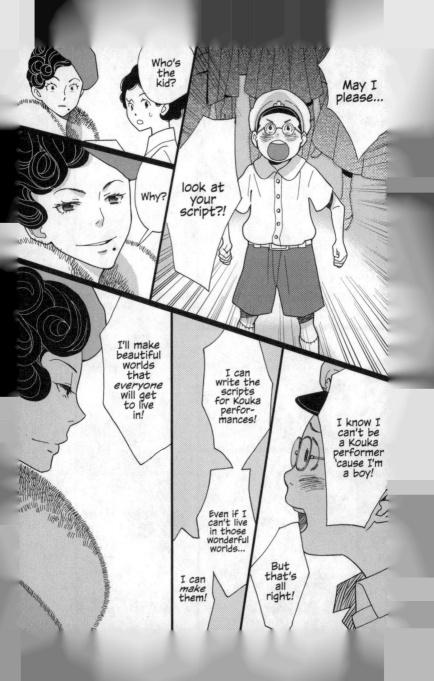

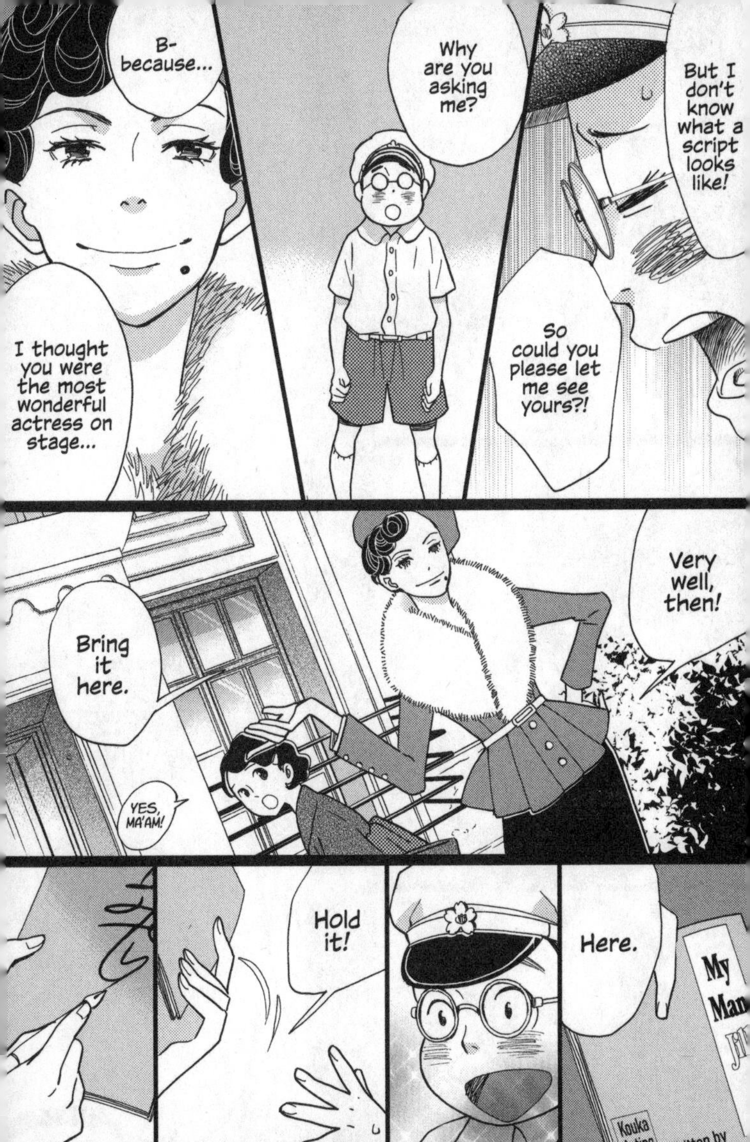
But I don't know what a script looks like!
So could you please let me see yours?!
Why are you asking me?
B- because...
I thought you were the most wonderful actress on stage...
Very well, then!
Bring it here.
YES, MA'AM!
Here.
Hold it!

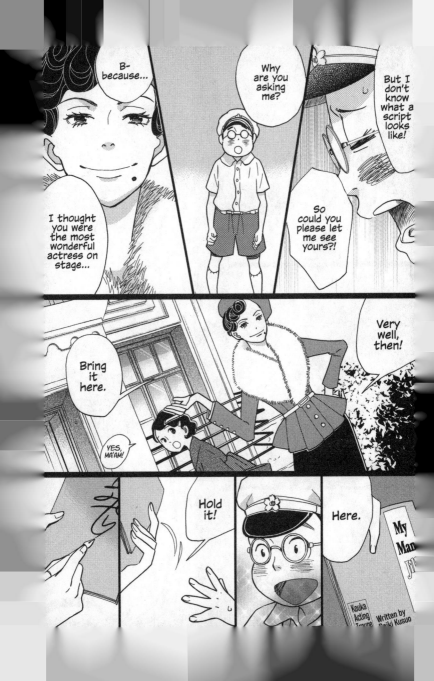

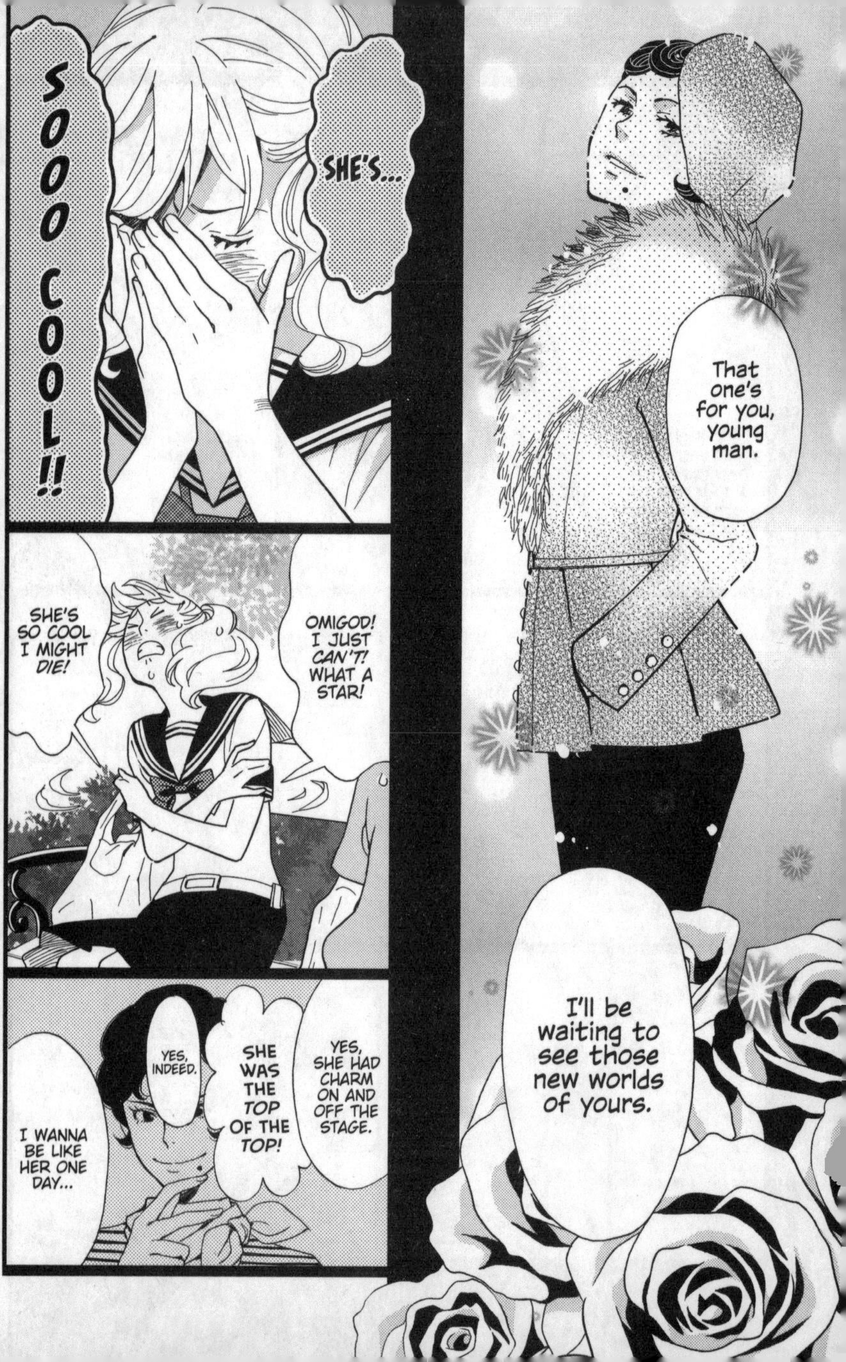
That one's for you, young man.
I'll be waiting to see those new worlds of yours.
SHE'S...
SOOOO COOL!!
OMIGOD! I JUST *CAN'T*! WHAT A STAR!
SHE'S SO COOL I MIGHT *DIE*!
YES, SHE HAD CHARM ON AND OFF THE STAGE.
SHE WAS THE *TOP* OF THE *TOP*!
YES, INDEED.
I WANNA BE LIKE HER ONE DAY...

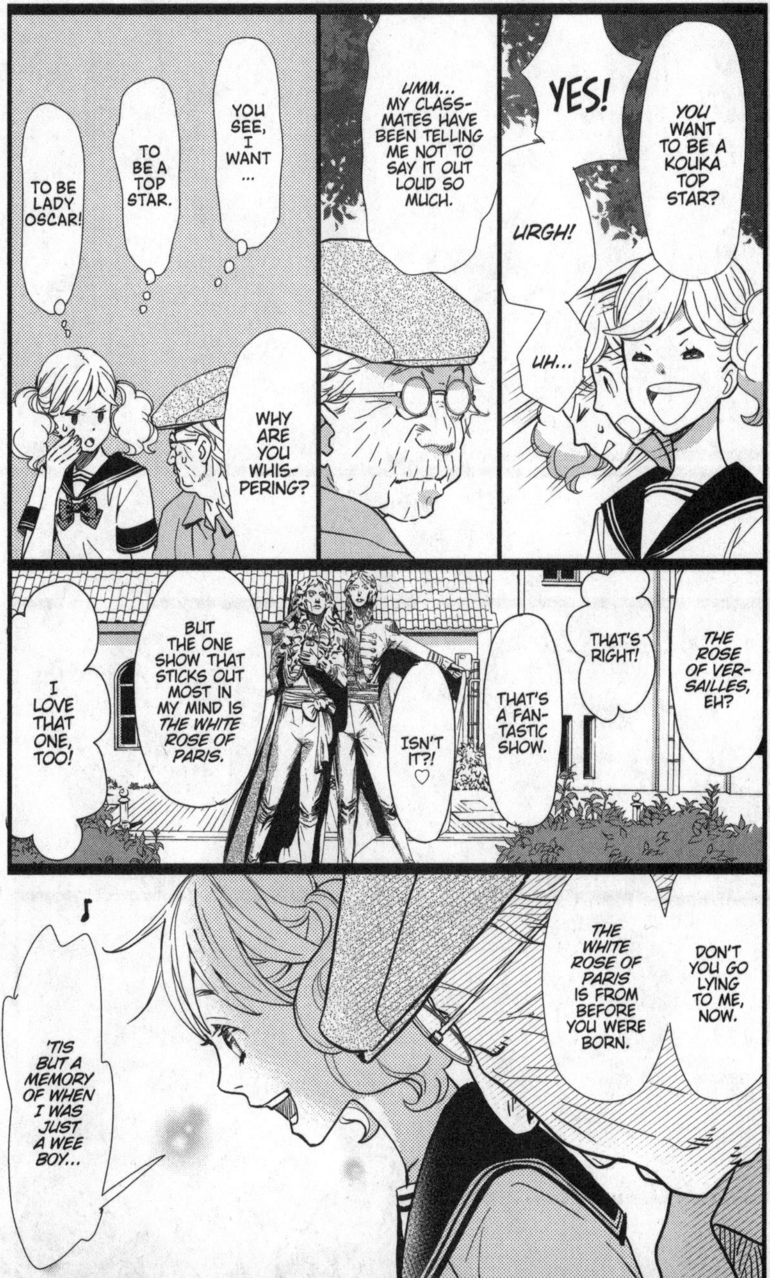
YOU WANT TO BE A KOUKA TOP STAR?
YES!
URGH!
UH...
UMM... MY CLASSMATES HAVE BEEN TELLING ME NOT TO SAY IT OUT LOUD SO MUCH.
YOU SEE, I WANT ...
TO BE A TOP STAR.
TO BE LADY OSCAR!
WHY ARE YOU WHISPERING?
THE ROSE OF VERSAILLES, EH?
THAT'S RIGHT!
THAT'S A FANTASTIC SHOW.
ISN'T IT?! ♡
BUT THE ONE SHOW THAT STICKS OUT MOST IN MY MIND IS THE WHITE ROSE OF PARIS.
I LOVE THAT ONE, TOO!
DON'T YOU GO LYING TO ME, NOW.
THE WHITE ROSE OF PARIS IS FROM BEFORE YOU WERE BORN.
'TIS BUT A MEMORY OF WHEN I WAS JUST A WEE BOY...

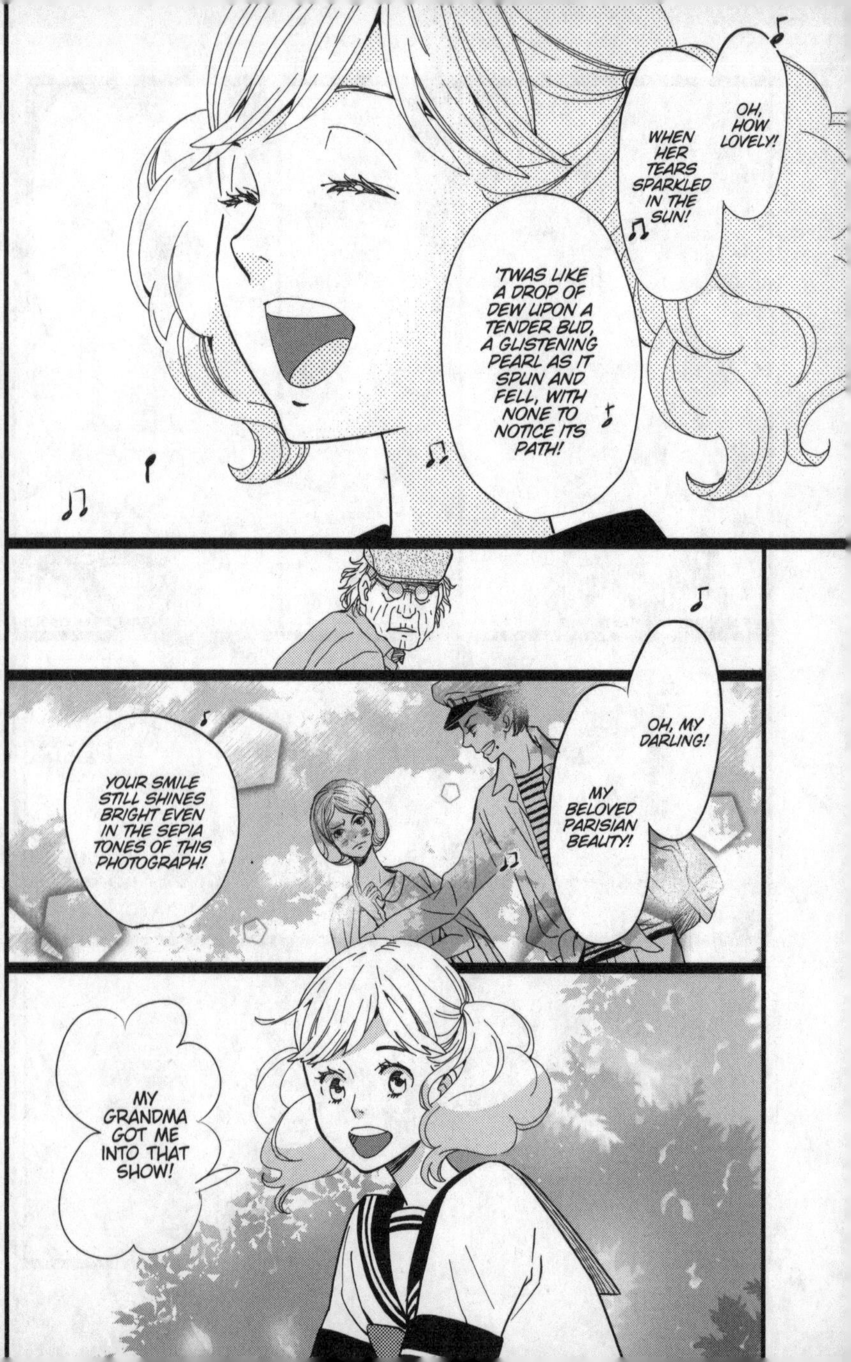

OH, HOW LOVELY!
WHEN HER TEARS SPARKLED IN THE SUN!
'TWAS LIKE A DROP OF DEW UPON A TENDER BUD, A GLISTENING PEARL AS IT SPUN AND FELL, WITH NONE TO NOTICE ITS PATH!
OH, MY DARLING!
MY BELOVED PARISIAN BEAUTY!
YOUR SMILE STILL SHINES BRIGHT EVEN IN THE SEPIA TONES OF THIS PHOTOGRAPH!
MY GRANDMA GOT ME INTO THAT SHOW!

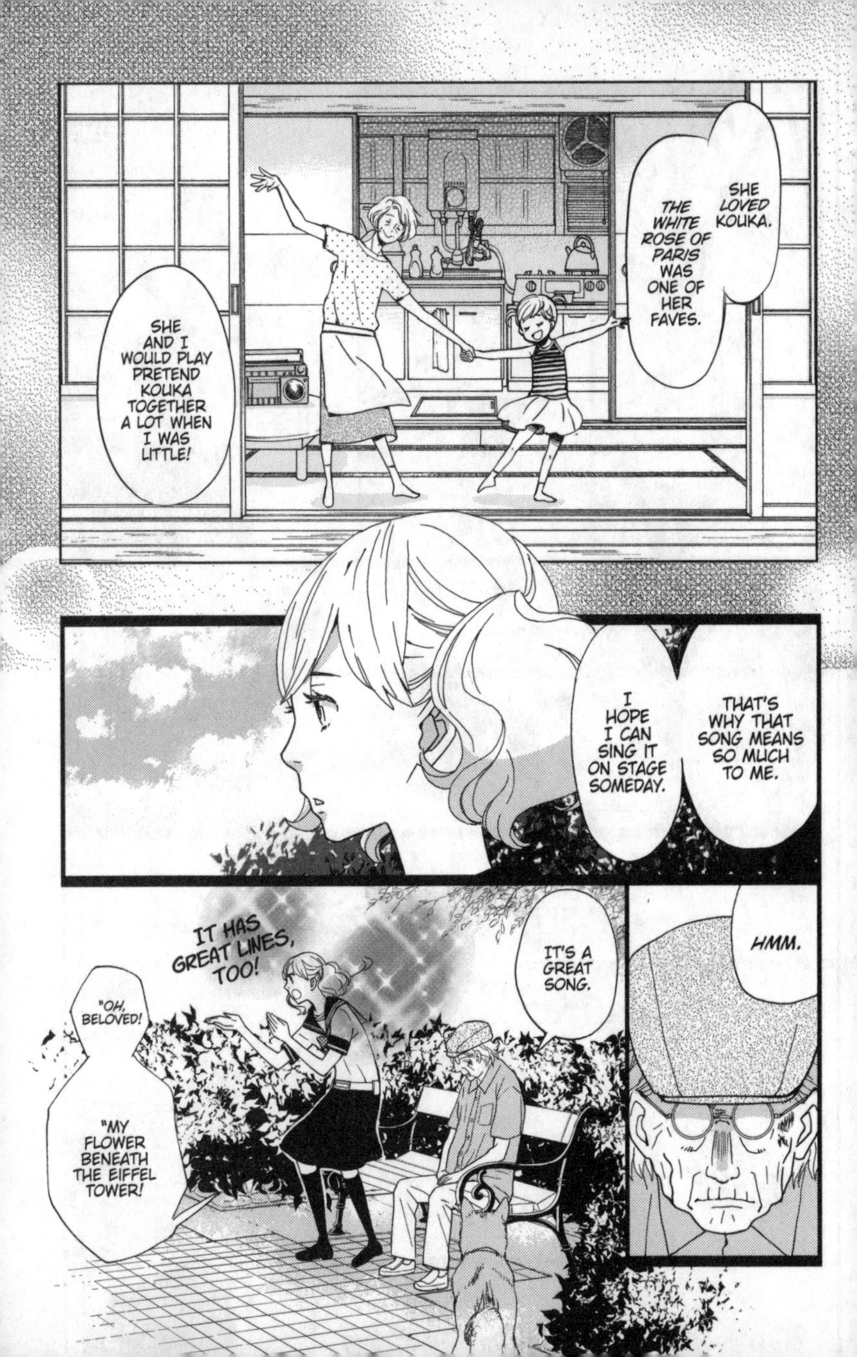
SHE LOVED KOUKA.
THE WHITE ROSE OF PARIS WAS ONE OF HER FAVES.
SHE AND I WOULD PLAY PRETEND KOUKA TOGETHER A LOT WHEN I WAS LITTLE!
THAT'S WHY THAT SONG MEANS SO MUCH TO ME.
I HOPE I CAN SING IT ON STAGE SOMEDAY.
HMM.
IT'S A GREAT SONG.
IT HAS GREAT LINES, TOO!
"OH, BELOVED!
"MY FLOWER BENEATH THE EIFFEL TOWER!

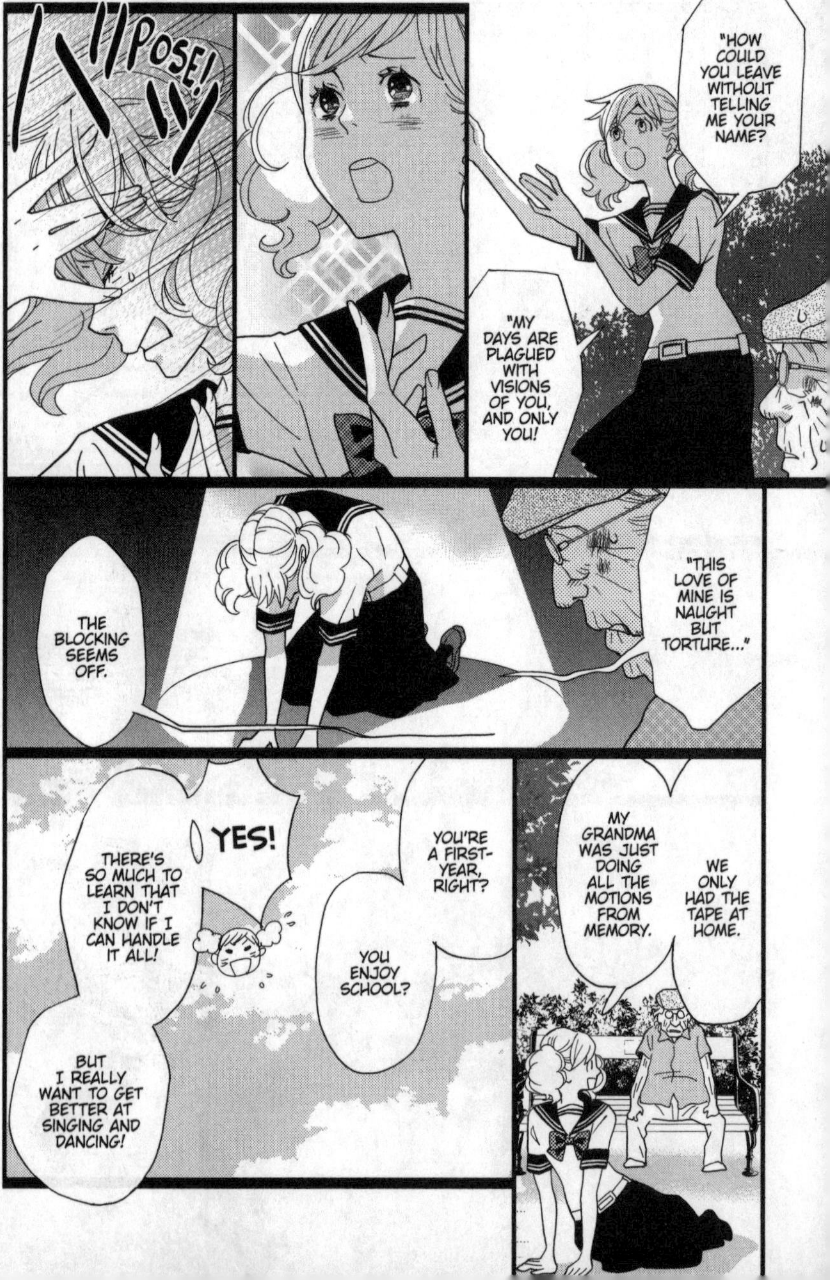
"HOW COULD YOU LEAVE WITHOUT TELLING ME YOUR NAME?
"MY DAYS ARE PLAGUED WITH VISIONS OF YOU, AND ONLY YOU!
POSE!
"THIS LOVE OF MINE IS NAUGHT BUT TORTURE..."
THE BLOCKING SEEMS OFF.
WE ONLY HAD THE TAPE AT HOME.
MY GRANDMA WAS JUST DOING ALL THE MOTIONS FROM MEMORY.
YOU'RE A FIRST-YEAR, RIGHT?
YOU ENJOY SCHOOL?
YES!
THERE'S SO MUCH TO LEARN THAT I DON'T KNOW IF I CAN HANDLE IT ALL!
BUT I REALLY WANT TO GET BETTER AT SINGING AND DANCING!

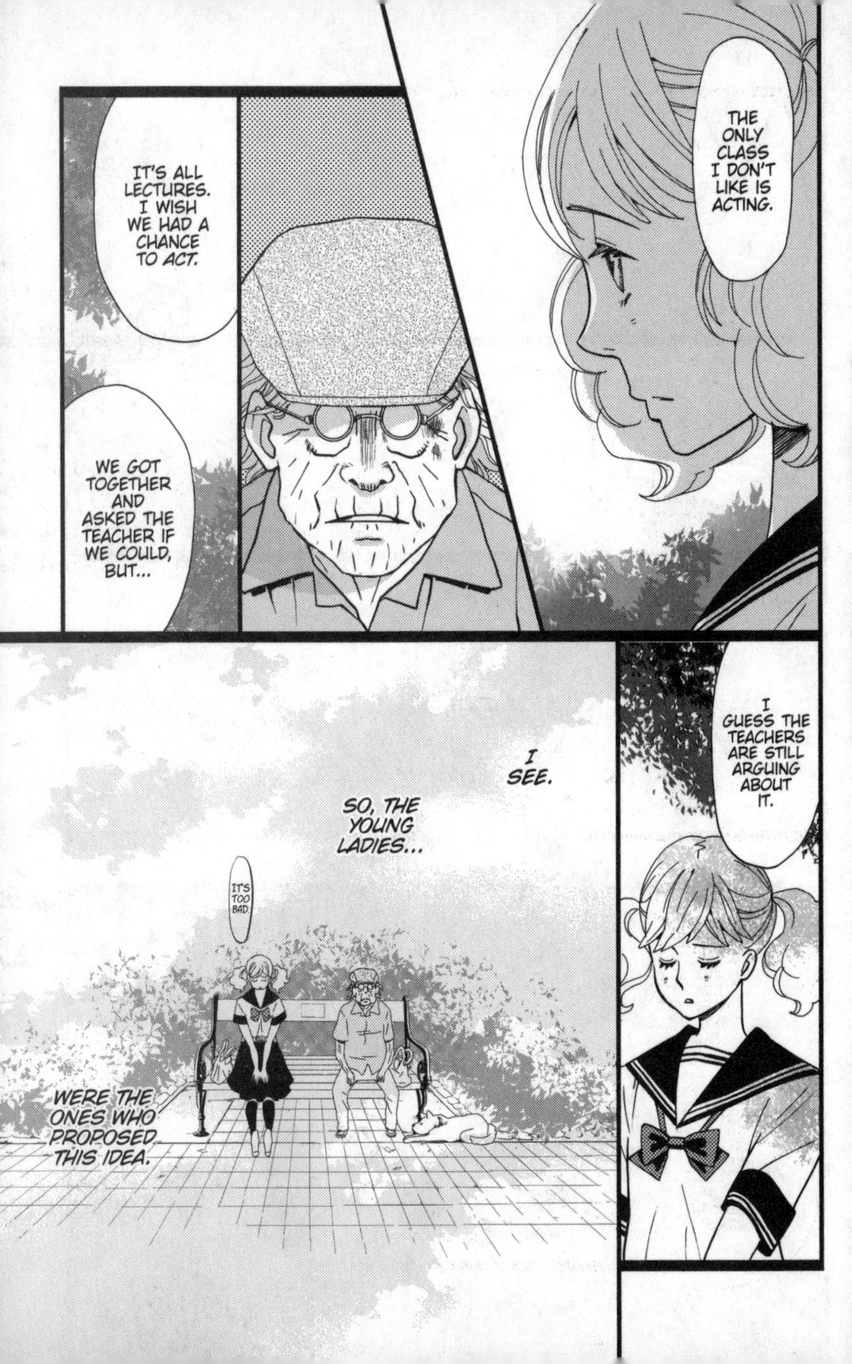
THE ONLY CLASS I DON'T LIKE IS ACTING.
IT'S ALL LECTURES. I WISH WE HAD A CHANCE TO ACT.
WE GOT TOGETHER AND ASKED THE TEACHER IF WE COULD, BUT...
I GUESS THE TEACHERS ARE STILL ARGUING ABOUT IT.
I SEE.
SO, THE YOUNG LADIES...
IT'S TOO BAD.
WERE THE ONES WHO PROPOSED THIS IDEA.

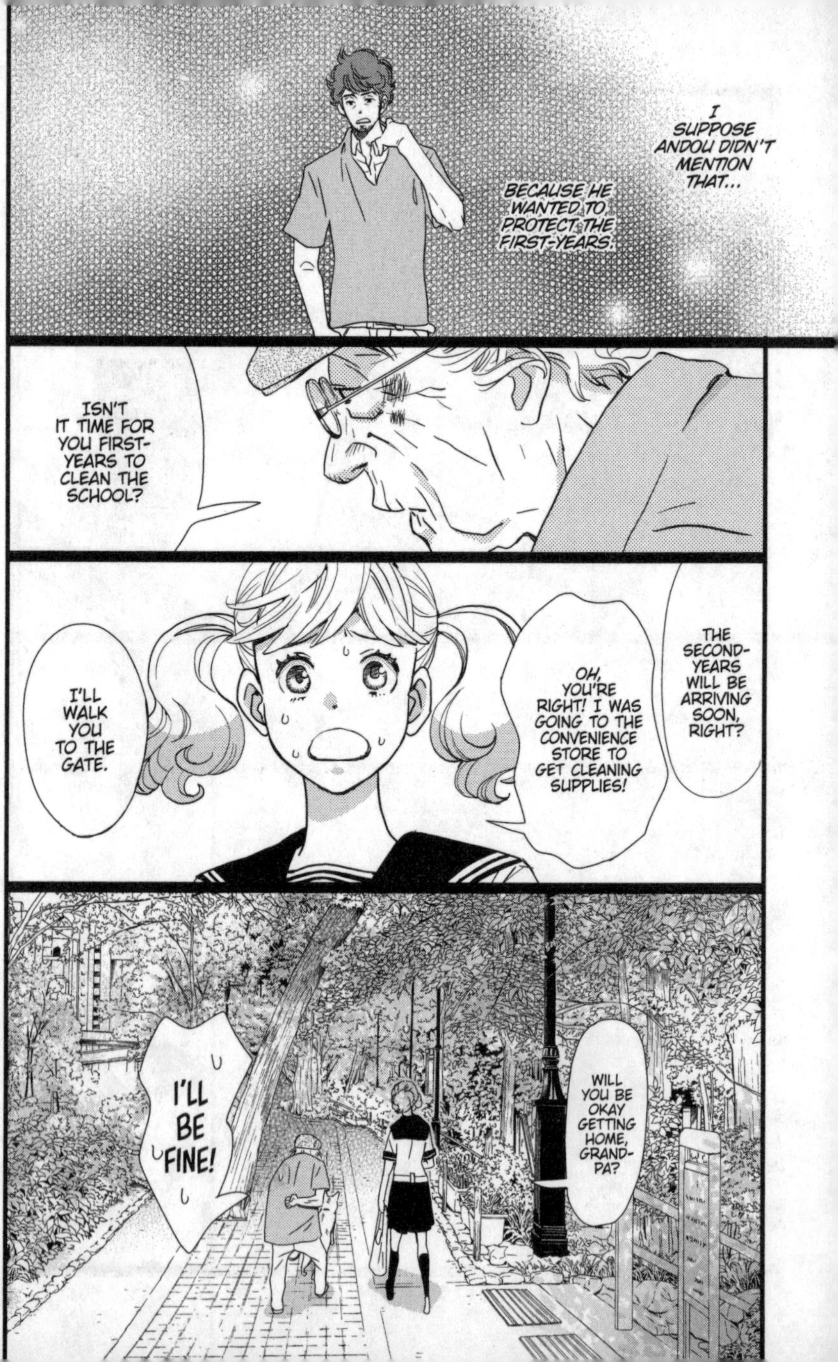
I SUPPOSE ANDOU DIDN'T MENTION THAT...
BECAUSE HE WANTED TO PROTECT THE FIRST-YEARS.
ISN'T IT TIME FOR YOU FIRST-YEARS TO CLEAN THE SCHOOL?
THE SECOND-YEARS WILL BE ARRIVING SOON, RIGHT?
OH, YOU'RE RIGHT! I WAS GOING TO THE CONVENIENCE STORE TO GET CLEANING SUPPLIES!
I'LL WALK YOU TO THE GATE.
WILL YOU BE OKAY GETTING HOME, GRANDPA?
I'LL BE FINE!

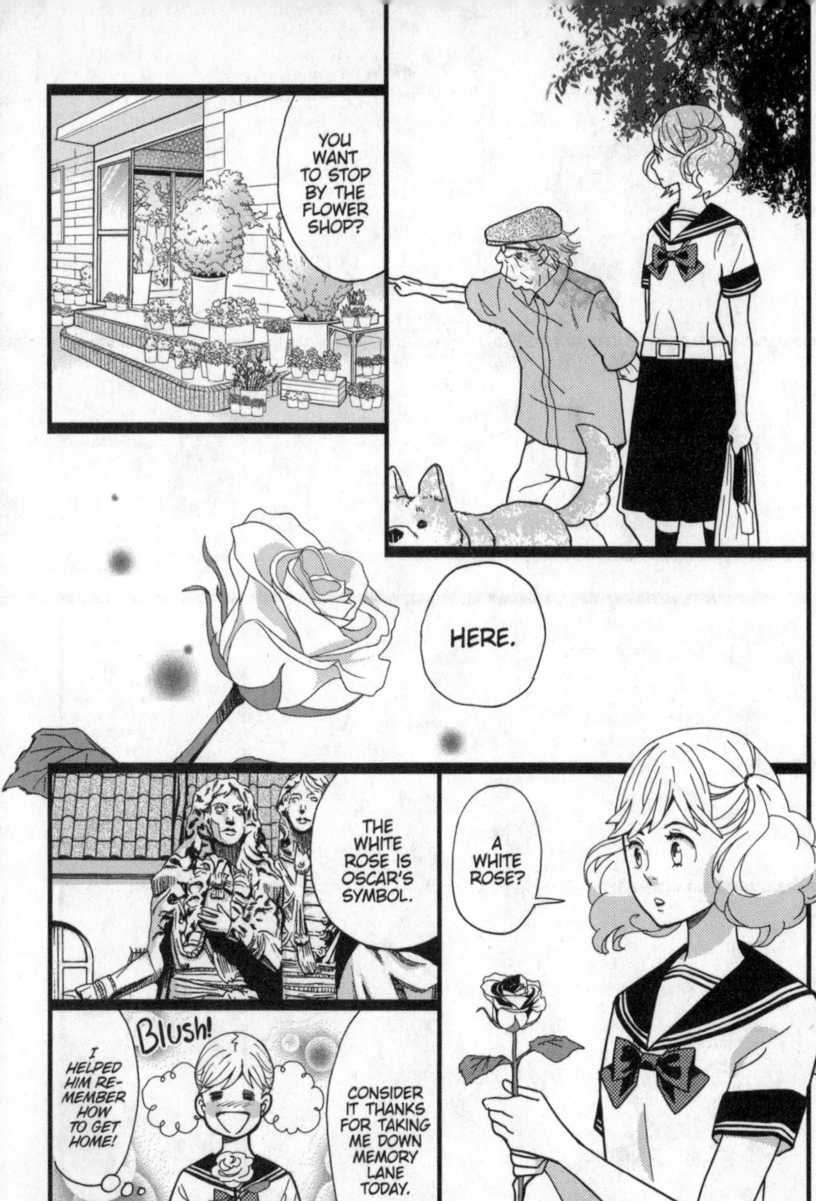
YOU WANT TO STOP BY THE FLOWER SHOP?
HERE.
A WHITE ROSE?
THE WHITE ROSE IS OSCAR'S SYMBOL.
CONSIDER IT THANKS FOR TAKING ME DOWN MEMORY LANE TODAY.
Blush!
I HELPED HIM RE-MEMBER HOW TO GET HOME!

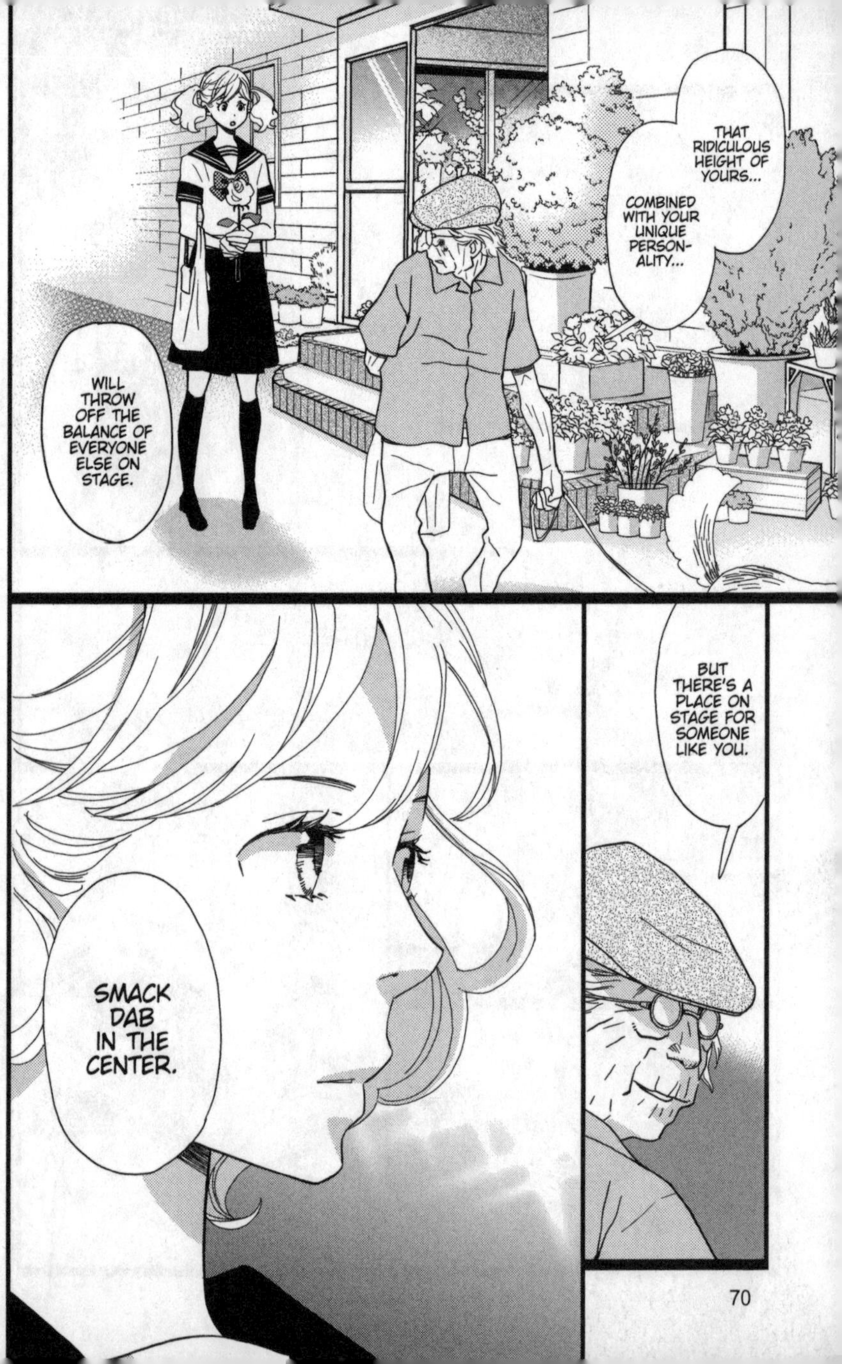
THAT RIDICULOUS HEIGHT OF YOURS...
COMBINED WITH YOUR UNIQUE PERSON-ALITY...
WILL THROW OFF THE BALANCE OF EVERYONE ELSE ON STAGE.
BUT THERE'S A PLACE ON STAGE FOR SOMEONE LIKE YOU.
SMACK DAB IN THE CENTER.

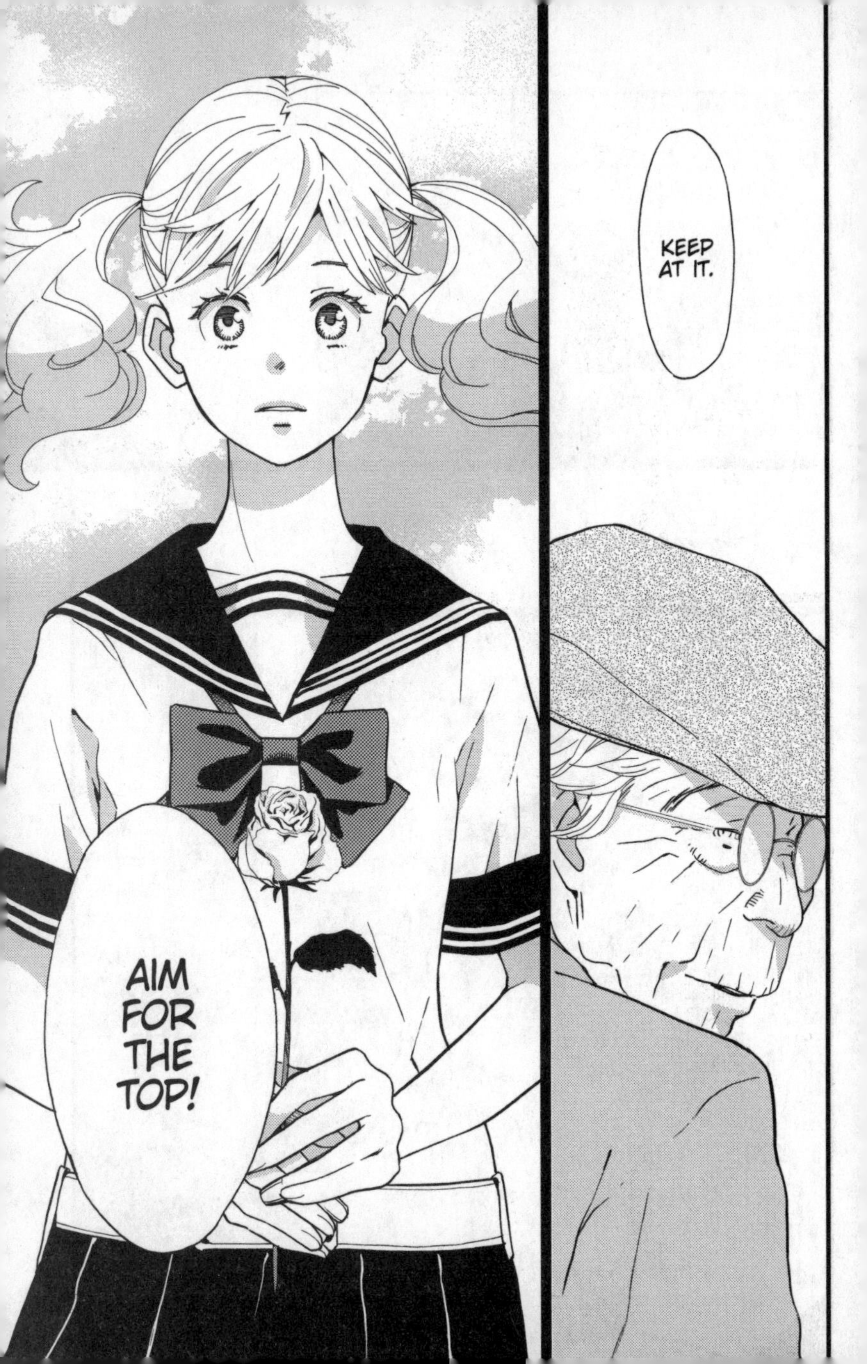
KEEP AT IT.
AIM FOR THE TOP!

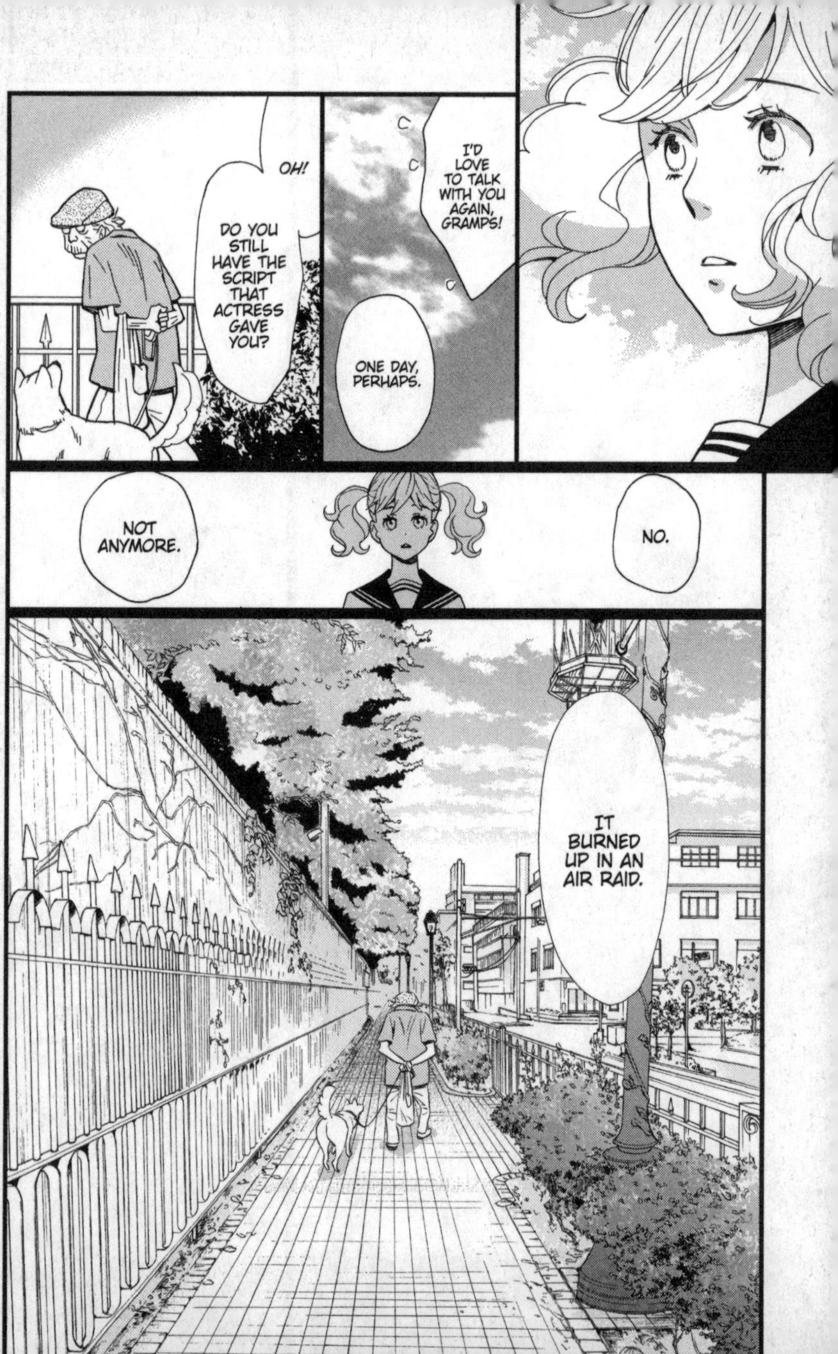
I'D LOVE TO TALK WITH YOU AGAIN, GRAMPS!
ONE DAY, PERHAPS.
OH!
DO YOU STILL HAVE THE SCRIPT THAT ACTRESS GAVE YOU?
NO.
NOT ANYMORE.
IT BURNED UP IN AN AIR RAID.

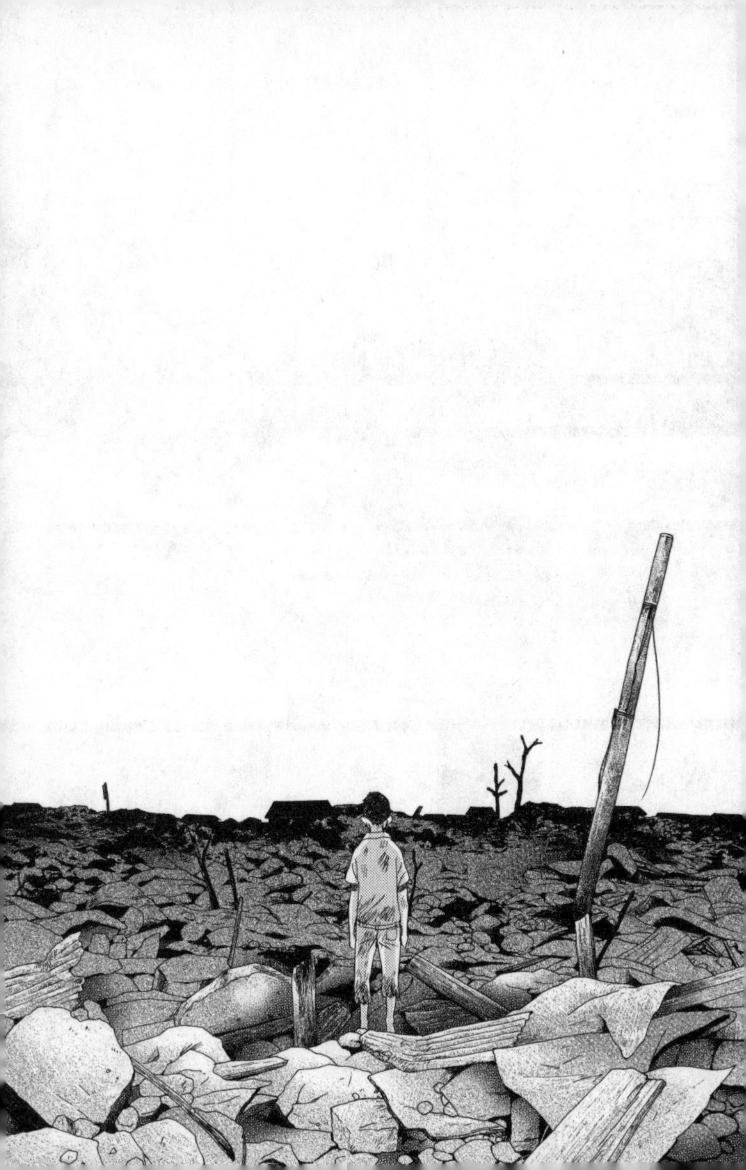

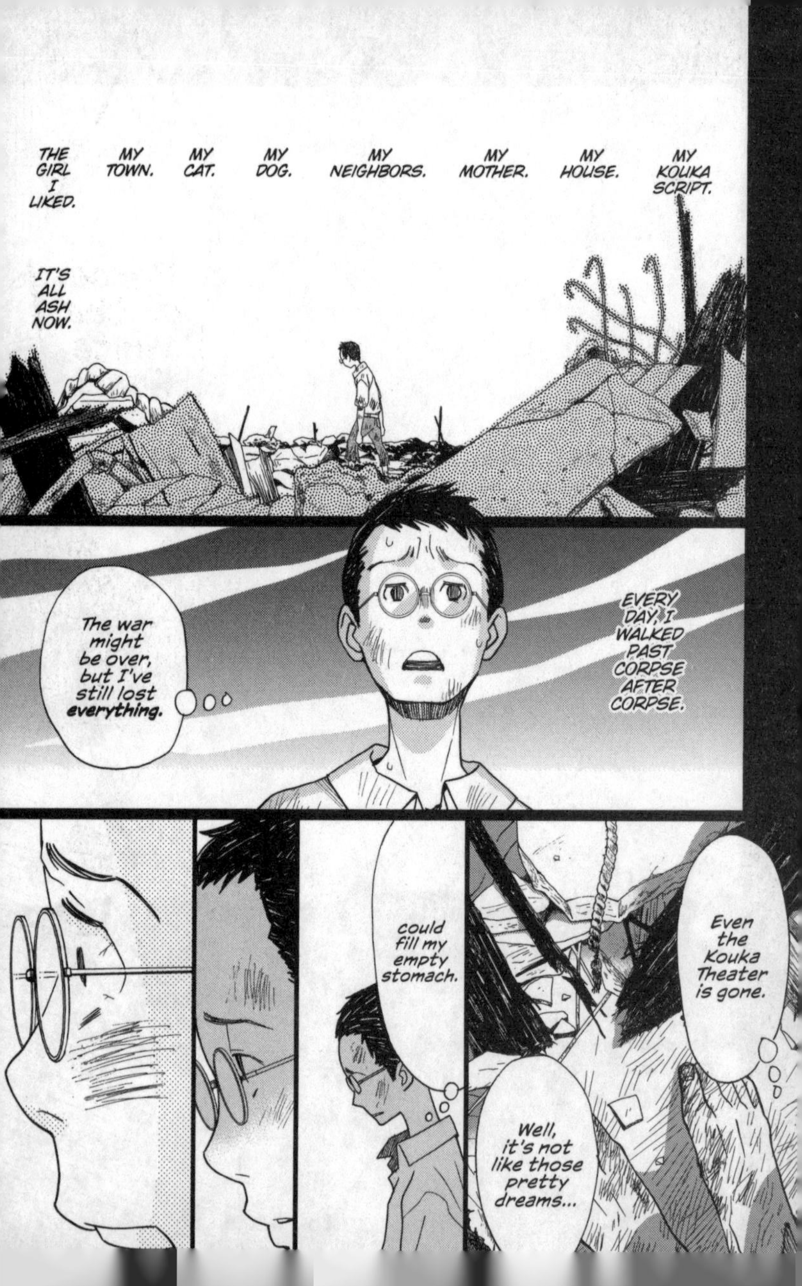
MY KOUKA SCRIPT.
MY HOUSE.
MY MOTHER.
MY NEIGHBORS.
MY DOG.
MY CAT.
MY TOWN.
THE GIRL I LIKED.
IT'S ALL ASH NOW.
EVERY DAY, I WALKED PAST CORPSE AFTER CORPSE.
The war might be over, but I've still lost **everything.**
Even the Kouka Theater is gone.
Well, it's not like those pretty dreams...
could fill my empty stomach.

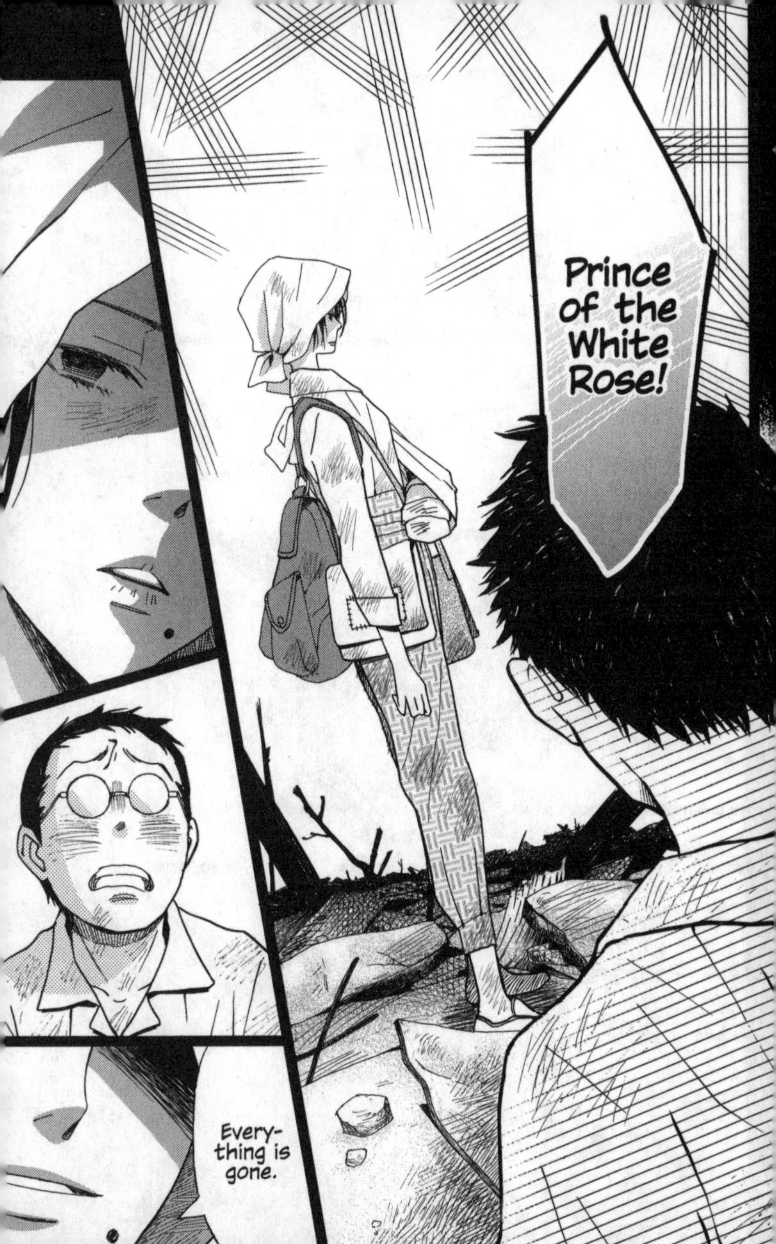
Prince of the White Rose!
Every-thing is gone.

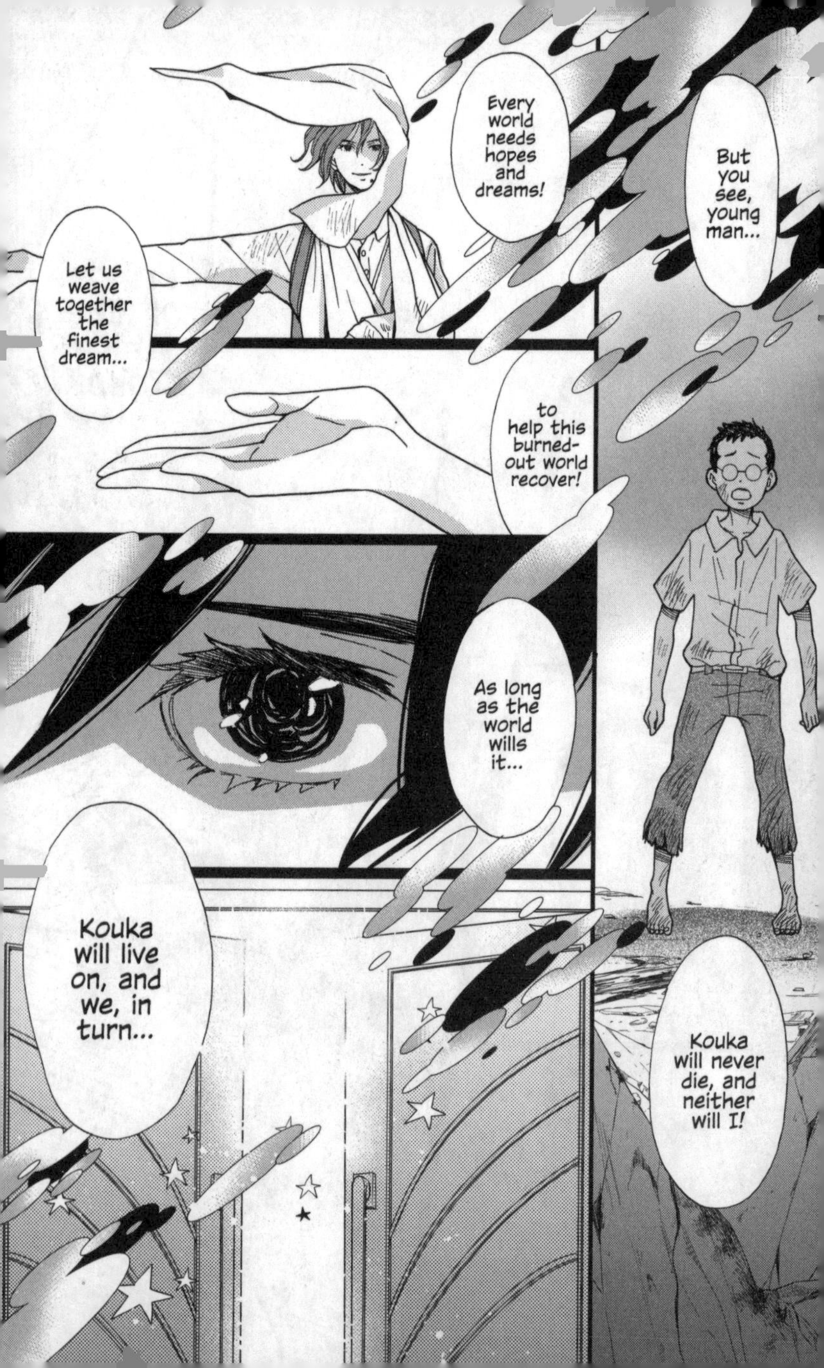
But you see, young man...
Every world needs hopes and dreams!
Let us weave together the finest dream...
to help this burned-out world recover!
As long as the world wills it...
Kouka will live on, and we, in turn...
Kouka will never die, and neither will I!

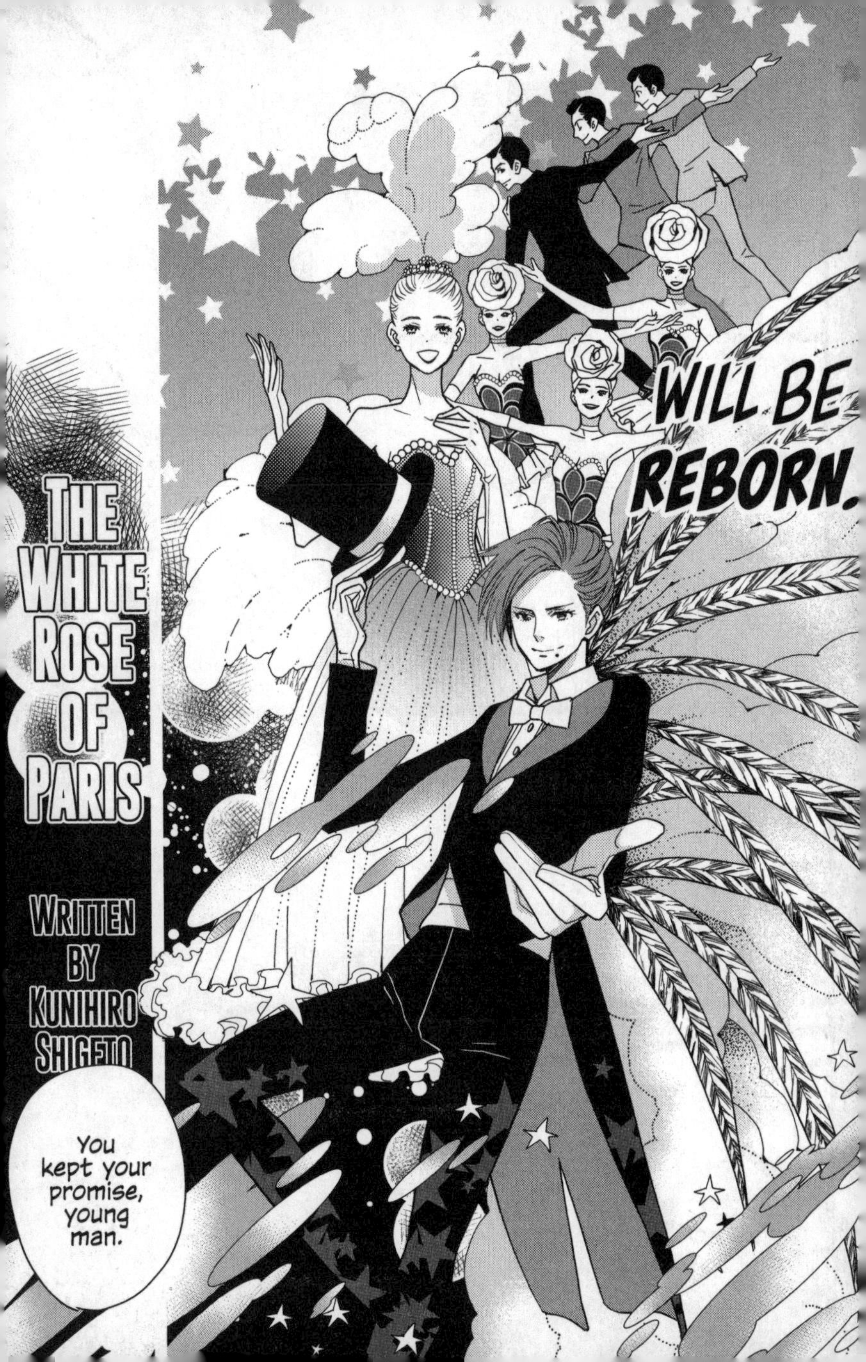
WILL BE REBORN.
THE WHITE ROSE OF PARIS
WRITTEN BY KUNIHIRO SHIGETO
You kept your promise, young man.

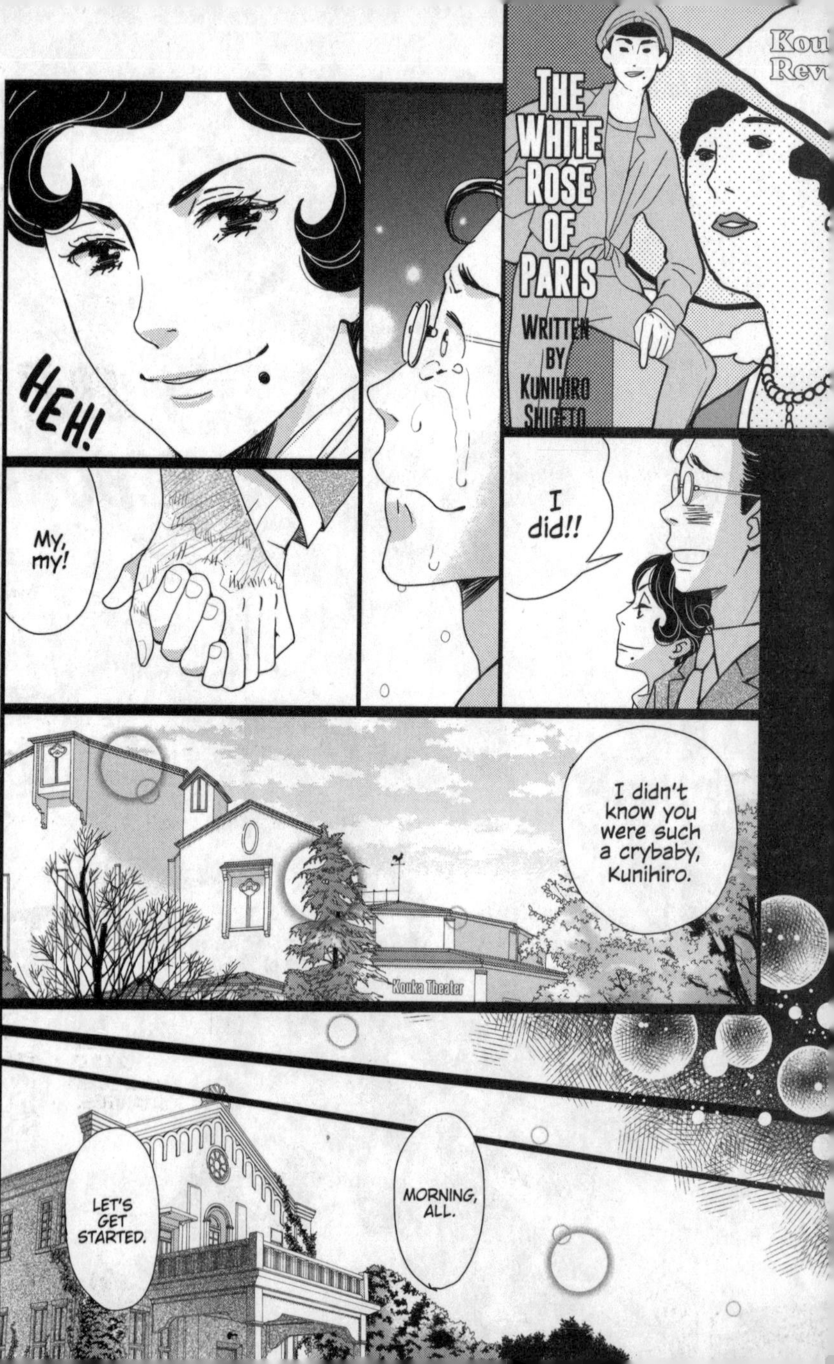
THE WHITE ROSE OF PARIS
WRITTEN BY KUNIHIRO SHIGETO
I did!!
HEH!
My, my!
I didn't know you were such a crybaby, Kunihiro.
Kouka Theater
MORNING, ALL.
LET'S GET STARTED.

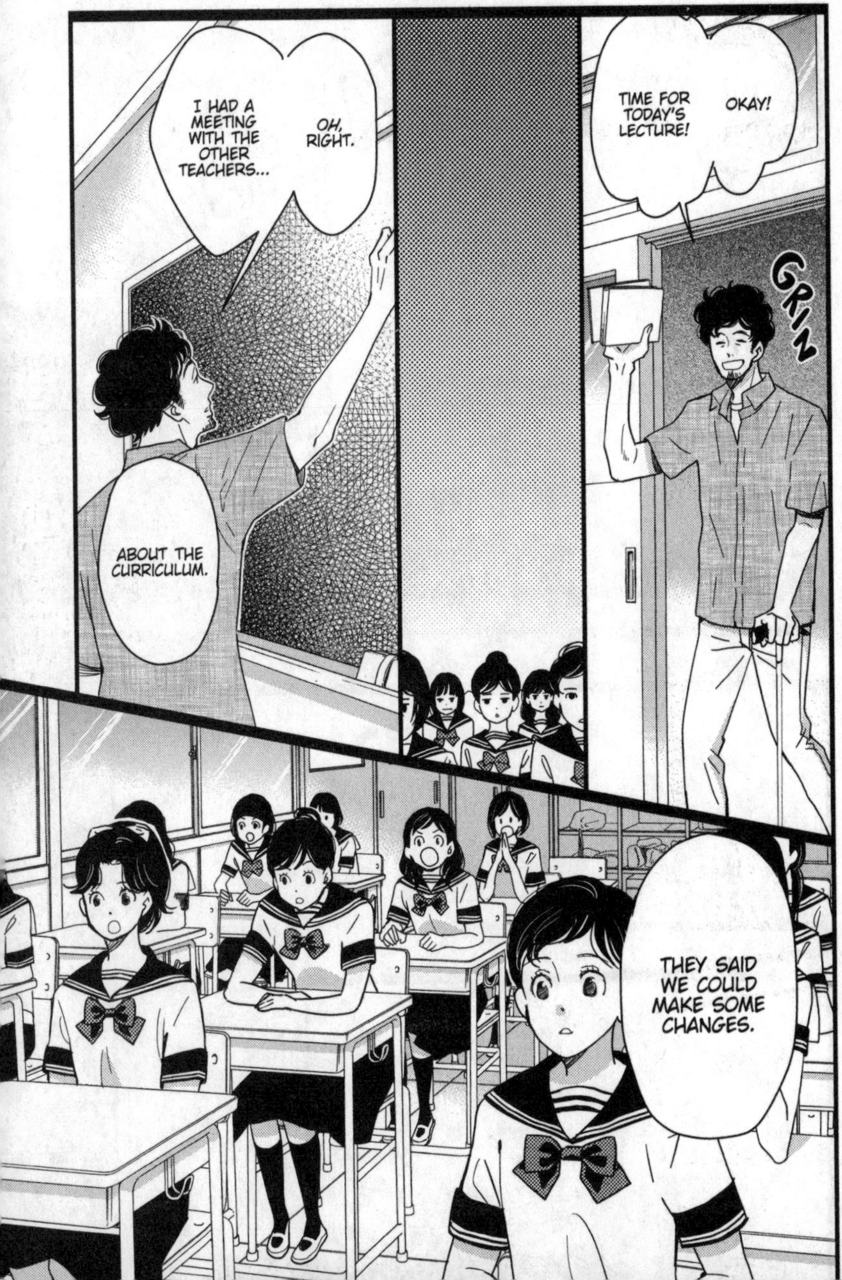
OKAY!
TIME FOR TODAY'S LECTURE!
GRIN
OH, RIGHT.
I HAD A MEETING WITH THE OTHER TEACHERS...
ABOUT THE CURRICULUM.
THEY SAID WE COULD MAKE SOME CHANGES.

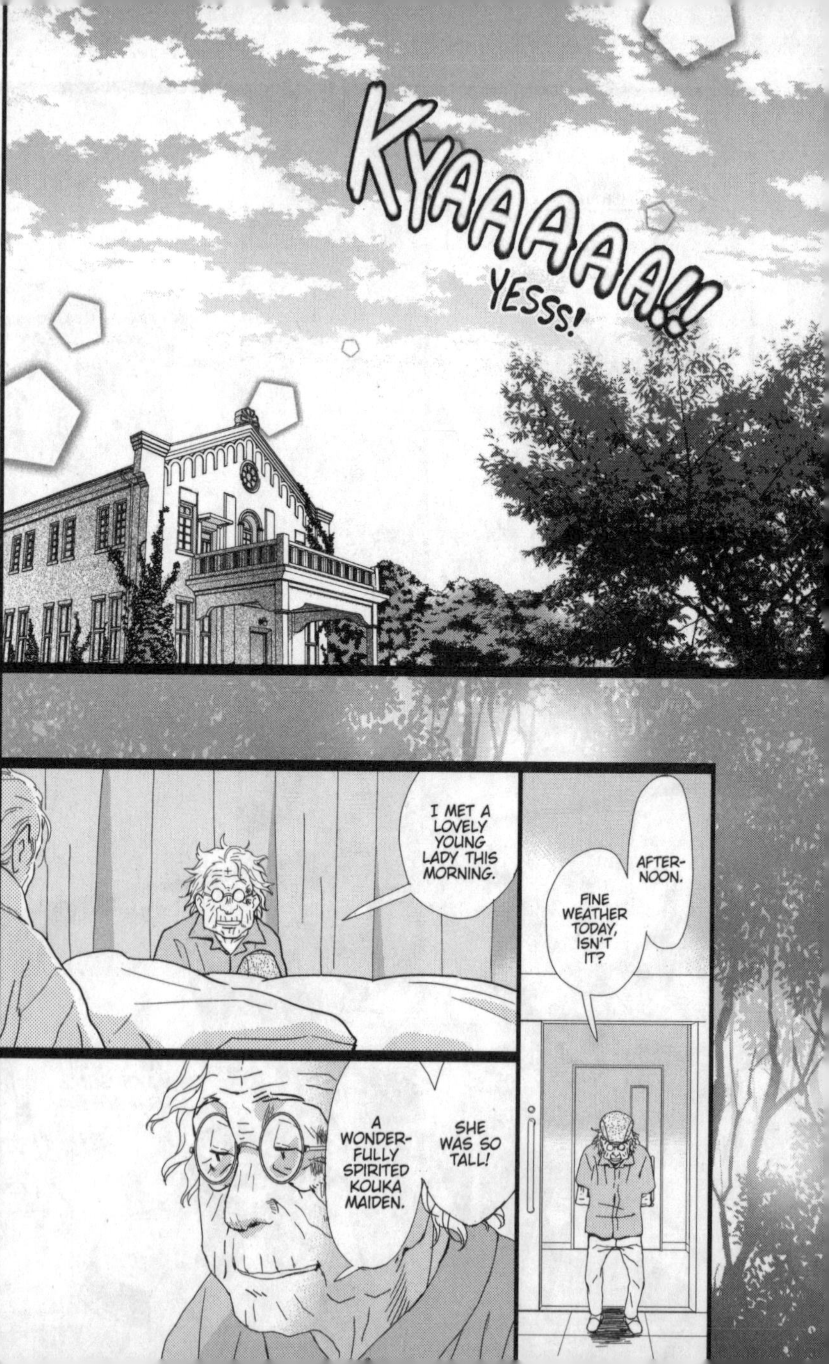
KYAAAAAA!!
YESSS!
AFTER-NOON.
FINE WEATHER TODAY, ISN'T IT?
I MET A LOVELY YOUNG LADY THIS MORNING.
SHE WAS SO TALL!
A WONDER-FULLY SPIRITED KOUKA MAIDEN.

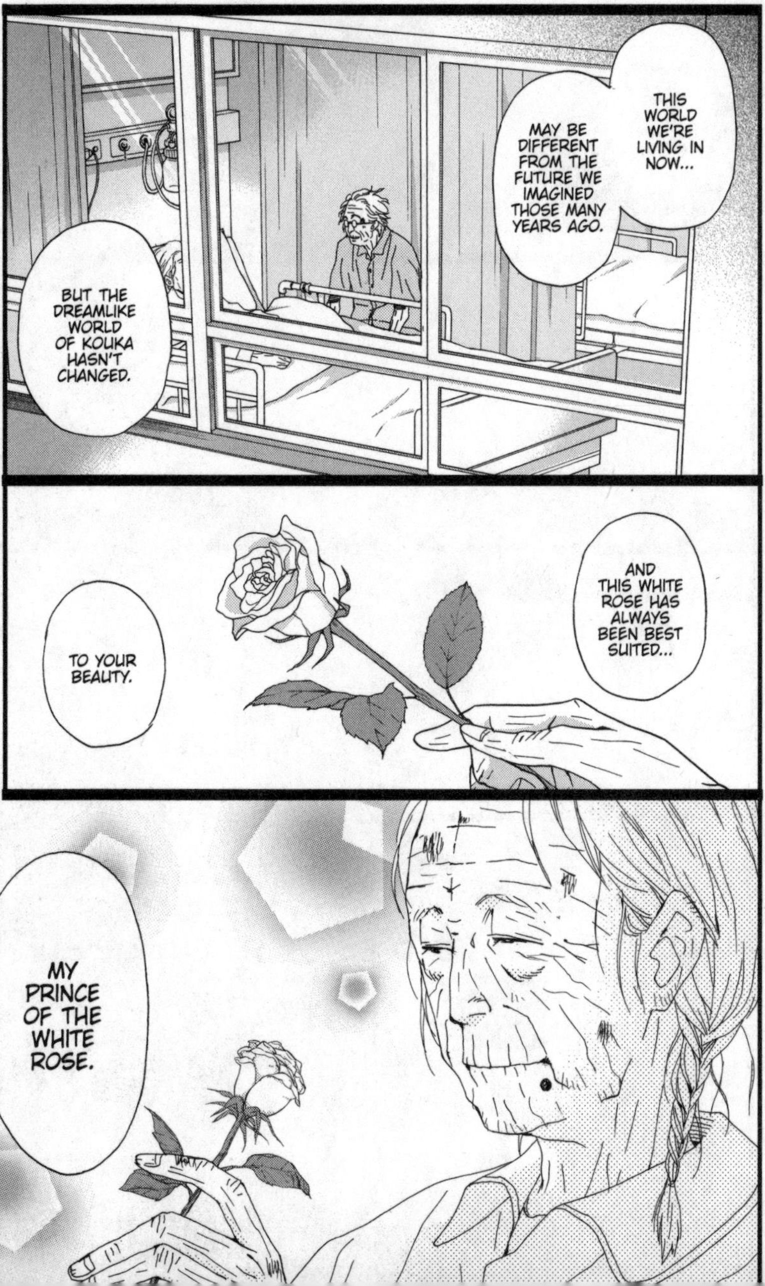
THIS WORLD WE'RE LIVING IN NOW...
MAY BE DIFFERENT FROM THE FUTURE WE IMAGINED THOSE MANY YEARS AGO.
BUT THE DREAMLIKE WORLD OF KOUKA HASN'T CHANGED.
AND THIS WHITE ROSE HAS ALWAYS BEEN BEST SUITED...
TO YOUR BEAUTY.
MY PRINCE OF THE WHITE ROSE.

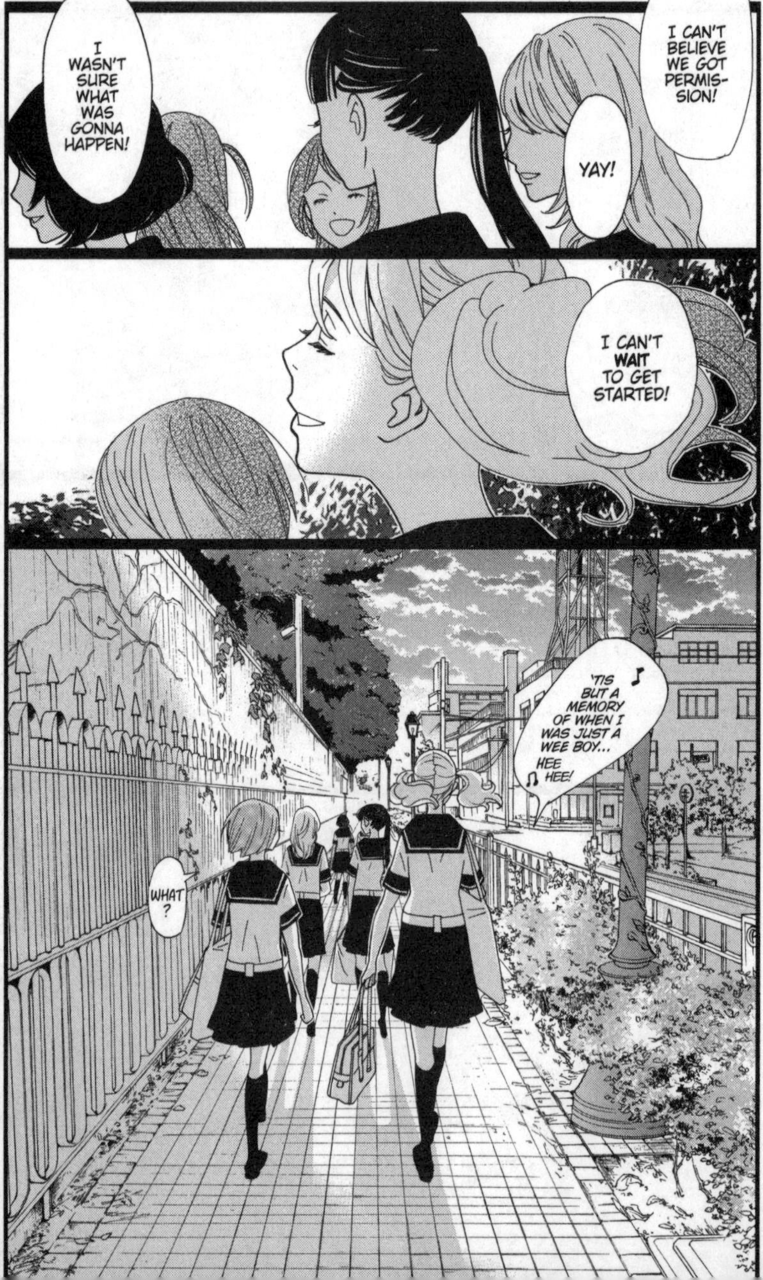
I CAN'T BELIEVE WE GOT PERMIS-SION!
YAY!
I WASN'T SURE WHAT WAS GONNA HAPPEN!
I CAN'T WAIT TO GET STARTED!
'TIS BUT A MEMORY OF WHEN I WAS JUST A WEE BOY... ♪
HEE HEE! ♫
WHAT?

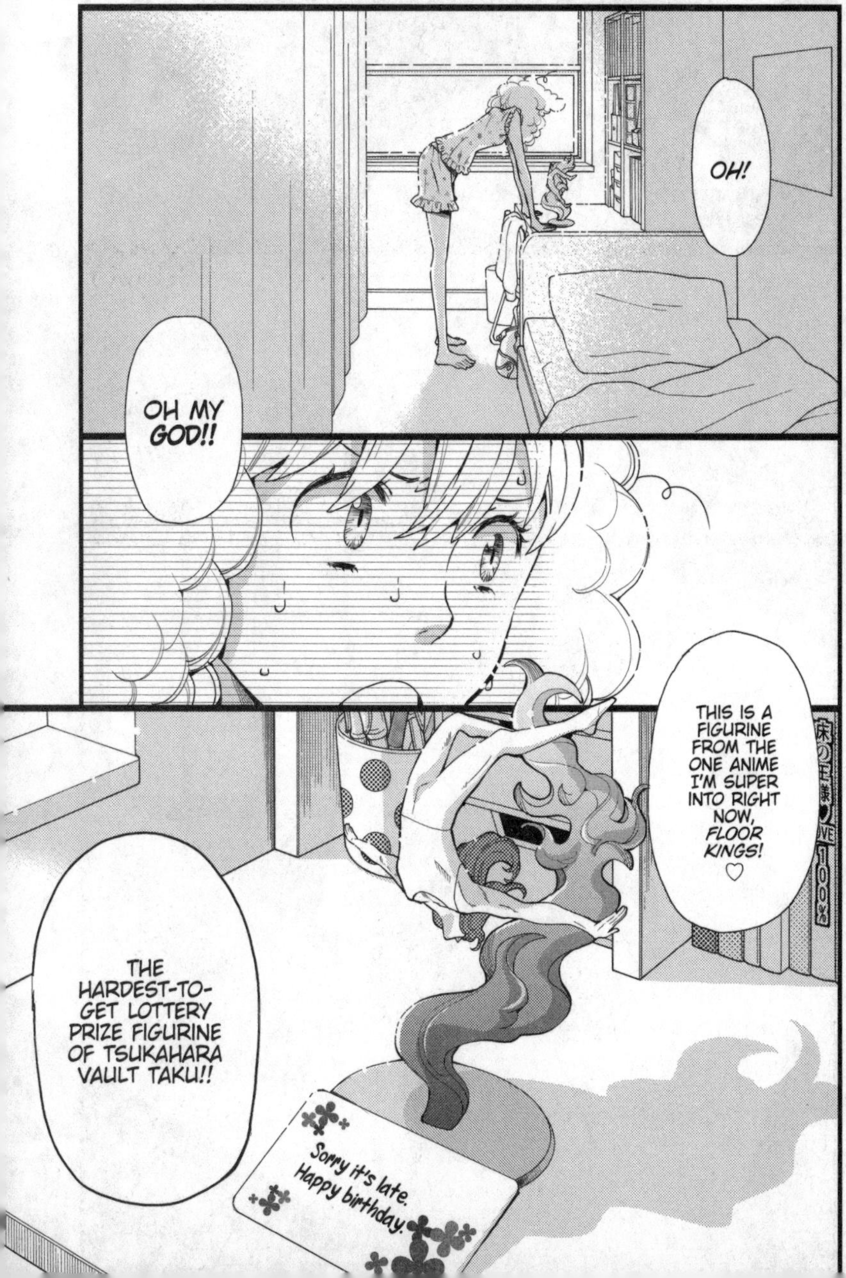
OH!
OH MY GOD!!
THIS IS A FIGURINE FROM THE ONE ANIME I'M SUPER INTO RIGHT NOW, *FLOOR KINGS!* ♡
THE HARDEST-TO-GET LOTTERY PRIZE FIGURINE OF TSUKAHARA VAULT TAKU!!
Sorry it's late. Happy birthday.

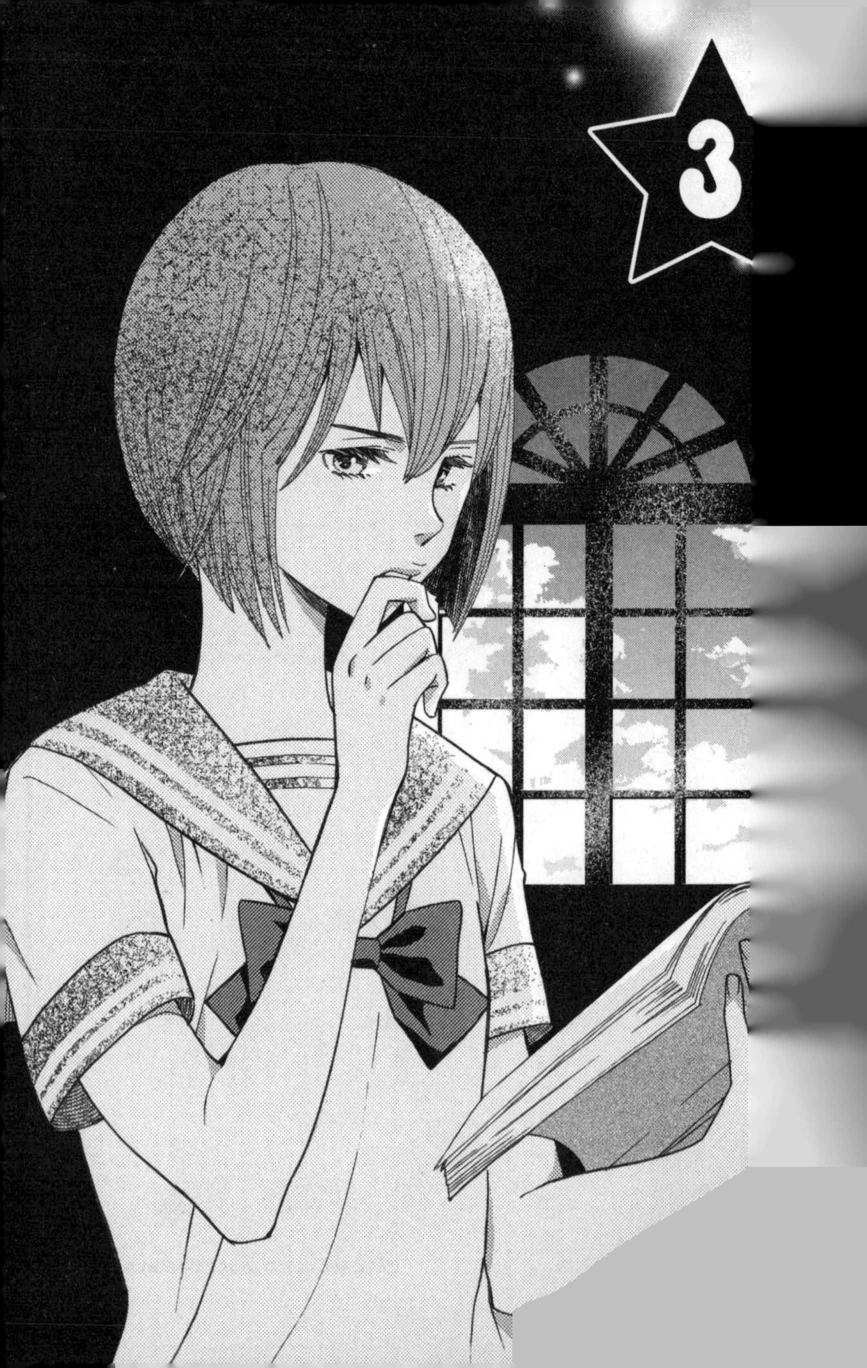
3

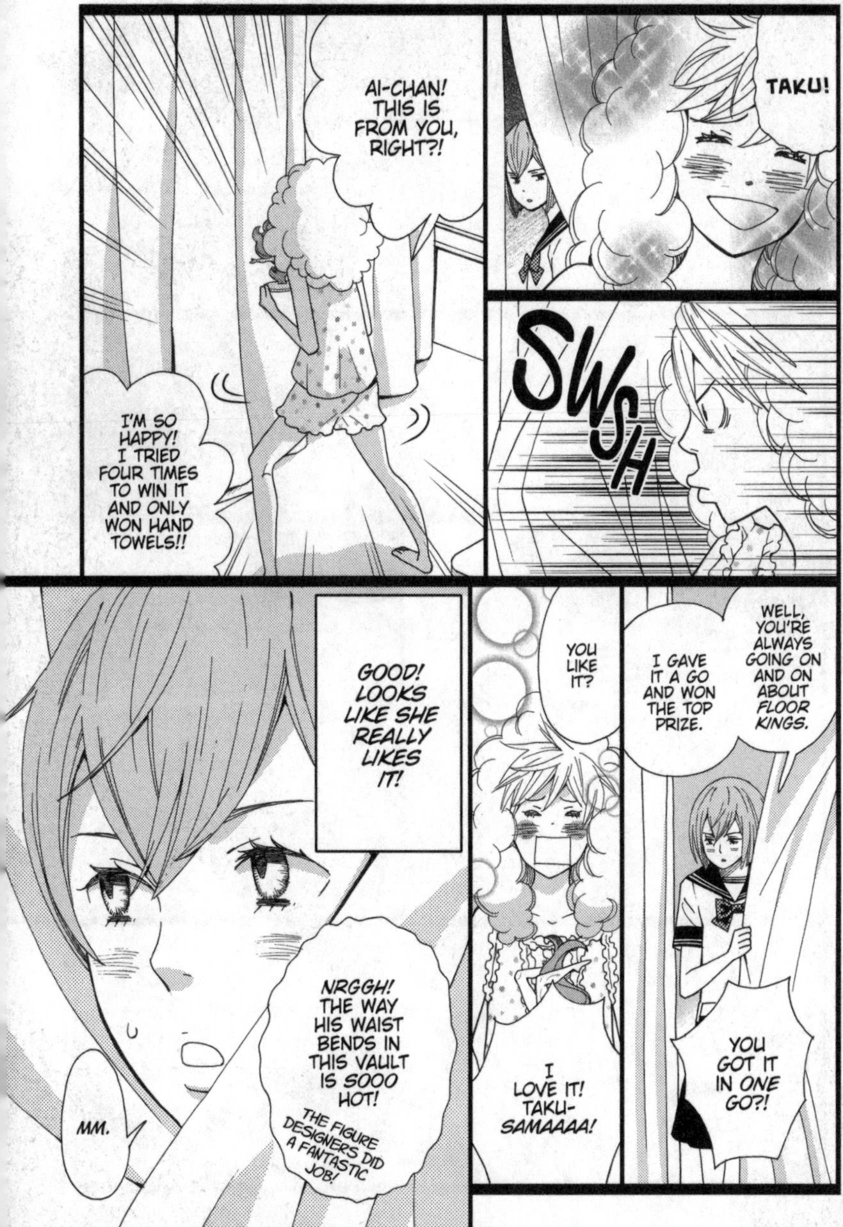
TAKU!
SWSH
AI-CHAN! THIS IS FROM YOU, RIGHT?!
I'M SO HAPPY! I TRIED FOUR TIMES TO WIN IT AND ONLY WON HAND TOWELS!!
WELL, YOU'RE ALWAYS GOING ON AND ON ABOUT *FLOOR KINGS.*
I GAVE IT A GO AND WON THE TOP PRIZE.
YOU GOT IT IN *ONE* GO?!
YOU LIKE IT?
I LOVE IT! TAKU-SAMAAAA!
GOOD! LOOKS LIKE SHE REALLY LIKES IT!
NRGGH! THE WAY HIS WAIST BENDS IN THIS VAULT IS *SOOO* HOT!
THE FIGURE DESIGNERS DID A FANTASTIC JOB!
MM.

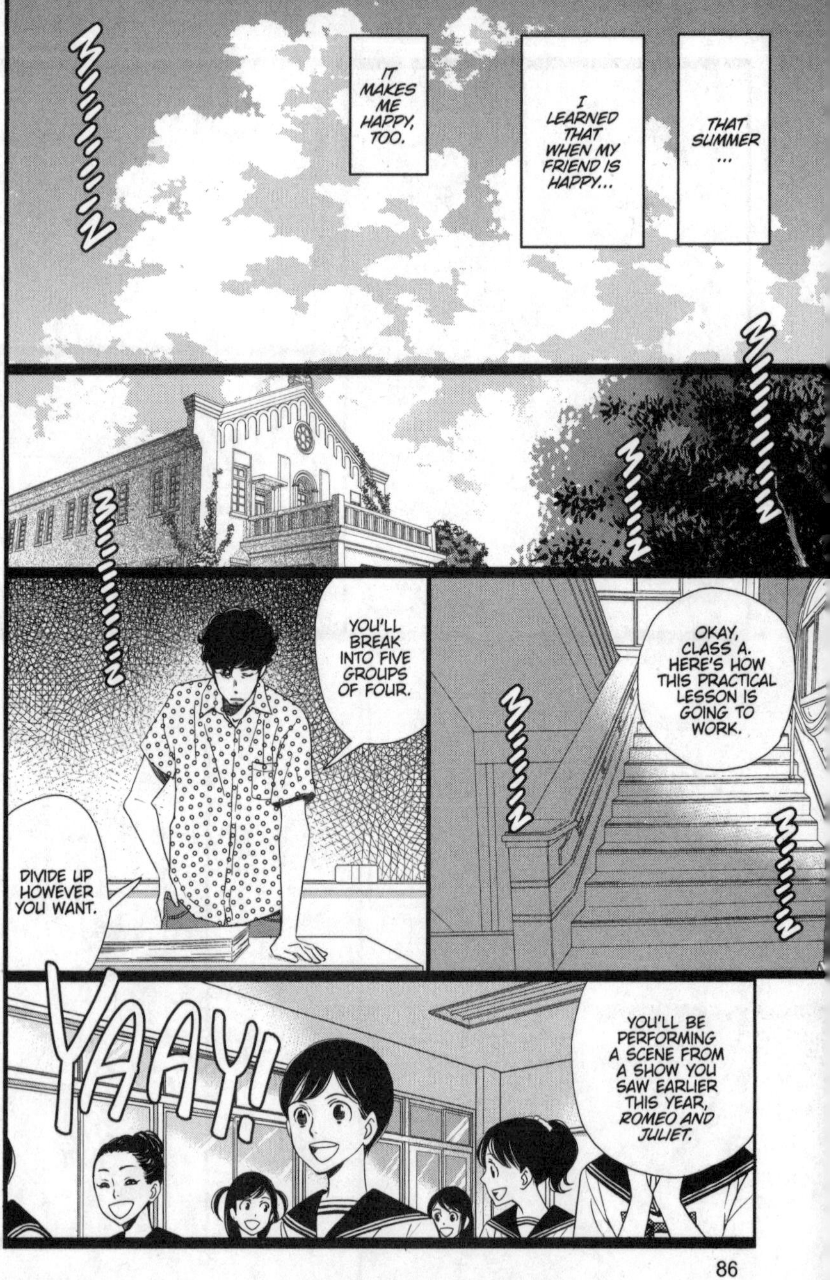
THAT SUMMER ...
I LEARNED THAT WHEN MY FRIEND IS HAPPY...
IT MAKES ME HAPPY, TOO.
MIIIIIIN
MIIIIIIIN
MIIIN
MIIIIIIIN
OKAY, CLASS A. HERE'S HOW THIS PRACTICAL LESSON IS GOING TO WORK.
MIIIIIN
MIIIN
YOU'LL BREAK INTO FIVE GROUPS OF FOUR.
DIVIDE UP HOWEVER YOU WANT.
YOU'LL BE PERFORMING A SCENE FROM A SHOW YOU SAW EARLIER THIS YEAR, *ROMEO AND JULIET.*
YAAY!

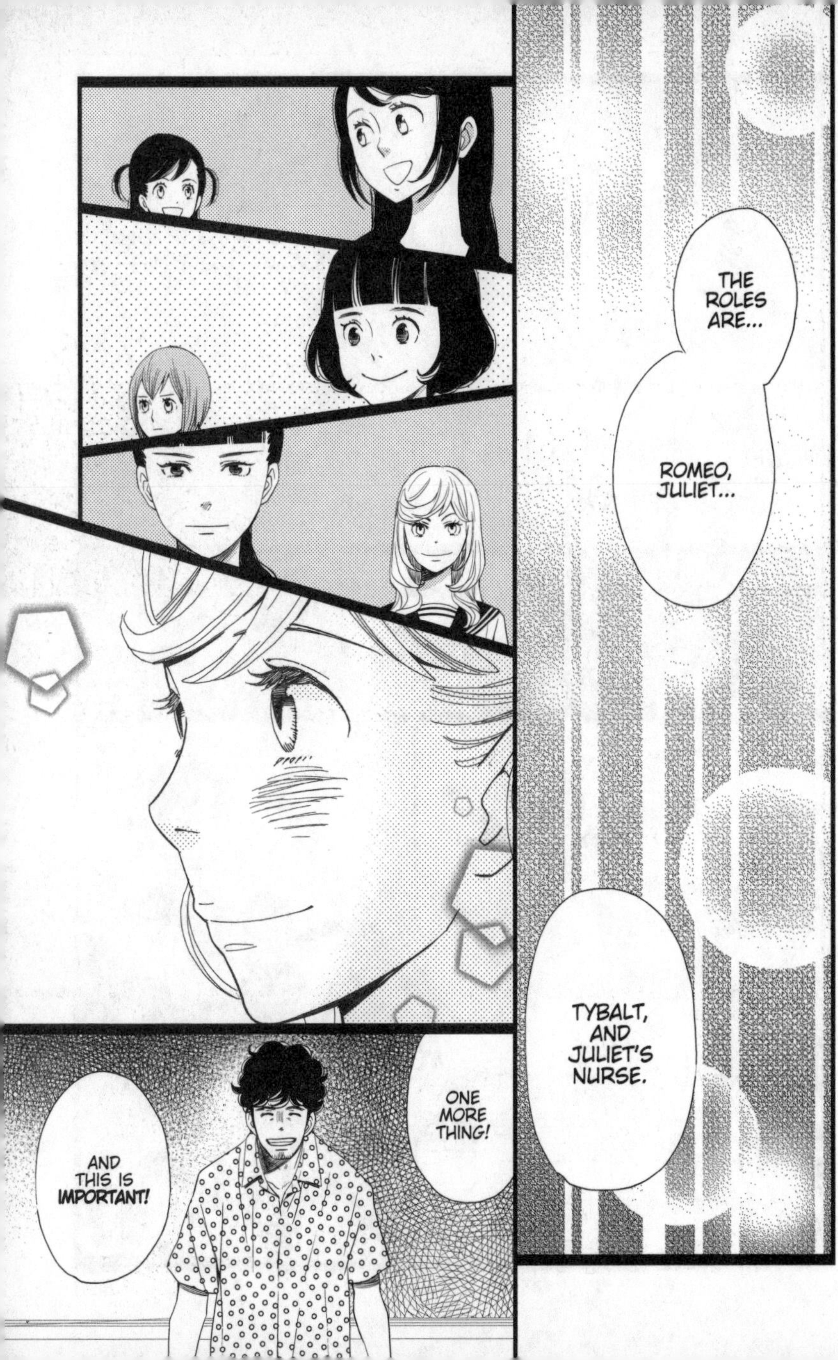
THE ROLES ARE...
ROMEO, JULIET...
TYBALT, AND JULIET'S NURSE.
ONE MORE THING!
AND THIS IS IMPORTANT!

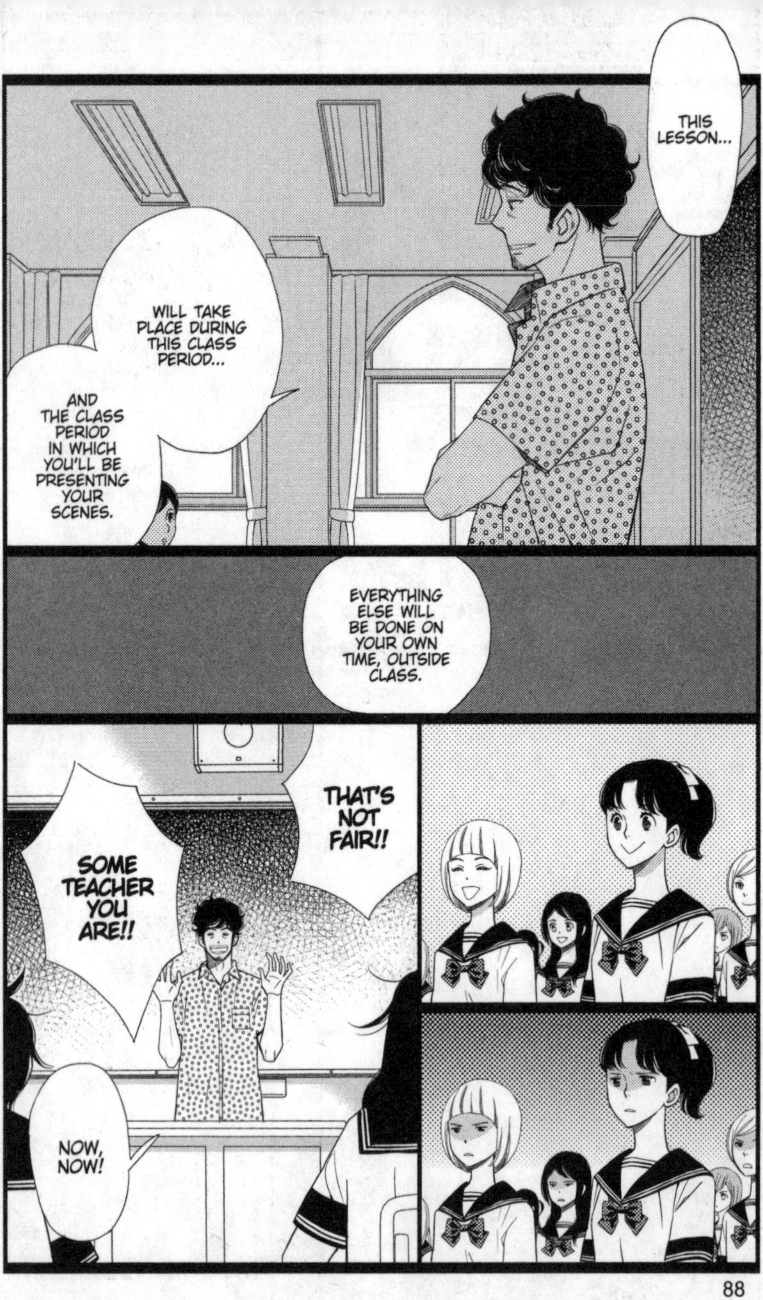
THIS LESSON...
WILL TAKE PLACE DURING THIS CLASS PERIOD...
AND THE CLASS PERIOD IN WHICH YOU'LL BE PRESENTING YOUR SCENES.
EVERYTHING ELSE WILL BE DONE ON YOUR OWN TIME, OUTSIDE CLASS.
THAT'S NOT FAIR!!
SOME TEACHER YOU ARE!!
NOW, NOW!

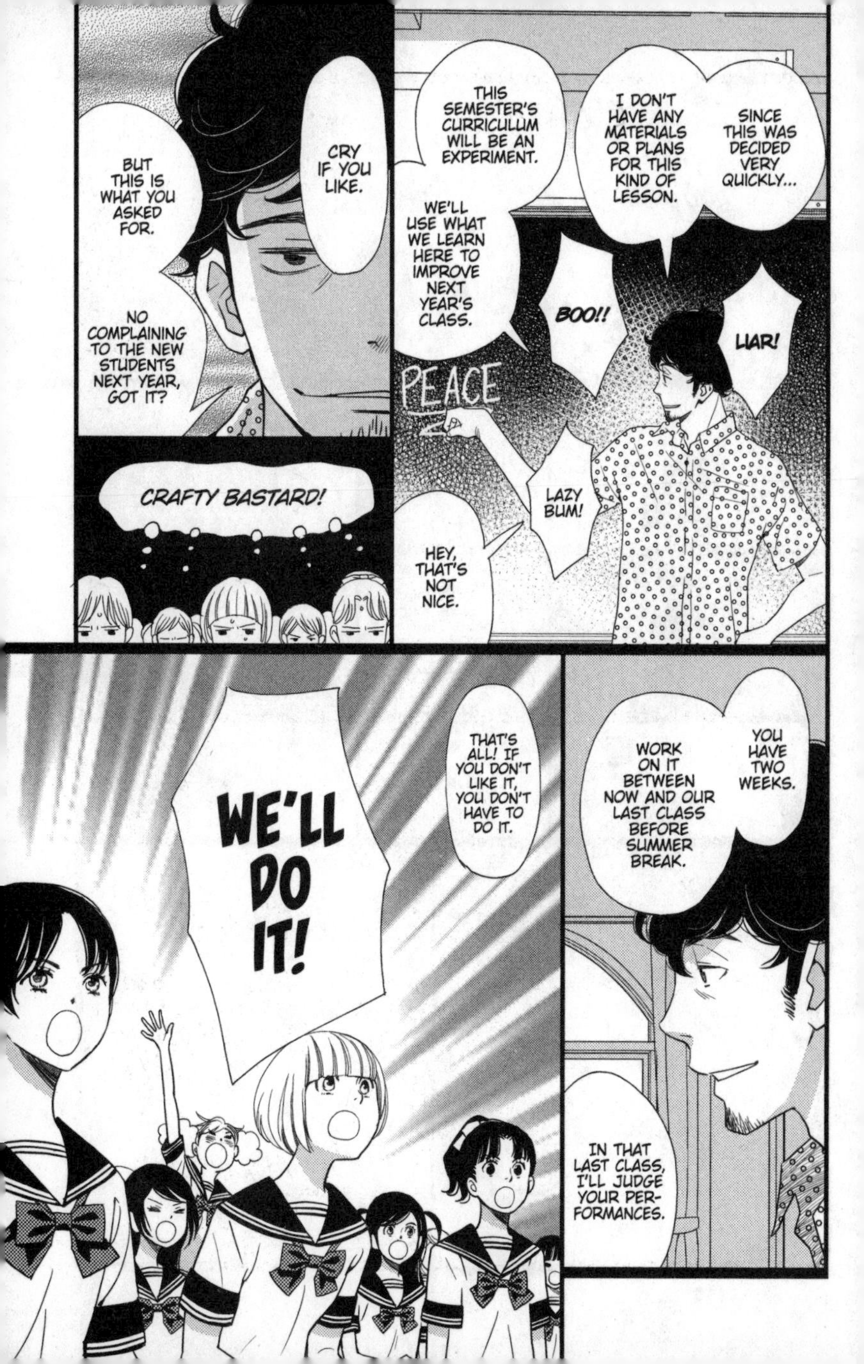
SINCE THIS WAS DECIDED VERY QUICKLY...
I DON'T HAVE ANY MATERIALS OR PLANS FOR THIS KIND OF LESSON.
THIS SEMESTER'S CURRICULUM WILL BE AN EXPERIMENT.
WE'LL USE WHAT WE LEARN HERE TO IMPROVE NEXT YEAR'S CLASS.
LIAR!
BOO!!
PEACE
LAZY BUM!
HEY, THAT'S NOT NICE.
CRY IF YOU LIKE.
BUT THIS IS WHAT YOU ASKED FOR.
NO COMPLAINING TO THE NEW STUDENTS NEXT YEAR, GOT IT?
CRAFTY BASTARD!
YOU HAVE TWO WEEKS.
WORK ON IT BETWEEN NOW AND OUR LAST CLASS BEFORE SUMMER BREAK.
IN THAT LAST CLASS, I'LL JUDGE YOUR PER-FORMANCES.
THAT'S ALL! IF YOU DON'T LIKE IT, YOU DON'T HAVE TO DO IT.
WE'LL DO IT!

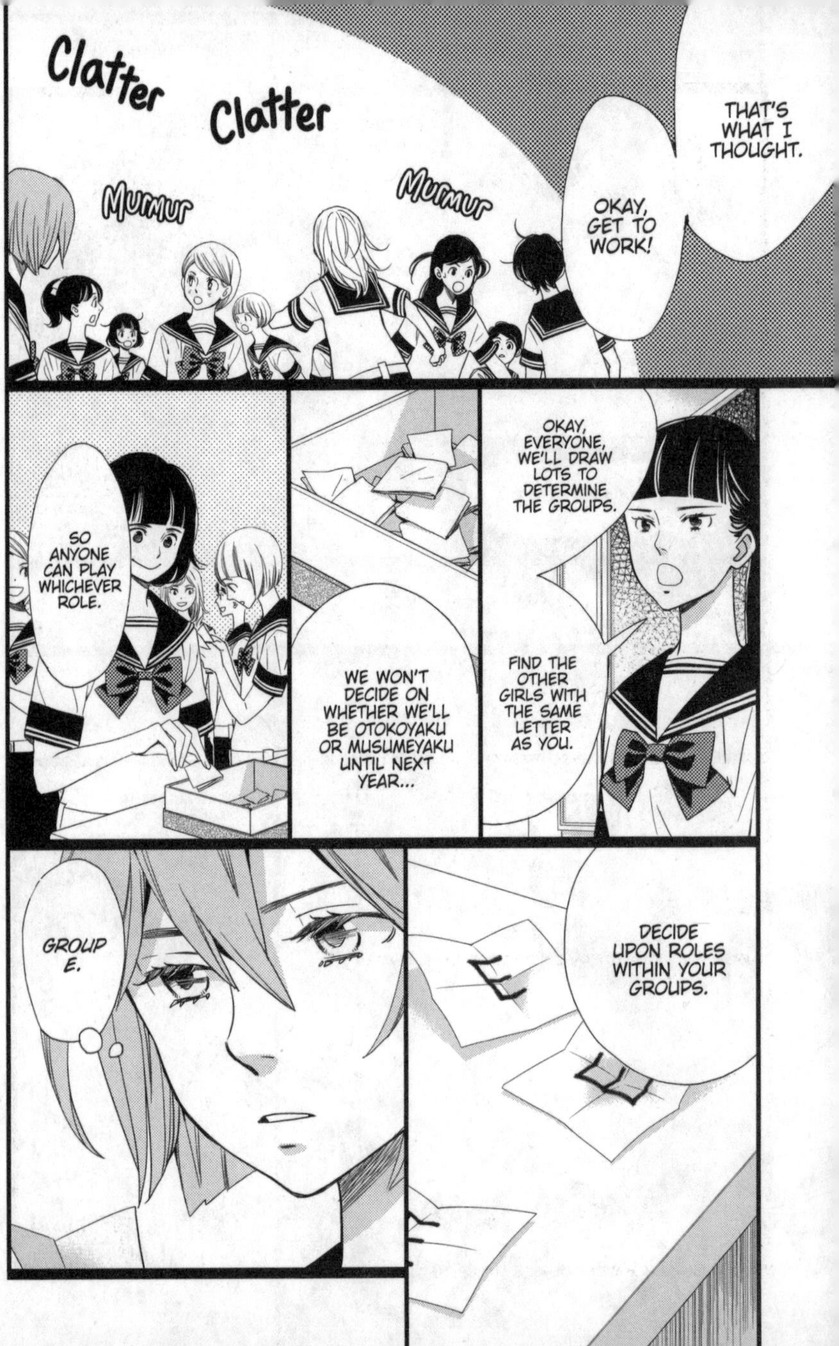
THAT'S WHAT I THOUGHT.
OKAY, GET TO WORK!
Murmur
Murmur
Clatter
Clatter
OKAY, EVERYONE, WE'LL DRAW LOTS TO DETERMINE THE GROUPS.
FIND THE OTHER GIRLS WITH THE SAME LETTER AS YOU.
WE WON'T DECIDE ON WHETHER WE'LL BE OTOKOYAKU OR MUSUMEYAKU UNTIL NEXT YEAR...
SO ANYONE CAN PLAY WHICHEVER ROLE.
DECIDE UPON ROLES WITHIN YOUR GROUPS.
GROUP E.

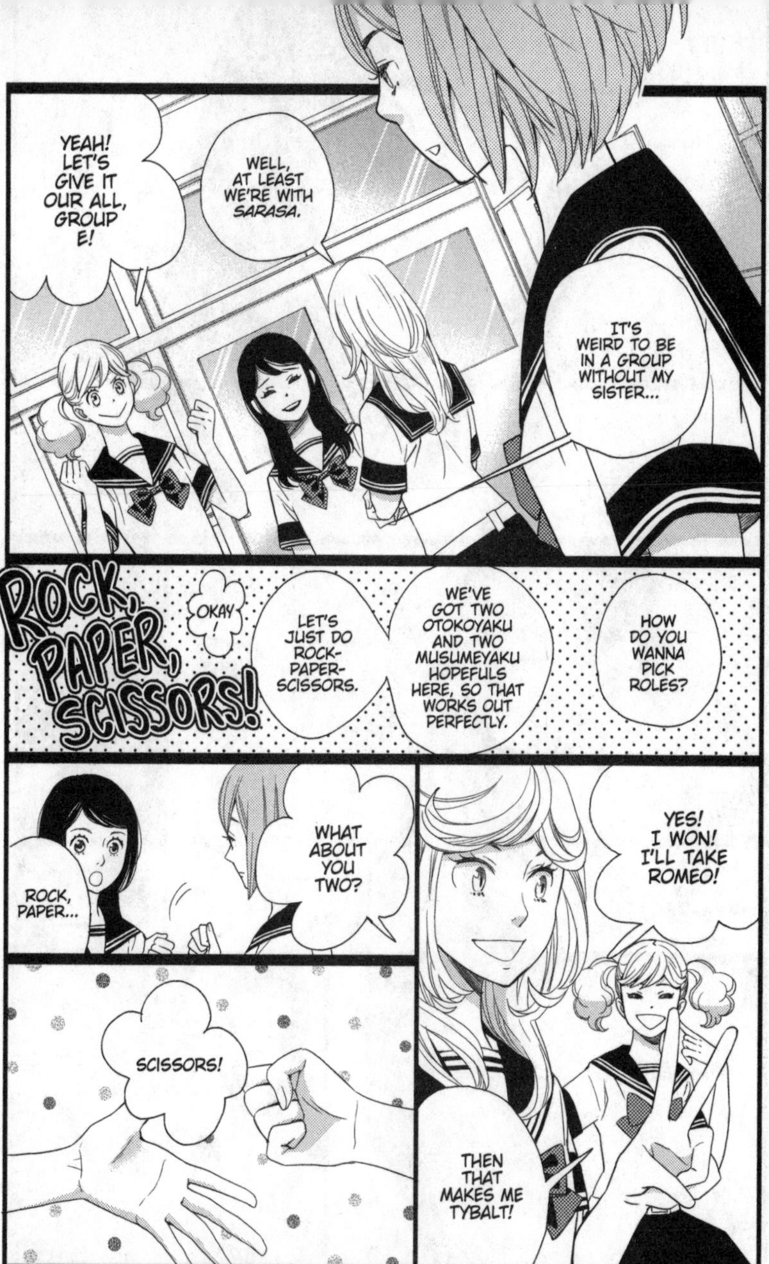
IT'S WEIRD TO BE IN A GROUP WITHOUT MY SISTER...
WELL, AT LEAST WE'RE WITH SARASA.
YEAH! LET'S GIVE IT OUR ALL, GROUP E!
HOW DO YOU WANNA PICK ROLES?
WE'VE GOT TWO OTOKOYAKU AND TWO MUSUMEYAKU HOPEFULS HERE, SO THAT WORKS OUT PERFECTLY.
LET'S JUST DO ROCK-PAPER-SCISSORS.
OKAY!
ROCK, PAPER, SCISSORS!
YES! I WON! I'LL TAKE ROMEO!
THEN THAT MAKES ME TYBALT!
WHAT ABOUT YOU TWO?
ROCK, PAPER...
SCISSORS!

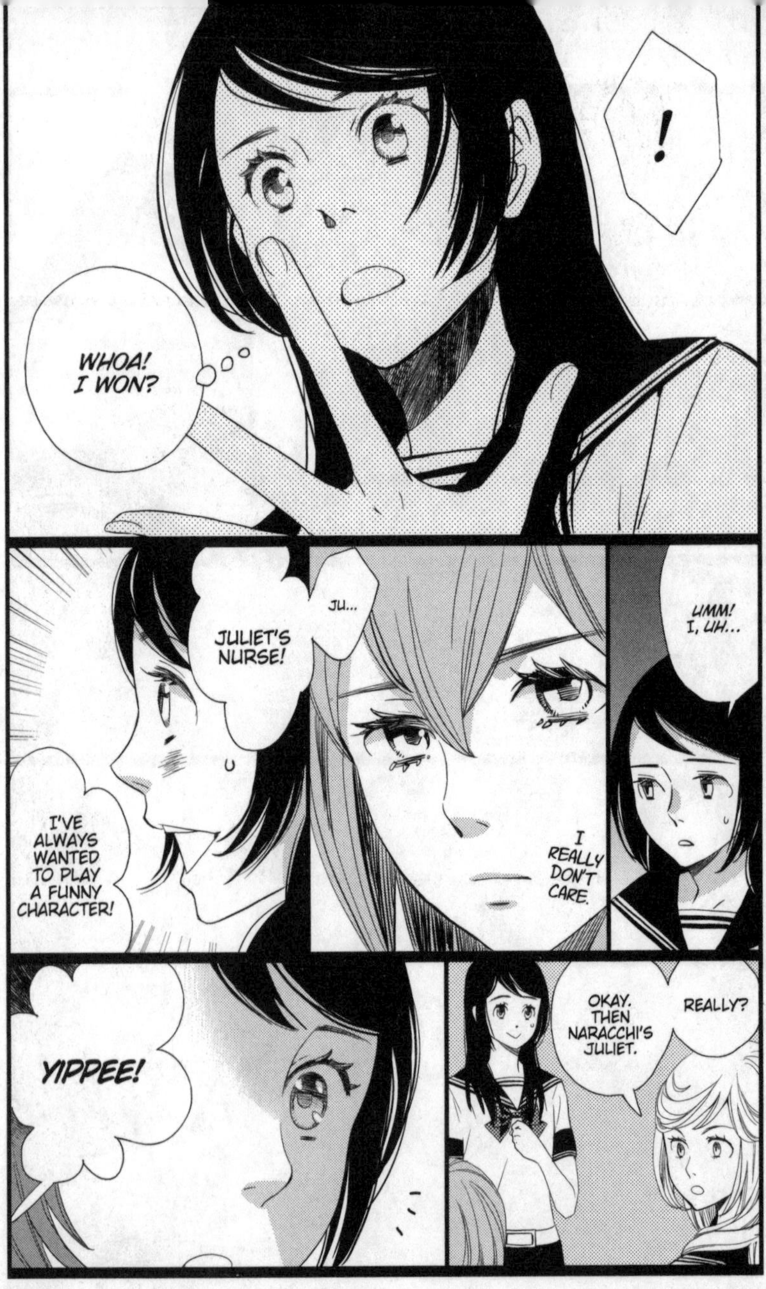
!
WHOA! I WON?
UMM! I, UH...
I REALLY DON'T CARE.
JU...
JULIET'S NURSE!
I'VE ALWAYS WANTED TO PLAY A FUNNY CHARACTER!
REALLY?
OKAY. THEN NARACCHI'S JULIET.
YIPPEE!

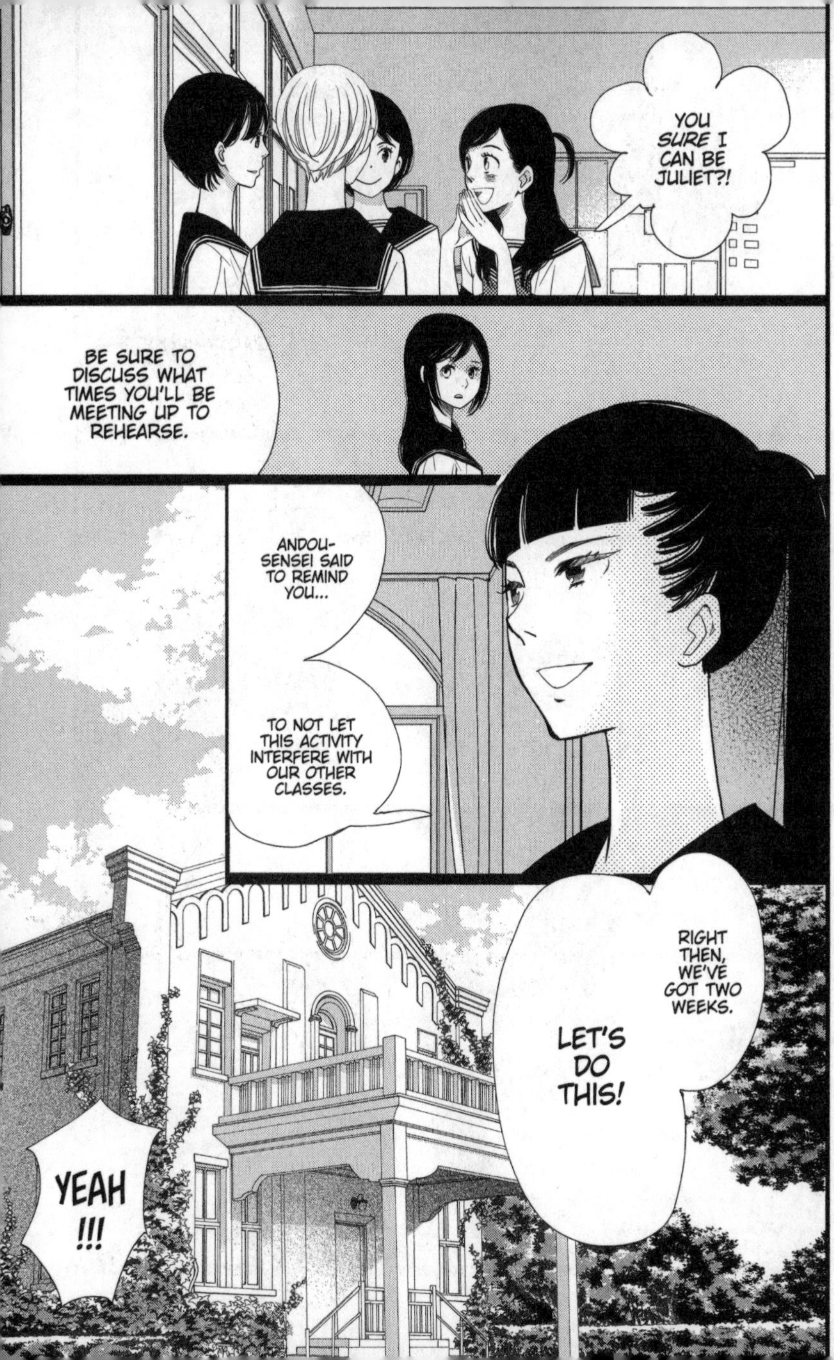
YOU SURE I CAN BE JULIET?!
BE SURE TO DISCUSS WHAT TIMES YOU'LL BE MEETING UP TO REHEARSE.
ANDOU-SENSEI SAID TO REMIND YOU...
TO NOT LET THIS ACTIVITY INTERFERE WITH OUR OTHER CLASSES.
RIGHT THEN, WE'VE GOT TWO WEEKS.
LET'S DO THIS!
YEAH !!!

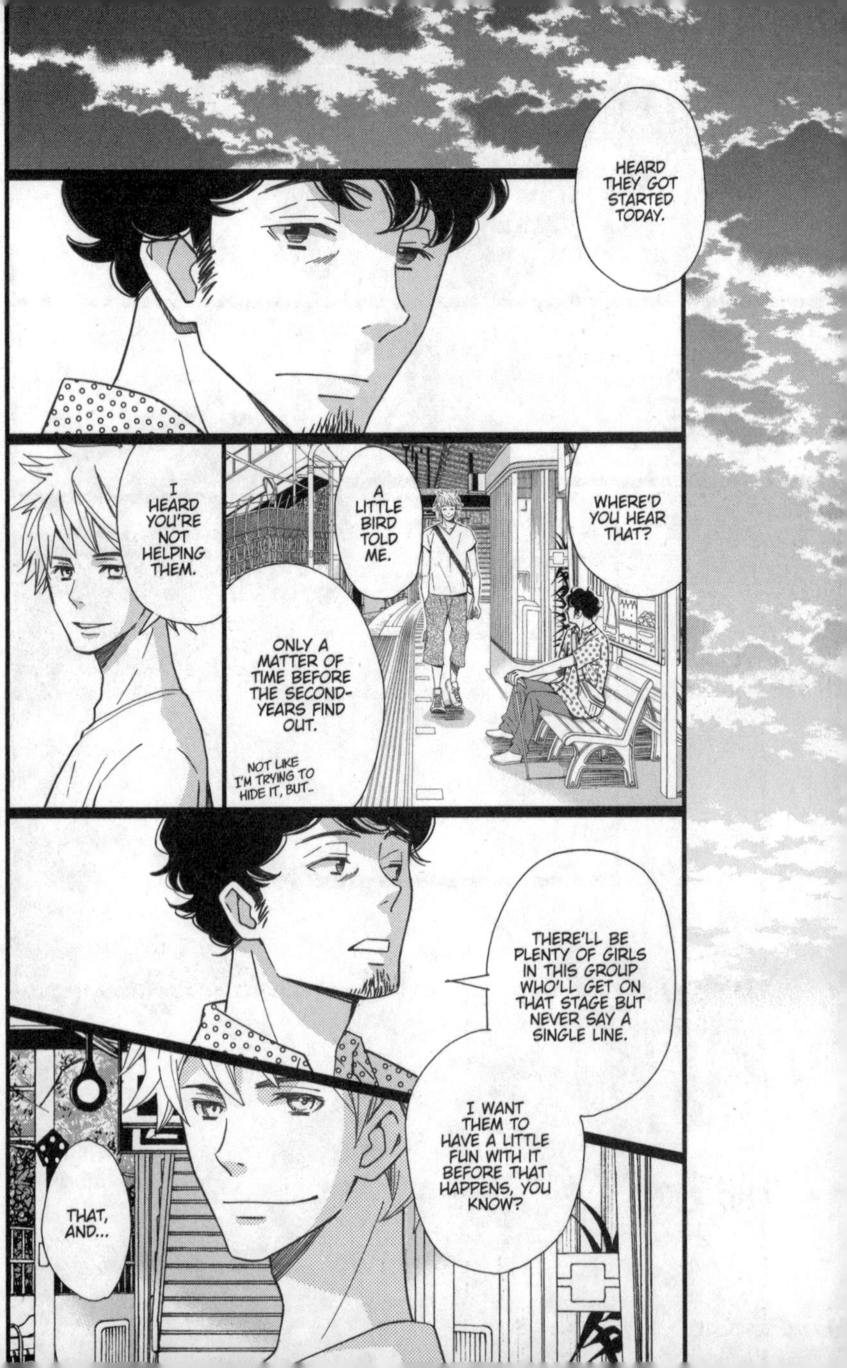
HEARD THEY GOT STARTED TODAY.
WHERE'D YOU HEAR THAT?
A LITTLE BIRD TOLD ME.
ONLY A MATTER OF TIME BEFORE THE SECOND-YEARS FIND OUT.
NOT LIKE I'M TRYING TO HIDE IT, BUT...
I HEARD YOU'RE NOT HELPING THEM.
THERE'LL BE PLENTY OF GIRLS IN THIS GROUP WHO'LL GET ON THAT STAGE BUT NEVER SAY A SINGLE LINE.
I WANT THEM TO HAVE A LITTLE FUN WITH IT BEFORE THAT HAPPENS, YOU KNOW?
THAT, AND...

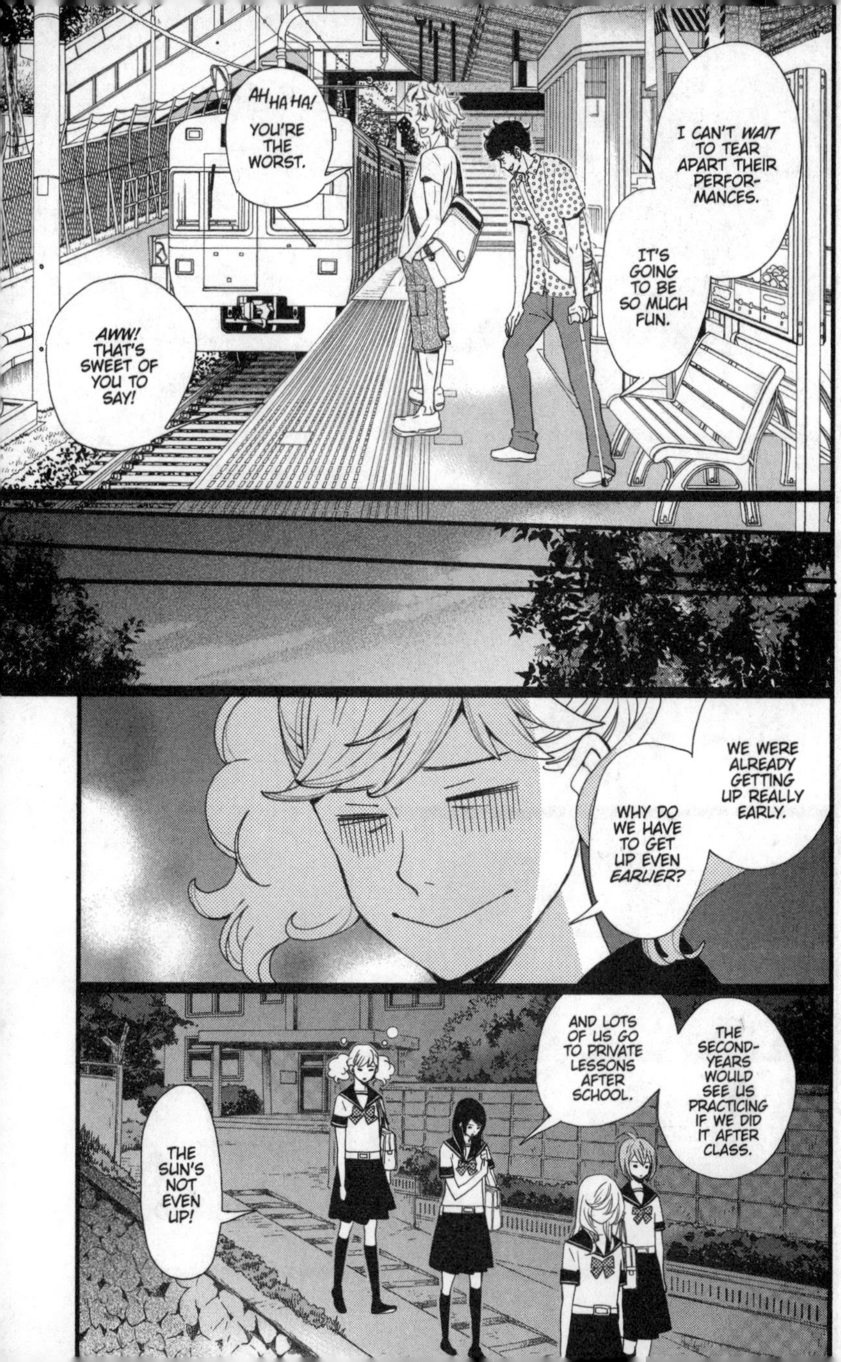
I CAN'T *WAIT* TO TEAR APART THEIR PERFORMANCES.
IT'S GOING TO BE SO MUCH FUN.
AH HA HA! YOU'RE THE WORST.
AWW! THAT'S SWEET OF YOU TO SAY!
WE WERE ALREADY GETTING UP REALLY EARLY.
WHY DO WE HAVE TO GET UP EVEN *EARLIER?*
THE SECOND-YEARS WOULD SEE US PRACTICING IF WE DID IT AFTER CLASS.
AND LOTS OF US GO TO PRIVATE LESSONS AFTER SCHOOL.
THE SUN'S NOT EVEN UP!

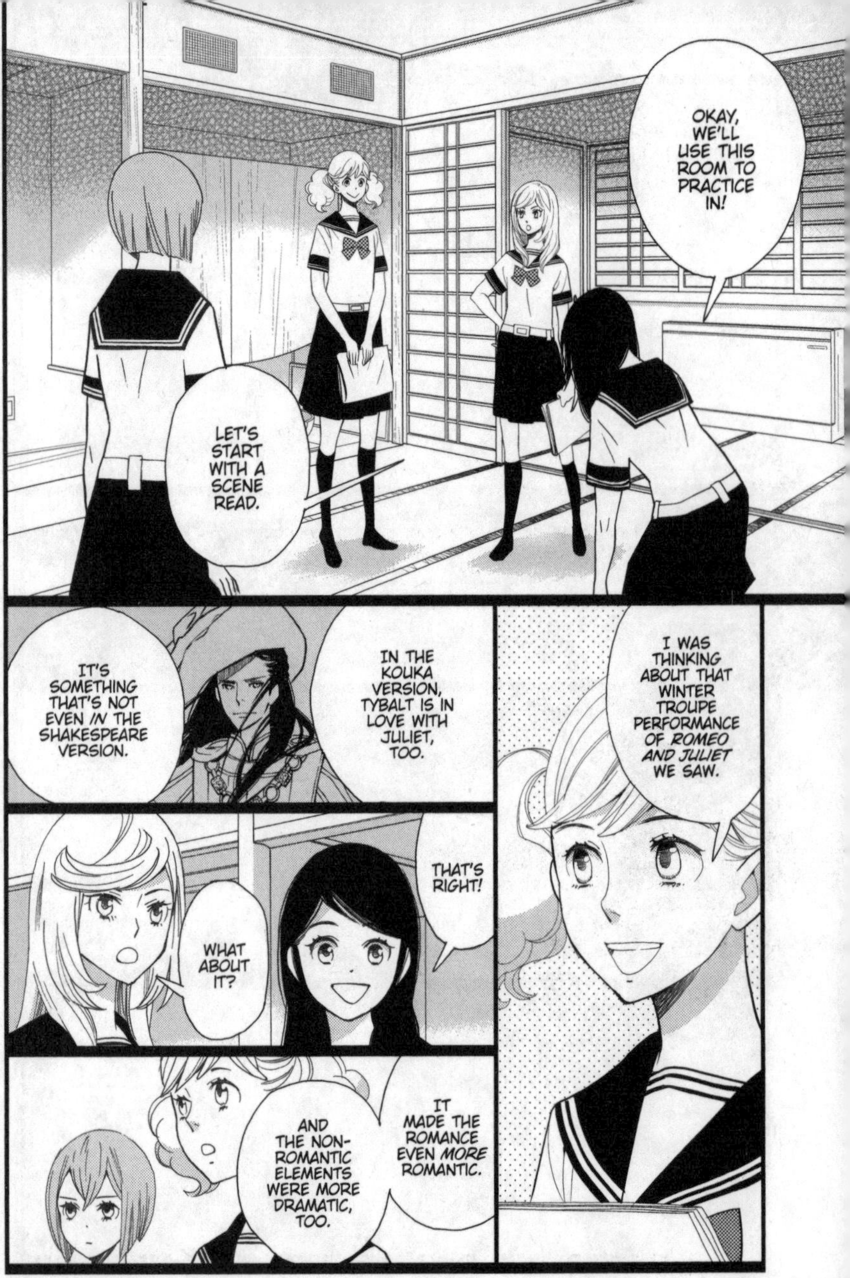
OKAY, WE'LL USE THIS ROOM TO PRACTICE IN!
LET'S START WITH A SCENE READ.
I WAS THINKING ABOUT THAT WINTER TROUPE PERFORMANCE OF *ROMEO AND JULIET* WE SAW.
IN THE KOUKA VERSION, TYBALT IS IN LOVE WITH JULIET, TOO.
IT'S SOMETHING THAT'S NOT EVEN *IN* THE SHAKESPEARE VERSION.
THAT'S RIGHT!
WHAT ABOUT IT?
IT MADE THE ROMANCE EVEN *MORE* ROMANTIC.
AND THE NON-ROMANTIC ELEMENTS WERE MORE DRAMATIC, TOO.

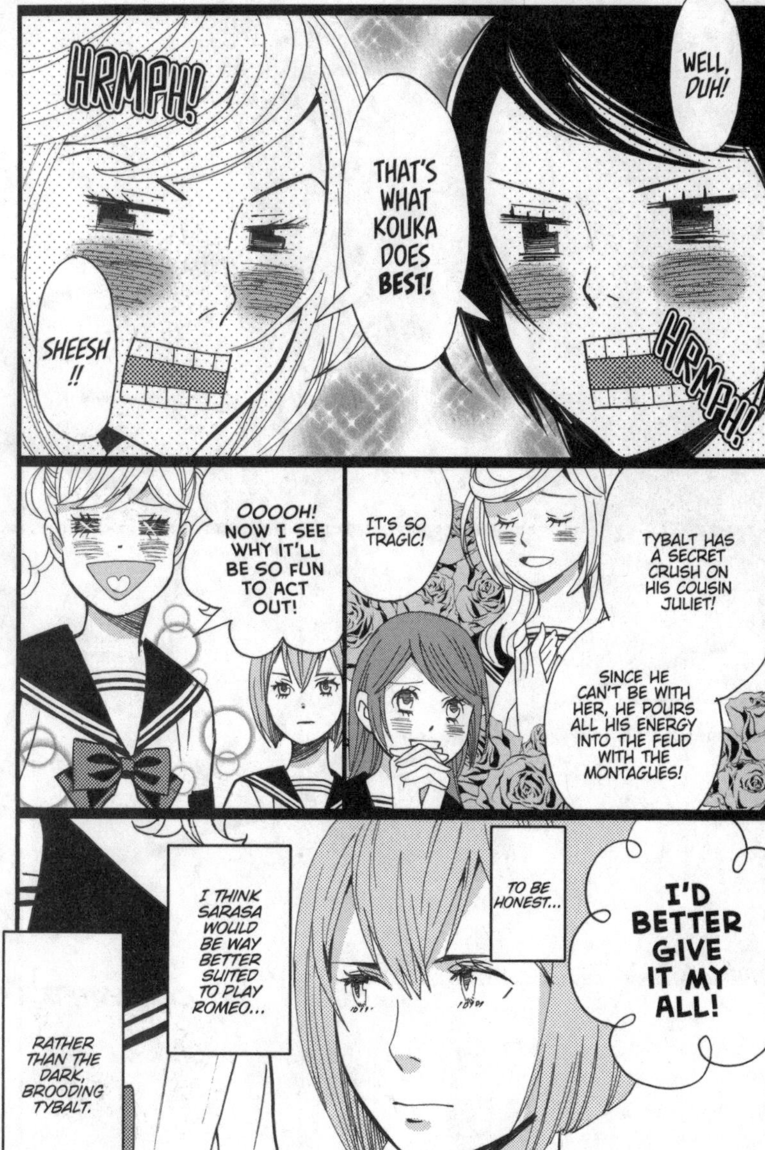
WELL, DUH!
THAT'S WHAT KOUKA DOES BEST!
HRMPH!!
HRMPH!
SHEESH!!
IT'S SO TRAGIC!
TYBALT HAS A SECRET CRUSH ON HIS COUSIN JULIET!
SINCE HE CAN'T BE WITH HER, HE POURS ALL HIS ENERGY INTO THE FEUD WITH THE MONTAGUES!
OOOOH! NOW I SEE WHY IT'LL BE SO FUN TO ACT OUT!
I'D BETTER GIVE IT MY ALL!
TO BE HONEST...
I THINK SARASA WOULD BE WAY BETTER SUITED TO PLAY ROMEO...
RATHER THAN THE DARK, BROODING TYBALT.

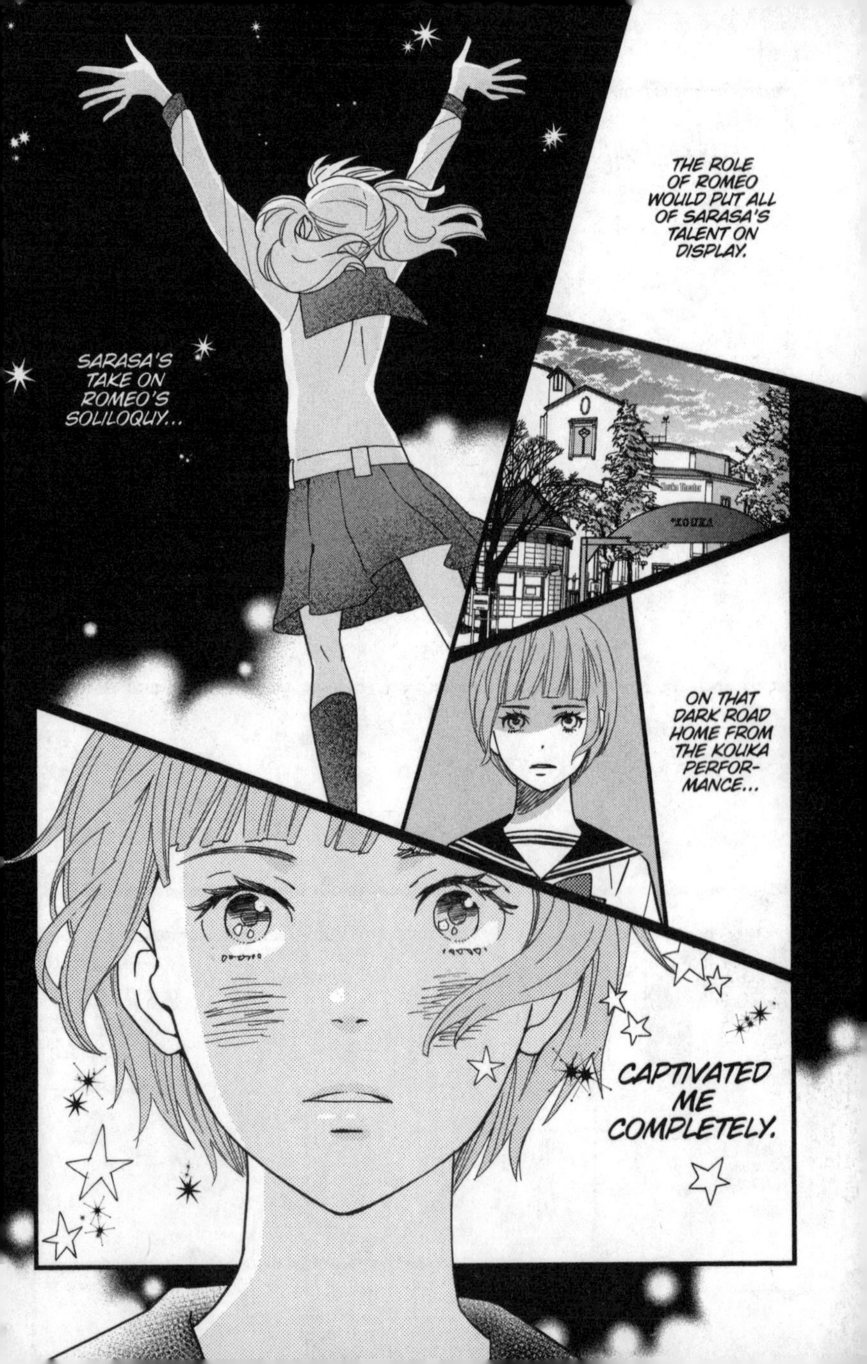
THE ROLE OF ROMEO WOULD PUT ALL OF SARASA'S TALENT ON DISPLAY.
SARASA'S TAKE ON ROMEO'S SOLILOQUY...
ON THAT DARK ROAD HOME FROM THE KOUKA PERFORMANCE...
CAPTIVATED ME COMPLETELY.

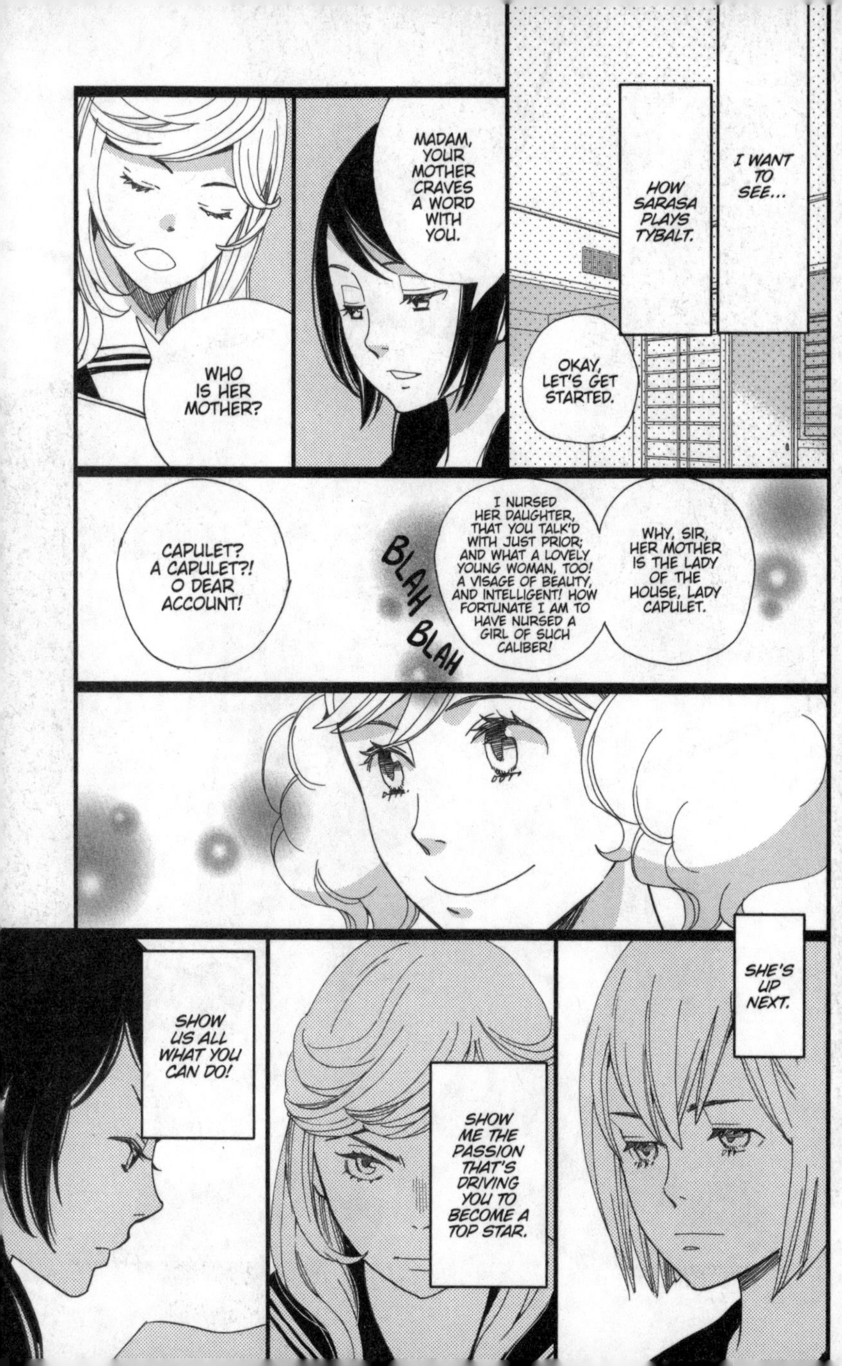
I WANT TO SEE...
HOW SARASA PLAYS TYBALT.
OKAY, LET'S GET STARTED.
MADAM, YOUR MOTHER CRAVES A WORD WITH YOU.
WHO IS HER MOTHER?
WHY, SIR, HER MOTHER IS THE LADY OF THE HOUSE, LADY CAPULET.
I NURSED HER DAUGHTER, THAT YOU TALK'D WITH JUST PRIOR; AND WHAT A LOVELY YOUNG WOMAN, TOO! A VISAGE OF BEAUTY, AND INTELLIGENT! HOW FORTUNATE I AM TO HAVE NURSED A GIRL OF SUCH CALIBER!
BLAH BLAH
CAPULET? A CAPULET?! O DEAR ACCOUNT!
SHE'S UP NEXT.
SHOW ME THE PASSION THAT'S DRIVING YOU TO BECOME A TOP STAR.
SHOW US ALL WHAT YOU CAN DO!

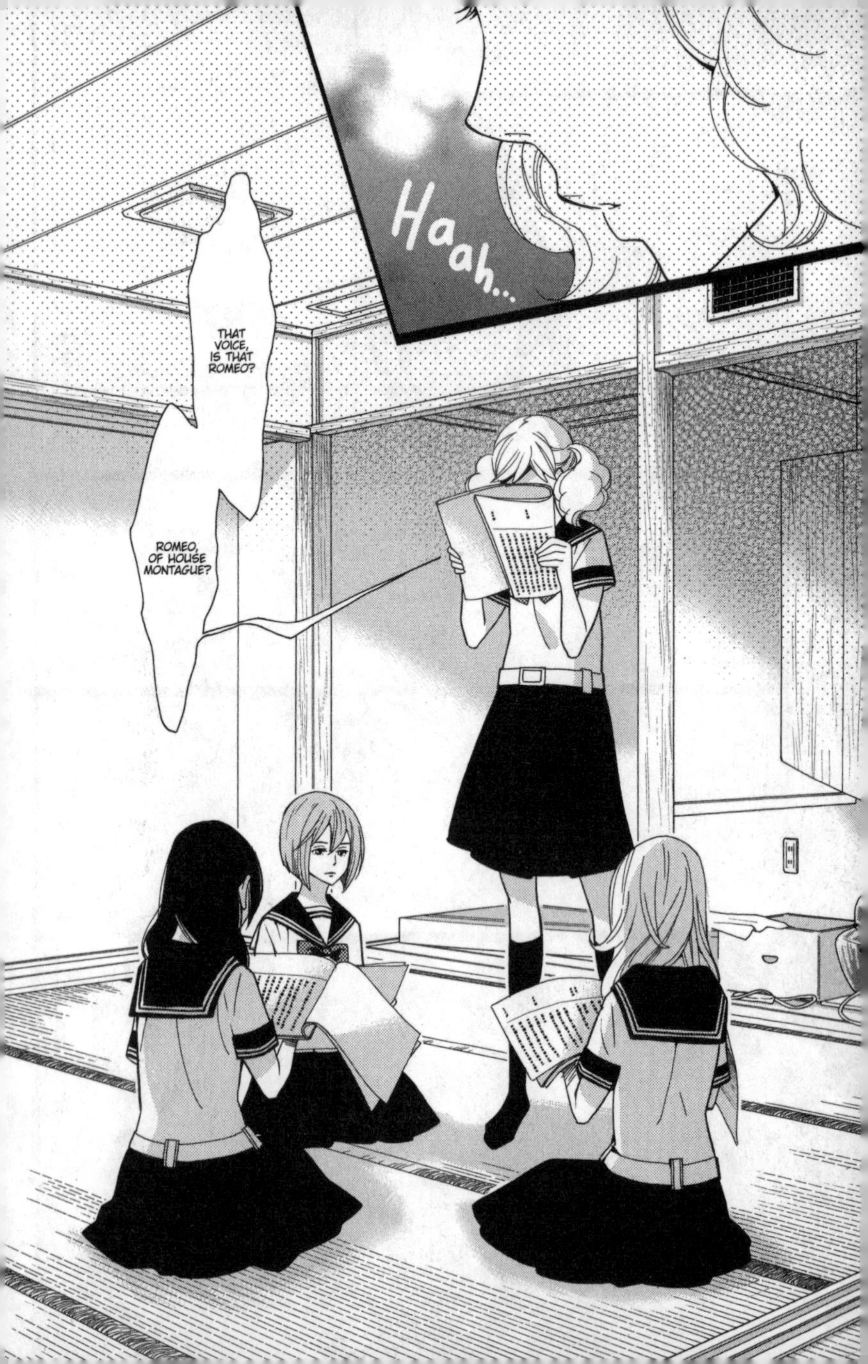
Haah...
THAT VOICE, IS THAT ROMEO?
ROMEO, OF HOUSE MONTAGUE?

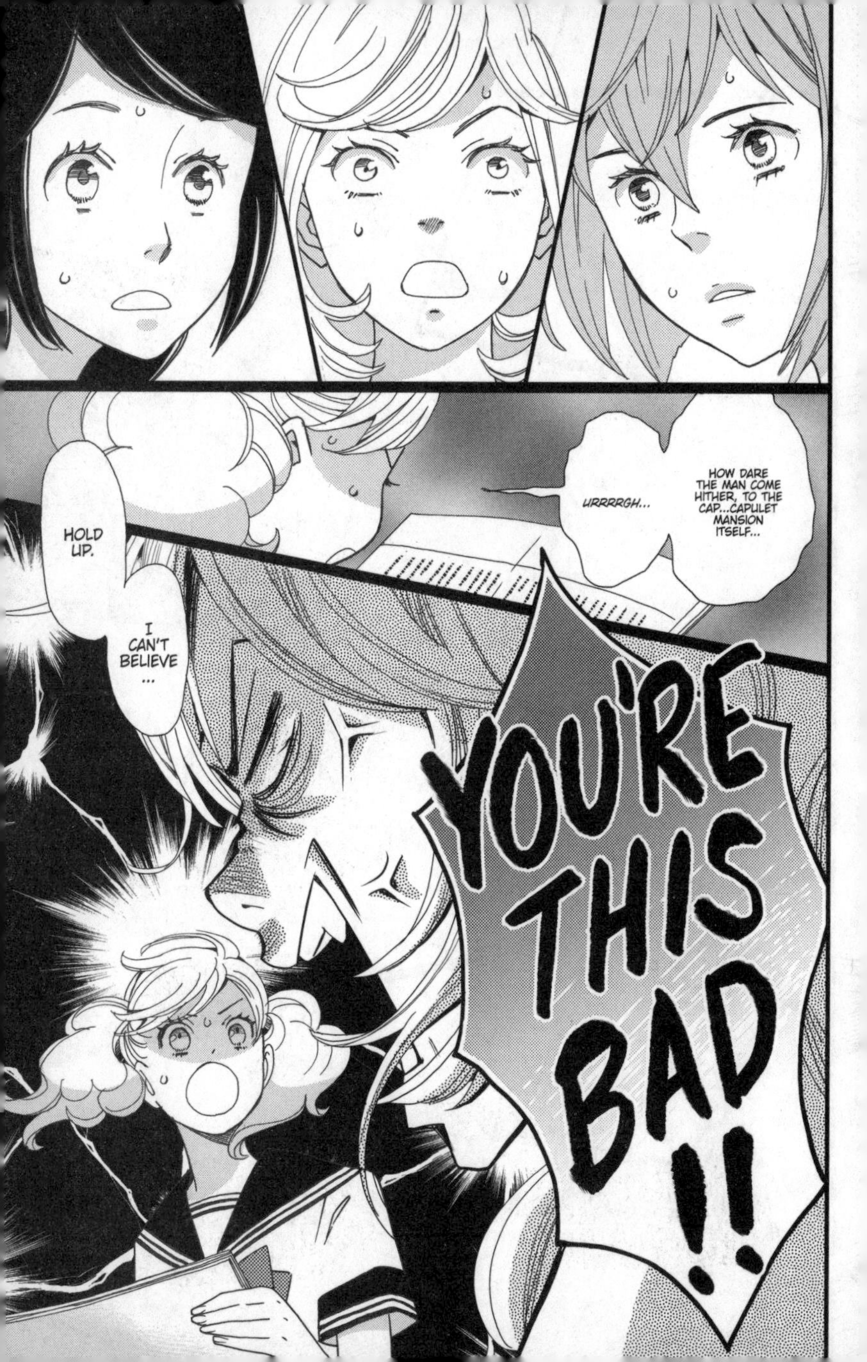
URRRRGH... HOW DARE THE MAN COME HITHER, TO THE CAP...CAPULET MANSION ITSELF...
HOLD UP.
I CAN'T BELIEVE ...
YOU'RE THIS BAD!!

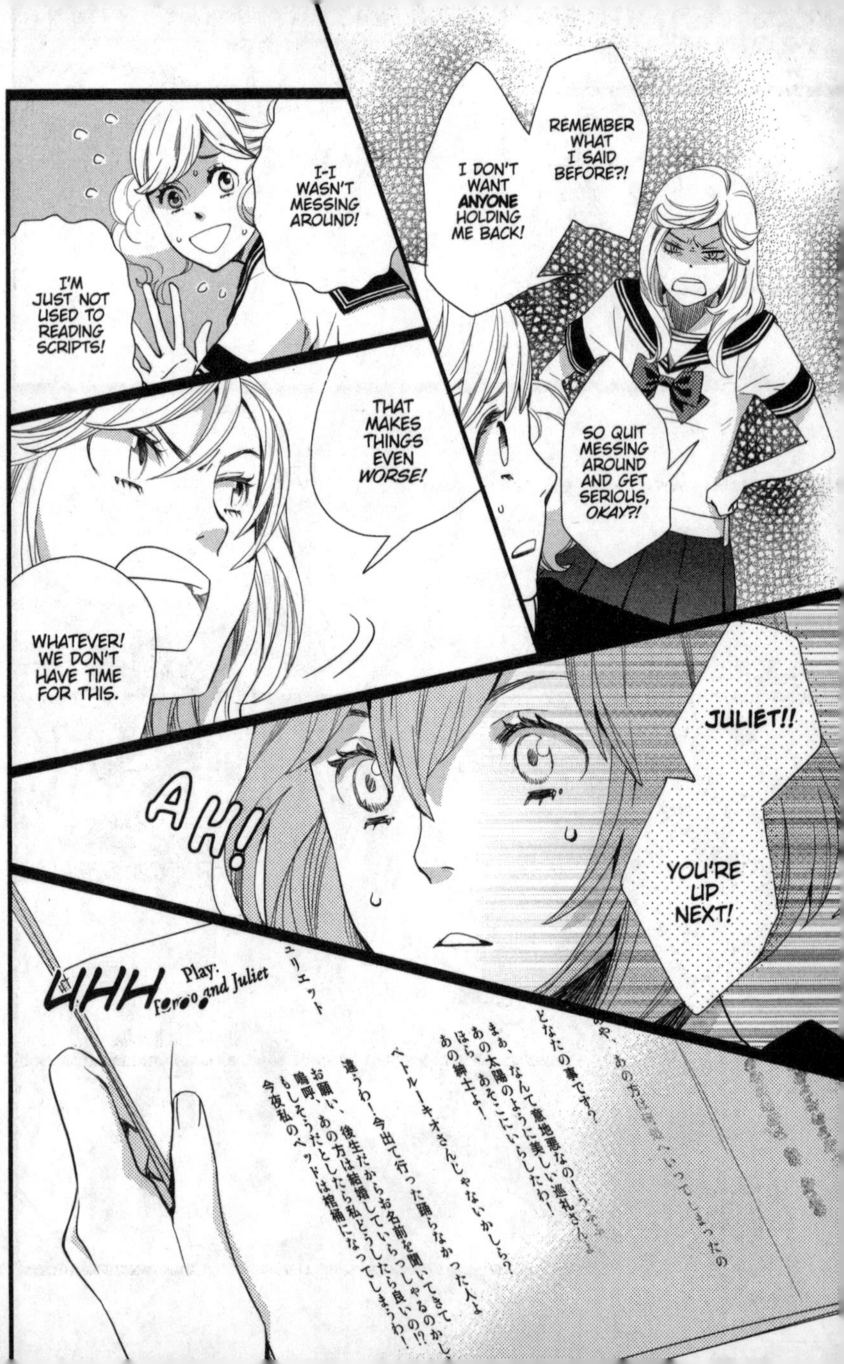
REMEMBER WHAT I SAID BEFORE?!
I DON'T WANT **ANYONE** HOLDING ME BACK!
SO QUIT MESSING AROUND AND GET SERIOUS, *OKAY?!*
I-I WASN'T MESSING AROUND!
I'M JUST NOT USED TO READING SCRIPTS!
THAT MAKES THINGS EVEN *WORSE!*
WHATEVER! WE DON'T HAVE TIME FOR THIS.
JULIET!!
YOU'RE UP NEXT!
AH!
UHH
Play:
and Juliet
どなたの事です？
まぁ、なんて意地悪なの！
あの太陽のように美しい巡礼さん
ほら、あそこにいらしたわ！
あの紳士よ！
ペトルーキオさんじゃないかしら？
違うわ！今出て行った踊らなかった人よ
お願い、後生だからお名前を聞いてきて
嗚呼、あの方は結婚していらっしゃるのかし
もしそうだとしたら私どうしたら良いの!?
今夜私のベッドは棺桶になってしまうわ！

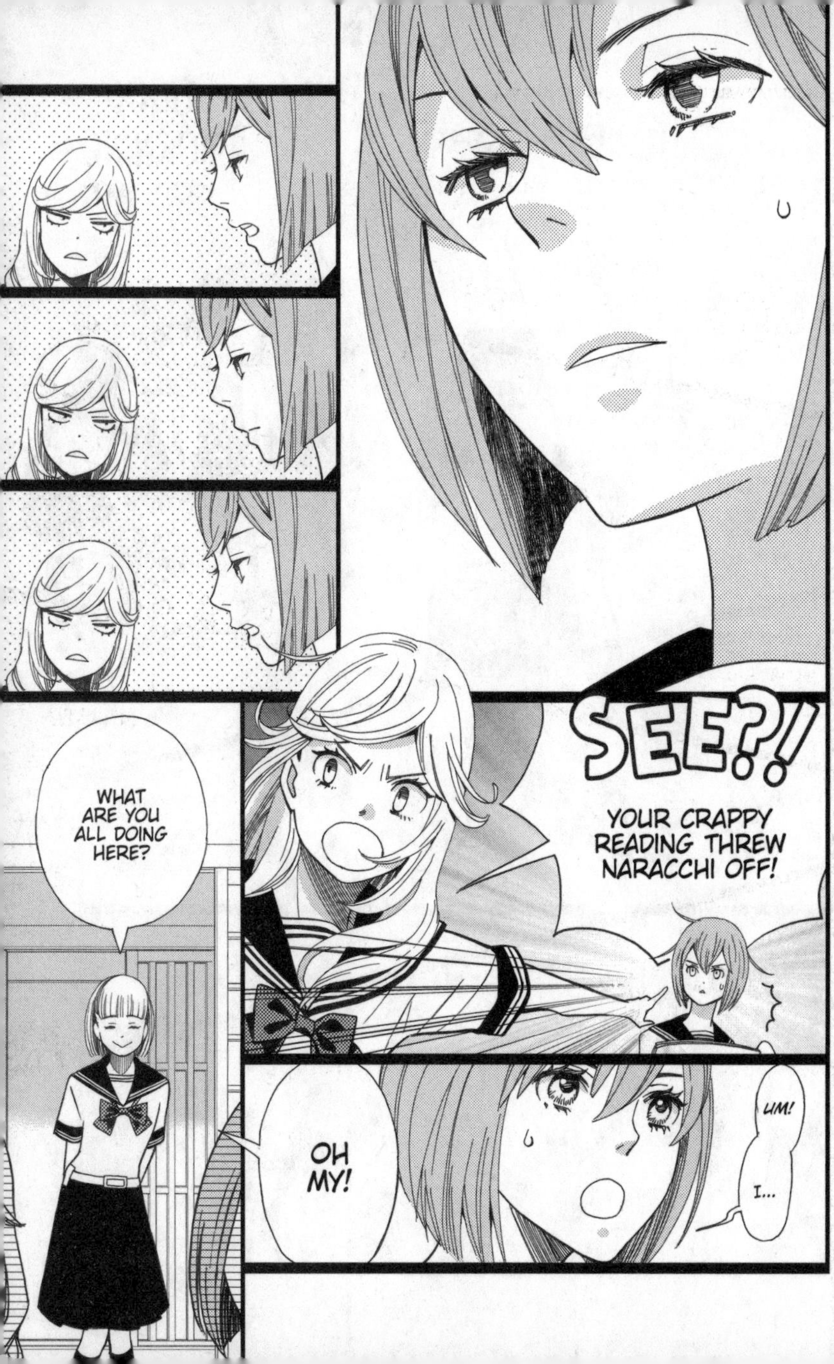
SEE?!
YOUR CRAPPY READING THREW NARACCHI OFF!
UM! I...
OH MY!
WHAT ARE YOU ALL DOING HERE?

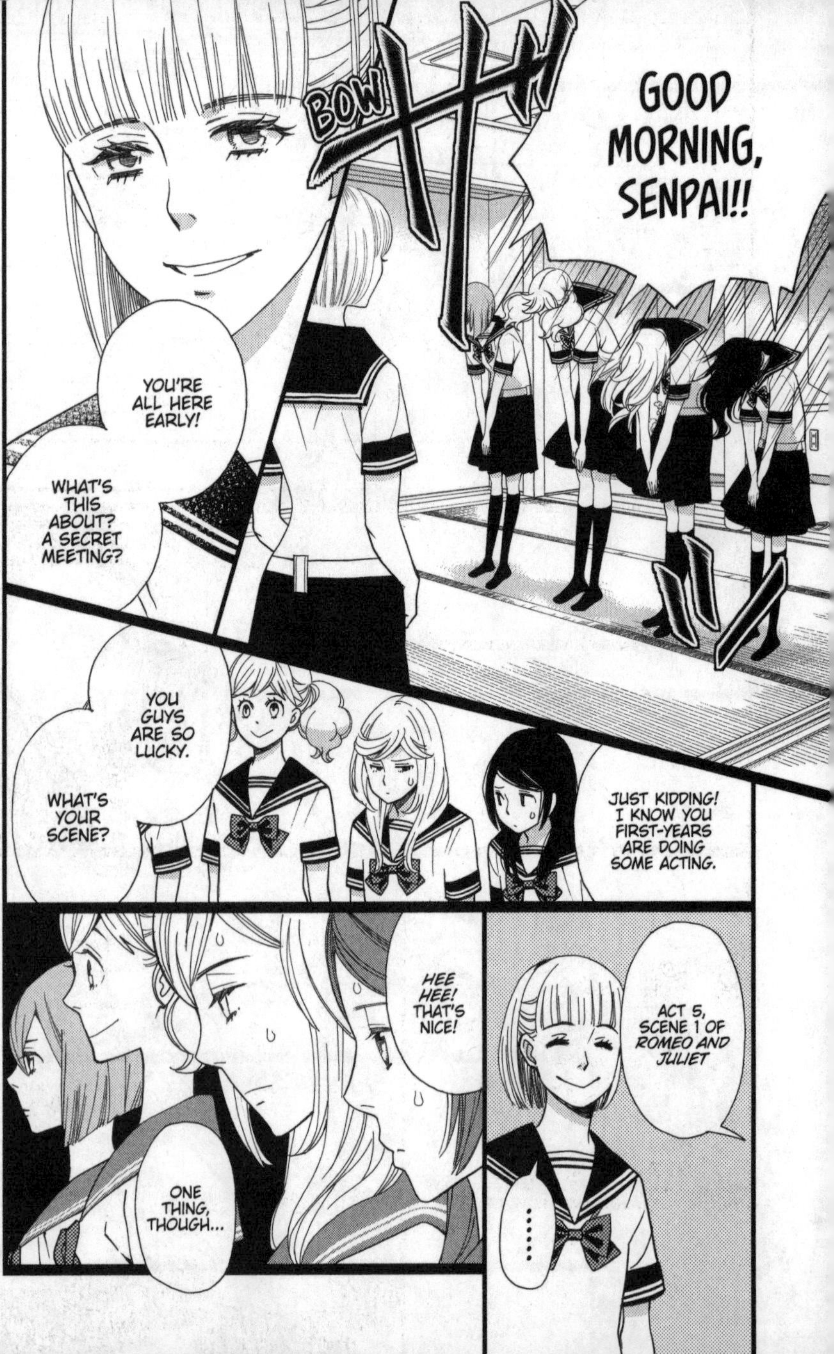
BOWWW
GOOD MORNING, SENPAI!!
YOU'RE ALL HERE EARLY!
WHAT'S THIS ABOUT? A SECRET MEETING?
JUST KIDDING! I KNOW YOU FIRST-YEARS ARE DOING SOME ACTING.
YOU GUYS ARE SO LUCKY.
WHAT'S YOUR SCENE?
ACT 5, SCENE 1 OF *ROMEO AND JULIET*
......
HEE HEE! THAT'S NICE!
ONE THING, THOUGH...

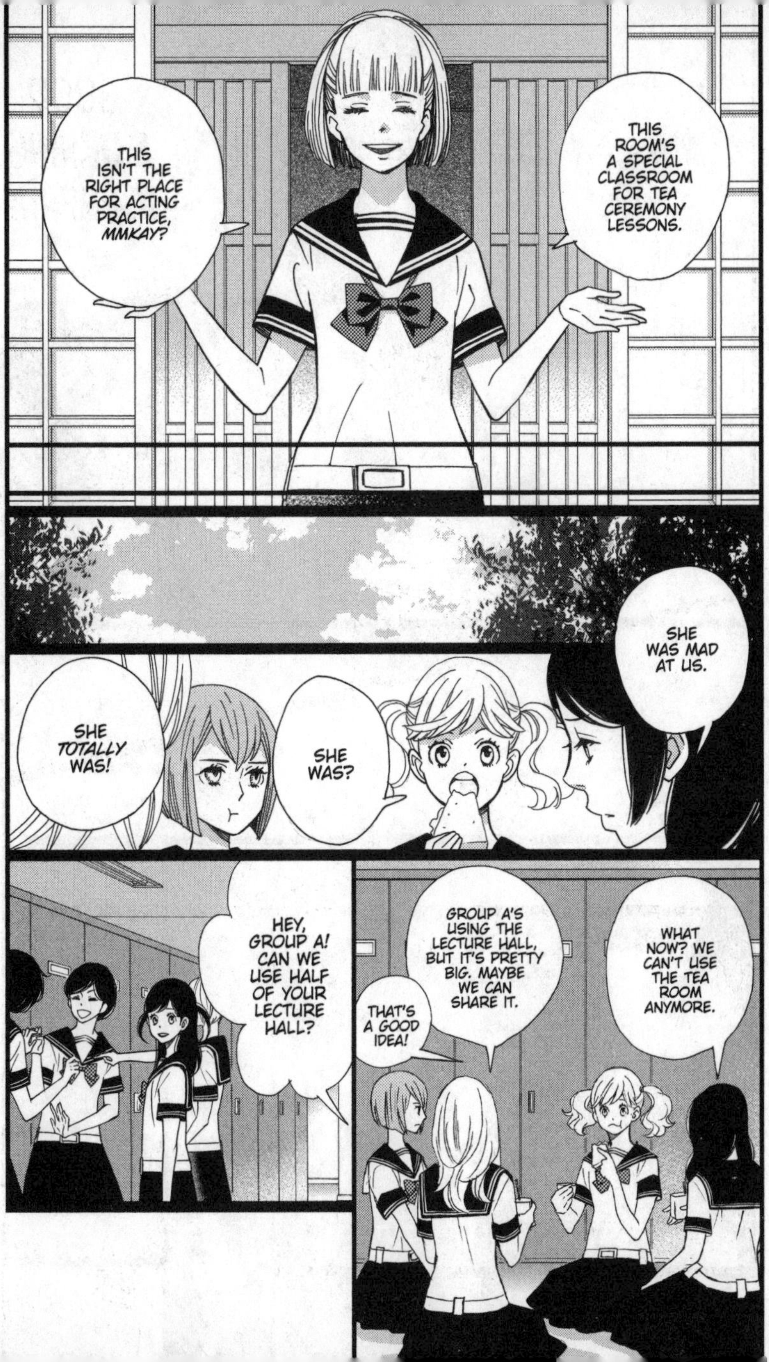
THIS ROOM'S A SPECIAL CLASSROOM FOR TEA CEREMONY LESSONS.
THIS ISN'T THE RIGHT PLACE FOR ACTING PRACTICE, *MMKAY?*
SHE WAS MAD AT US.
SHE WAS?
SHE *TOTALLY* WAS!
WHAT NOW? WE CAN'T USE THE TEA ROOM ANYMORE.
GROUP A'S USING THE LECTURE HALL, BUT IT'S PRETTY BIG. MAYBE WE CAN SHARE IT.
THAT'S A GOOD IDEA!
HEY, GROUP A! CAN WE USE HALF OF YOUR LECTURE HALL?

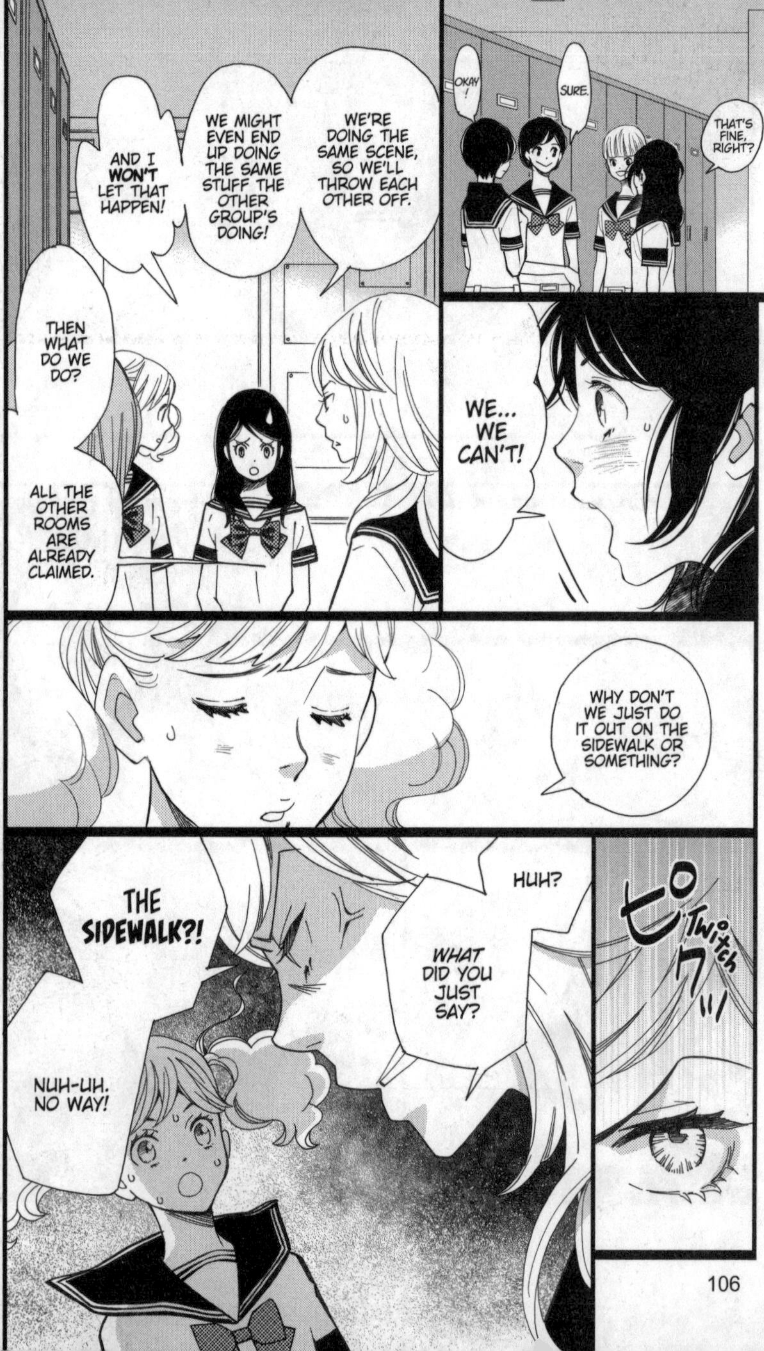
THAT'S FINE, RIGHT?
SURE.
OKAY!
WE... WE CAN'T!
WE'RE DOING THE SAME SCENE, SO WE'LL THROW EACH OTHER OFF.
WE MIGHT EVEN END UP DOING THE SAME STUFF THE OTHER GROUP'S DOING!
AND I **WON'T** LET THAT HAPPEN!
THEN WHAT DO WE DO?
ALL THE OTHER ROOMS ARE ALREADY CLAIMED.
WHY DON'T WE JUST DO IT OUT ON THE SIDEWALK OR SOMETHING?
ピクッ
Twitch
HUH?
WHAT DID YOU JUST SAY?
THE SIDEWALK?!
NUH-UH. NO WAY!

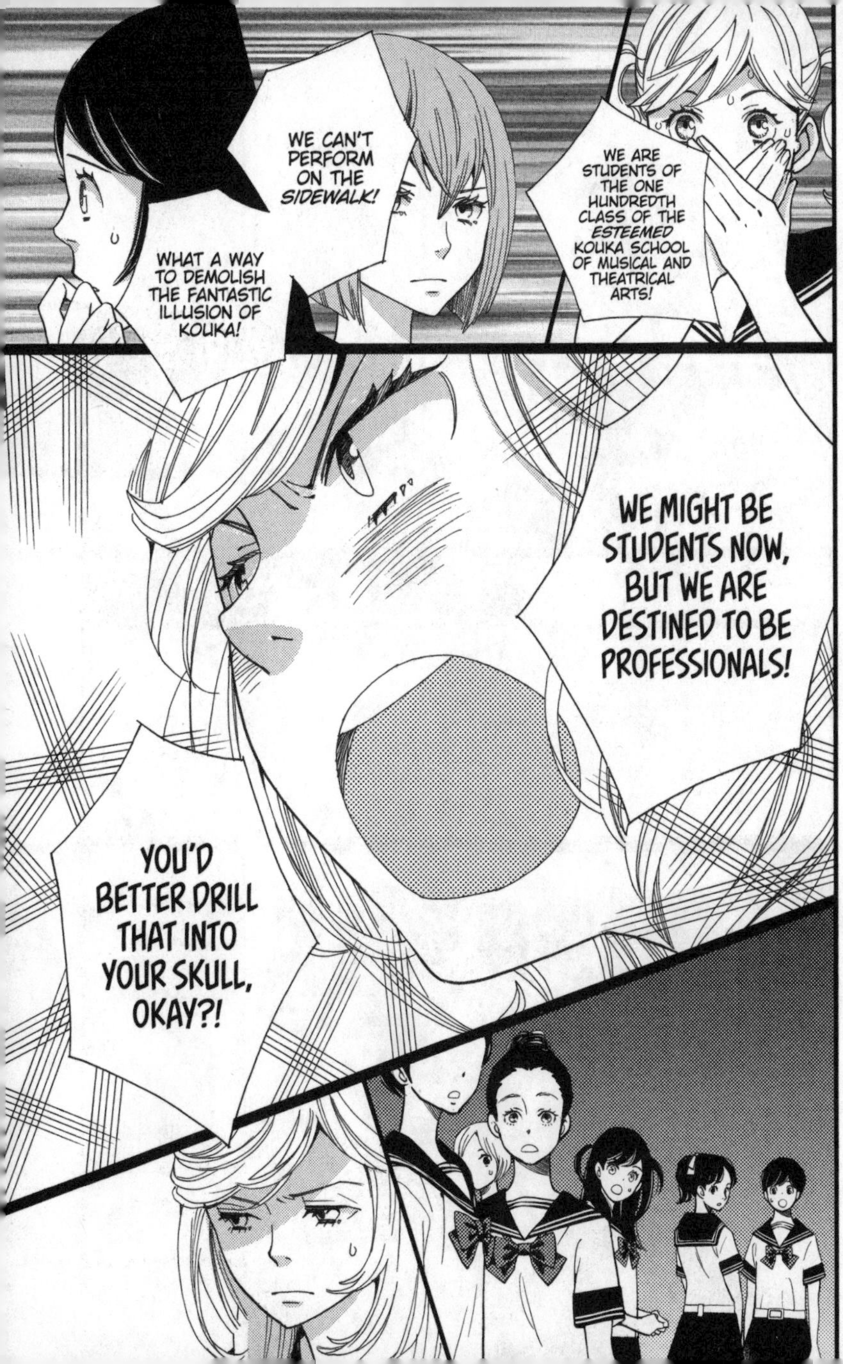
WE ARE STUDENTS OF THE ONE HUNDREDTH CLASS OF THE *ESTEEMED* KOUKA SCHOOL OF MUSICAL AND THEATRICAL ARTS!
WE CAN'T PERFORM ON THE *SIDEWALK!*
WHAT A WAY TO DEMOLISH THE FANTASTIC ILLUSION OF KOUKA!
WE MIGHT BE STUDENTS NOW, BUT WE ARE DESTINED TO BE PROFESSIONALS!
YOU'D BETTER DRILL THAT INTO YOUR SKULL, OKAY?!

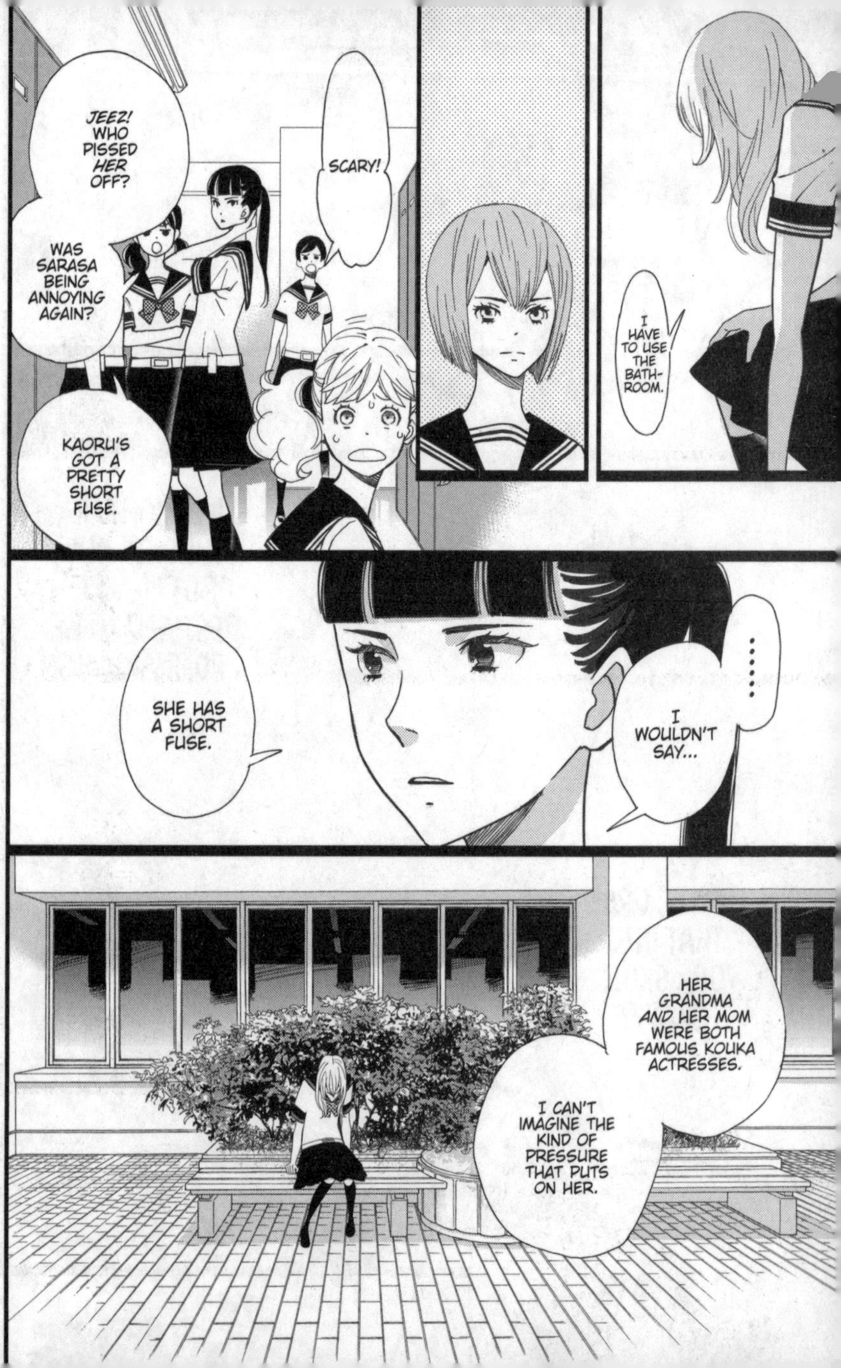
I HAVE TO USE THE BATH-ROOM.
SCARY!
JEEZ! WHO PISSED HER OFF?
WAS SARASA BEING ANNOYING AGAIN?
KAORU'S GOT A PRETTY SHORT FUSE.
......
I WOULDN'T SAY...
SHE HAS A SHORT FUSE.
HER GRANDMA AND HER MOM WERE BOTH FAMOUS KOUKA ACTRESSES.
I CAN'T IMAGINE THE KIND OF PRESSURE THAT PUTS ON HER.

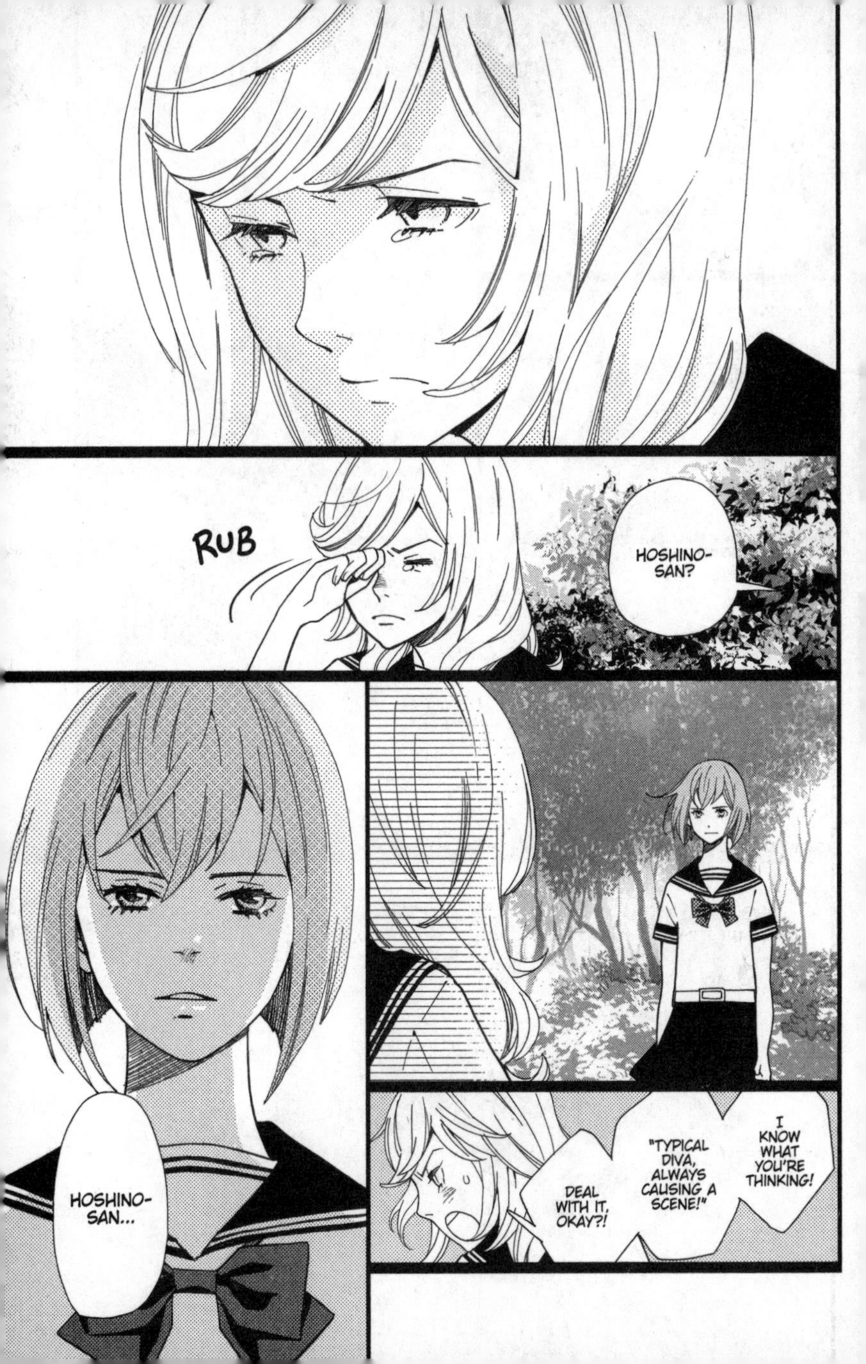
HOSHINO-SAN?
RUB
I KNOW WHAT YOU'RE THINKING!
"TYPICAL DIVA, ALWAYS CAUSING A SCENE!"
DEAL WITH IT, OKAY?!
HOSHINO-SAN...

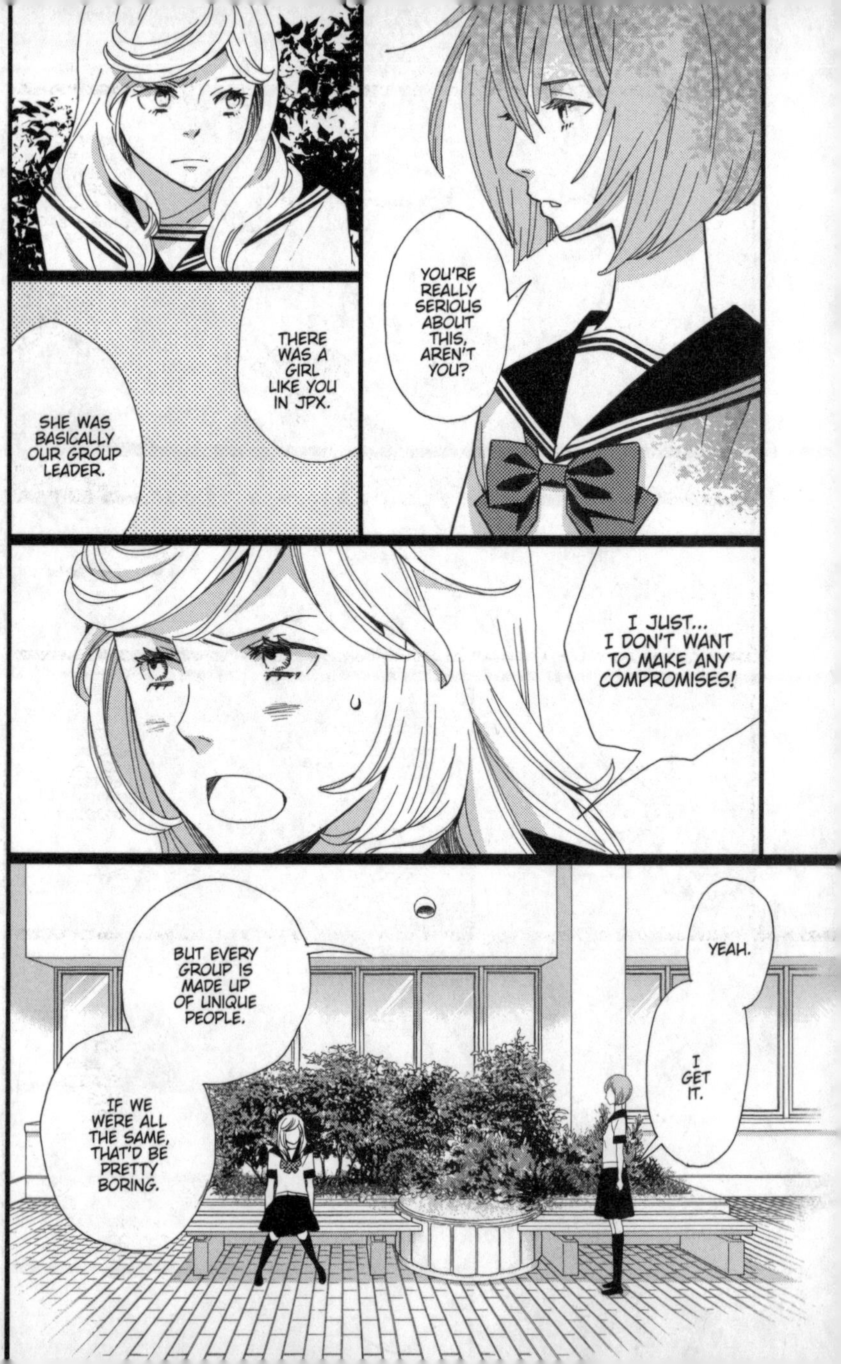
YOU'RE REALLY SERIOUS ABOUT THIS, AREN'T YOU?
THERE WAS A GIRL LIKE YOU IN JPX.
SHE WAS BASICALLY OUR GROUP LEADER.
I JUST... I DON'T WANT TO MAKE ANY COMPROMISES!
YEAH.
I GET IT.
BUT EVERY GROUP IS MADE UP OF UNIQUE PEOPLE.
IF WE WERE ALL THE SAME, THAT'D BE PRETTY BORING.

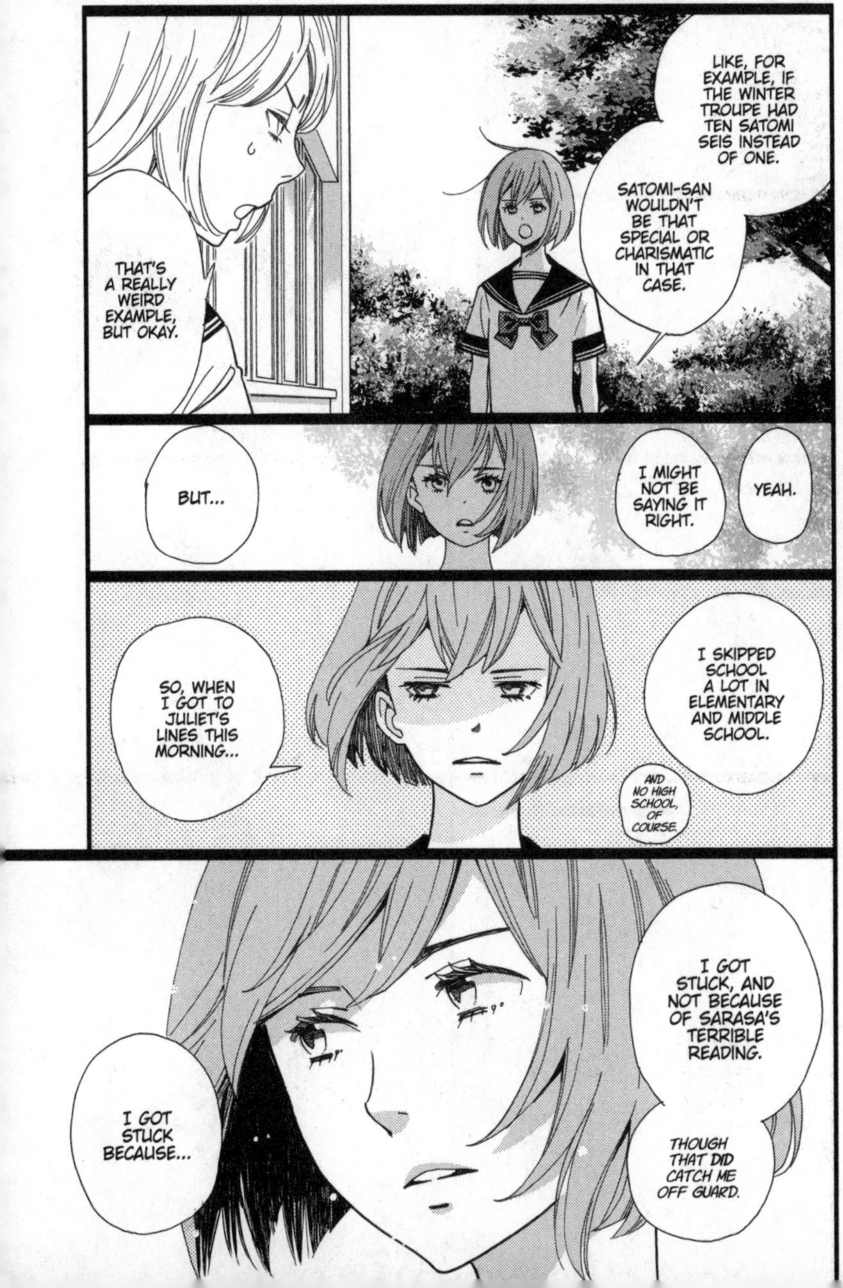
LIKE, FOR EXAMPLE, IF THE WINTER TROUPE HAD TEN SATOMI SEIS INSTEAD OF ONE.
SATOMI-SAN WOULDN'T BE THAT SPECIAL OR CHARISMATIC IN THAT CASE.
THAT'S A REALLY WEIRD EXAMPLE, BUT OKAY.
YEAH.
I MIGHT NOT BE SAYING IT RIGHT.
BUT...
I SKIPPED SCHOOL A LOT IN ELEMENTARY AND MIDDLE SCHOOL.
AND NO HIGH SCHOOL, OF COURSE.
SO, WHEN I GOT TO JULIET'S LINES THIS MORNING...
I GOT STUCK, AND NOT BECAUSE OF SARASA'S TERRIBLE READING.
THOUGH THAT DID CATCH ME OFF GUARD.
I GOT STUCK BECAUSE...

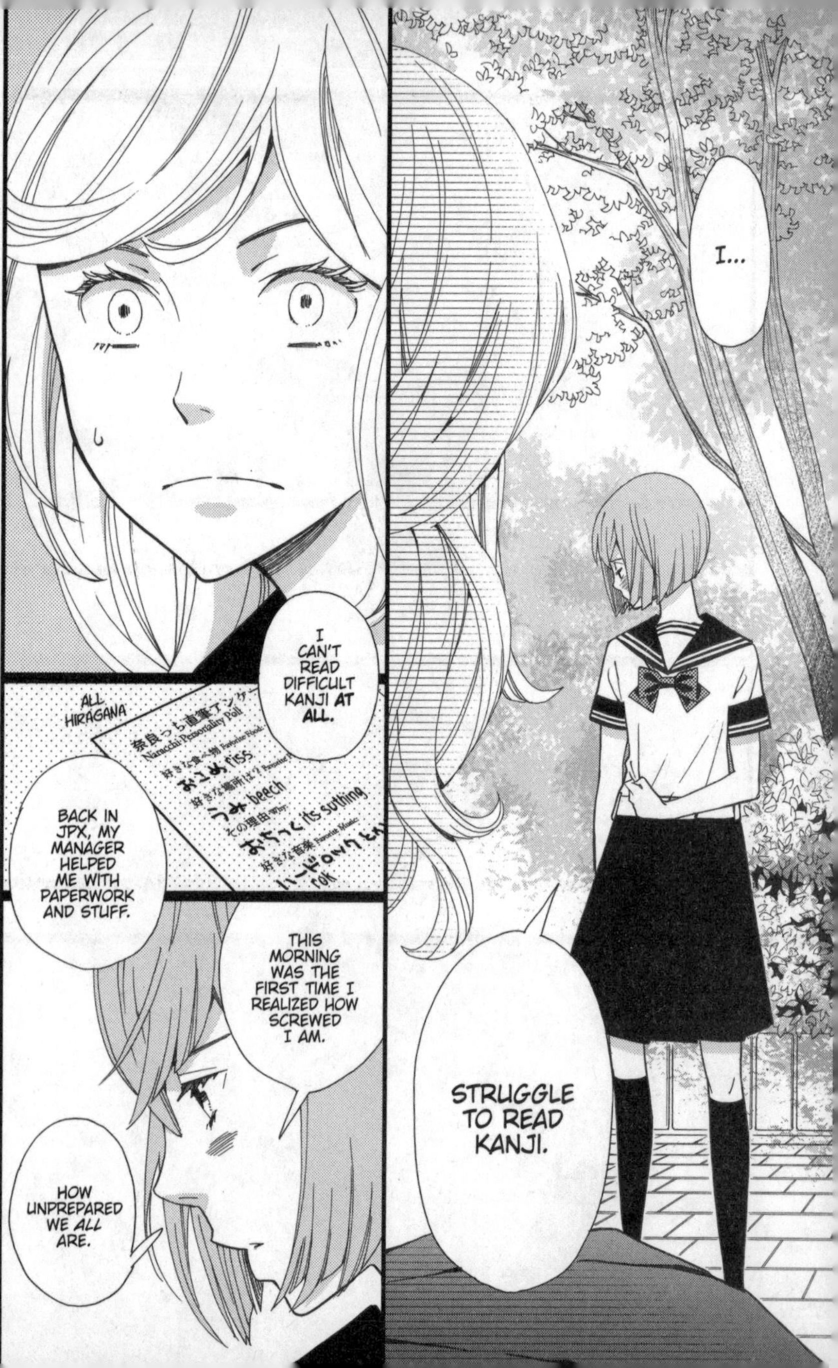
I...
STRUGGLE TO READ KANJI.
I CAN'T READ DIFFICULT KANJI AT ALL.
ALL HIRAGANA
奈良っち直筆アンケー
Naracchi: Personality Poll
Favorite Food:
fiss
beech
its suthing
Favorite Music:
rok
BACK IN JPX, MY MANAGER HELPED ME WITH PAPERWORK AND STUFF.
THIS MORNING WAS THE FIRST TIME I REALIZED HOW SCREWED I AM.
HOW UNPREPARED WE ALL ARE.

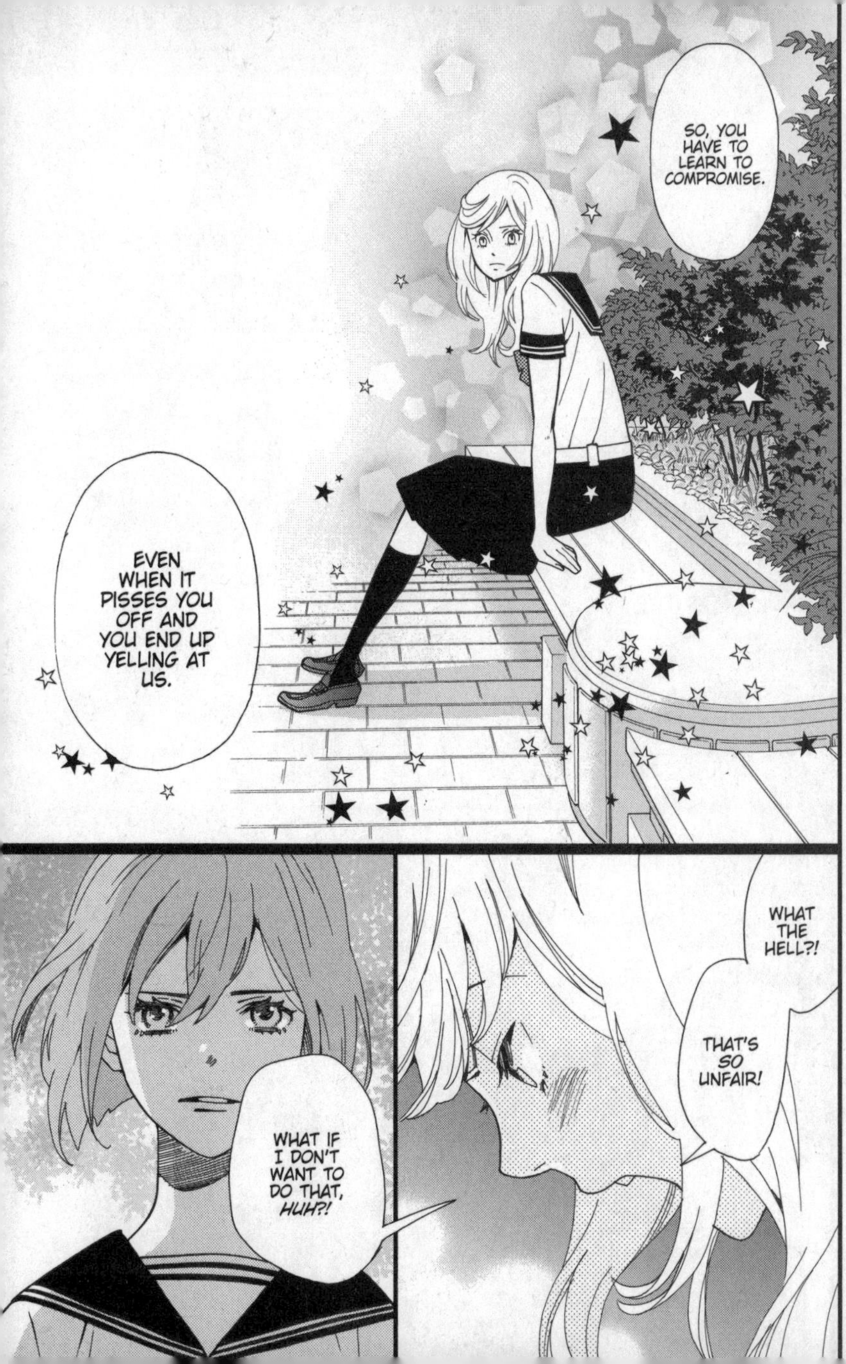
SO, YOU HAVE TO LEARN TO COMPROMISE.
EVEN WHEN IT PISSES YOU OFF AND YOU END UP YELLING AT US.
WHAT THE HELL?!
THAT'S SO UNFAIR!
WHAT IF I DON'T WANT TO DO THAT, *HUH?!*

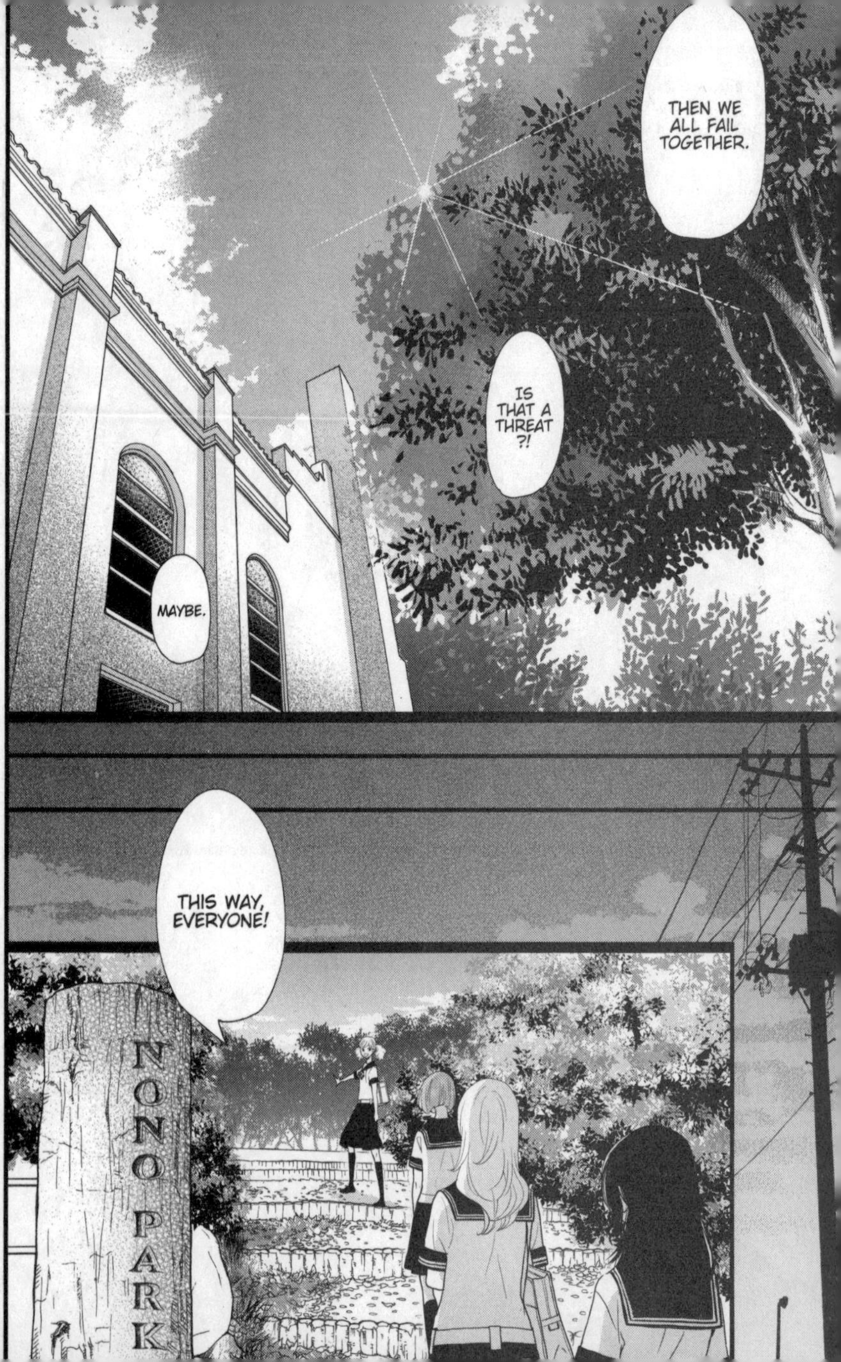
THEN WE ALL FAIL TOGETHER.
IS THAT A THREAT?!
MAYBE.
THIS WAY, EVERYONE!
NONO PARK

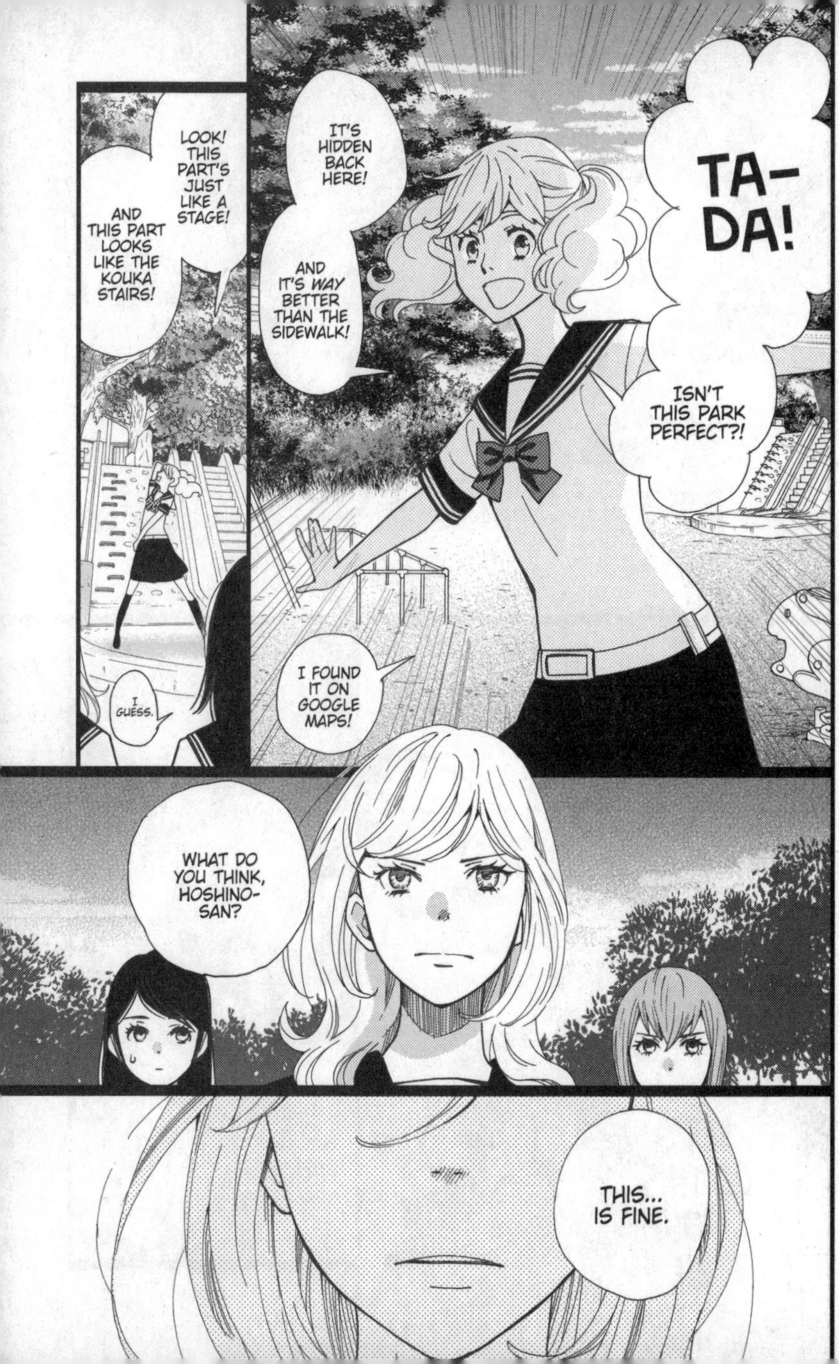
TA-DA!
ISN'T THIS PARK PERFECT?!
IT'S HIDDEN BACK HERE!
AND IT'S *WAY* BETTER THAN THE SIDEWALK!
I FOUND IT ON GOOGLE MAPS!
LOOK! THIS PART'S JUST LIKE A STAGE!
AND THIS PART LOOKS LIKE THE KOUKA STAIRS!
I GUESS.
WHAT DO YOU THINK, HOSHINO-SAN?
THIS... IS FINE.

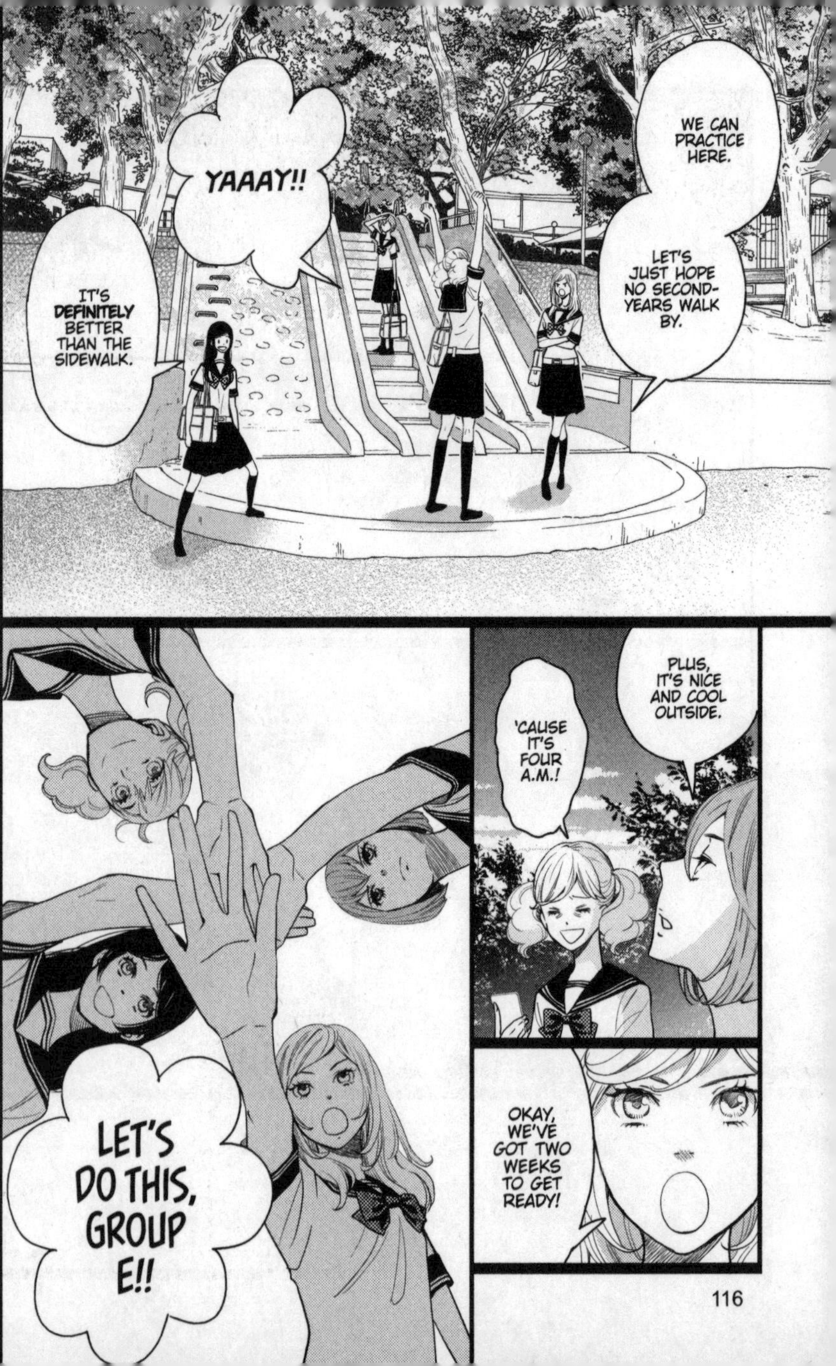
WE CAN PRACTICE HERE.
LET'S JUST HOPE NO SECOND-YEARS WALK BY.
YAAAY!!
IT'S DEFINITELY BETTER THAN THE SIDEWALK.
PLUS, IT'S NICE AND COOL OUTSIDE.
'CAUSE IT'S FOUR A.M.!
OKAY, WE'VE GOT TWO WEEKS TO GET READY!
LET'S DO THIS, GROUP E!!

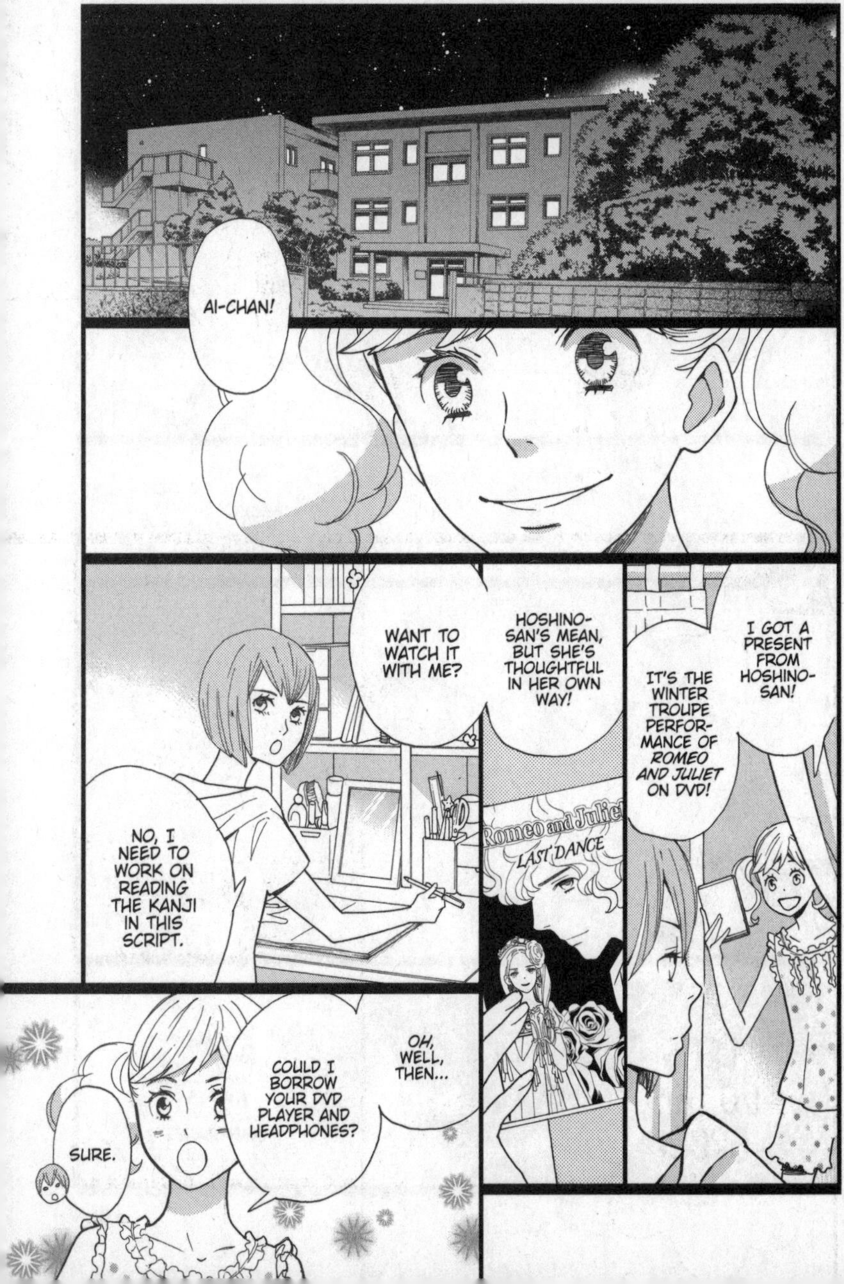
AI-CHAN!
I GOT A PRESENT FROM HOSHINO-SAN!
IT'S THE WINTER TROUPE PERFORMANCE OF *ROMEO AND JULIET* ON DVD!
Romeo and Juliet
LAST DANCE
HOSHINO-SAN'S MEAN, BUT SHE'S THOUGHTFUL IN HER OWN WAY!
WANT TO WATCH IT WITH ME?
NO, I NEED TO WORK ON READING THE KANJI IN THIS SCRIPT.
OH, WELL, THEN...
COULD I BORROW YOUR DVD PLAYER AND HEADPHONES?
SURE.

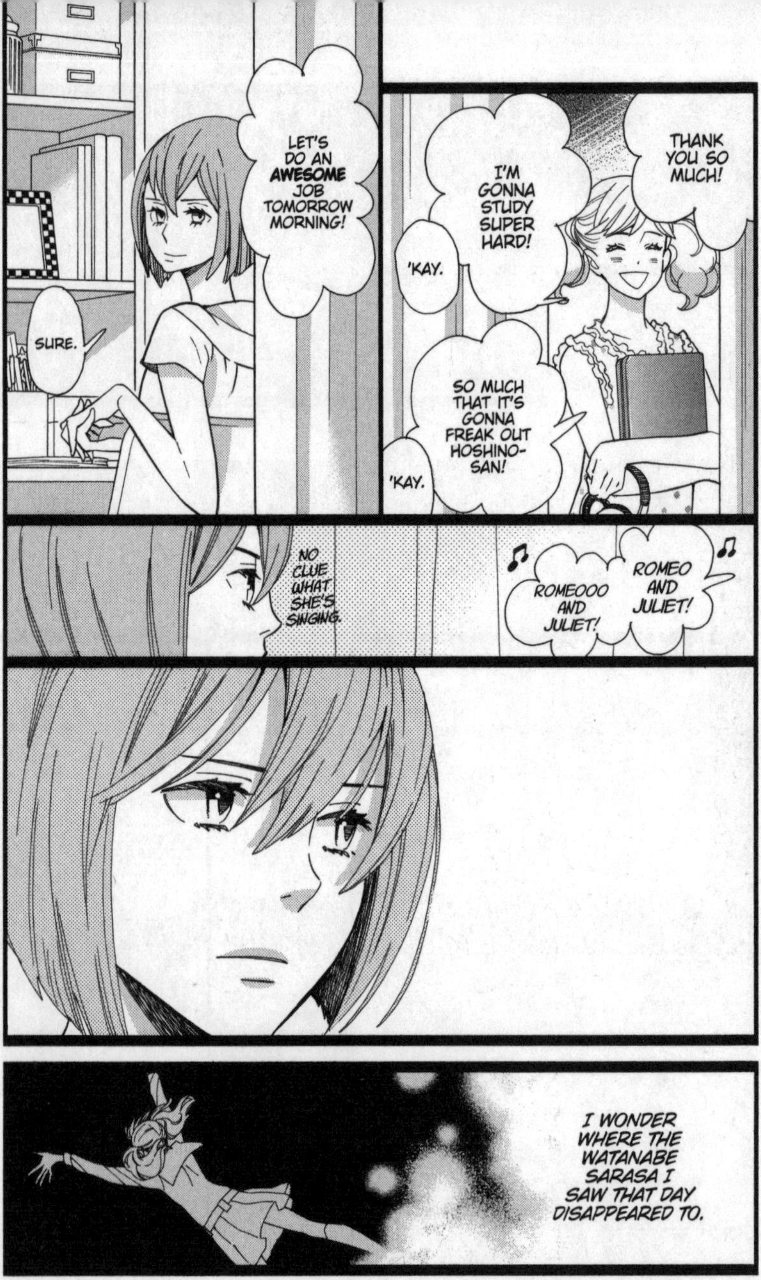
THANK YOU SO MUCH!
I'M GONNA STUDY SUPER HARD!
'KAY.
SO MUCH THAT IT'S GONNA FREAK OUT HOSHINO-SAN!
'KAY.
LET'S DO AN **AWESOME** JOB TOMORROW MORNING!
SURE.
ROMEO AND JULIET!
ROMEOOO AND JULIET!
NO CLUE WHAT SHE'S SINGING.
I WONDER WHERE THE WATANABE SARASA I SAW THAT DAY DISAPPEARED TO.

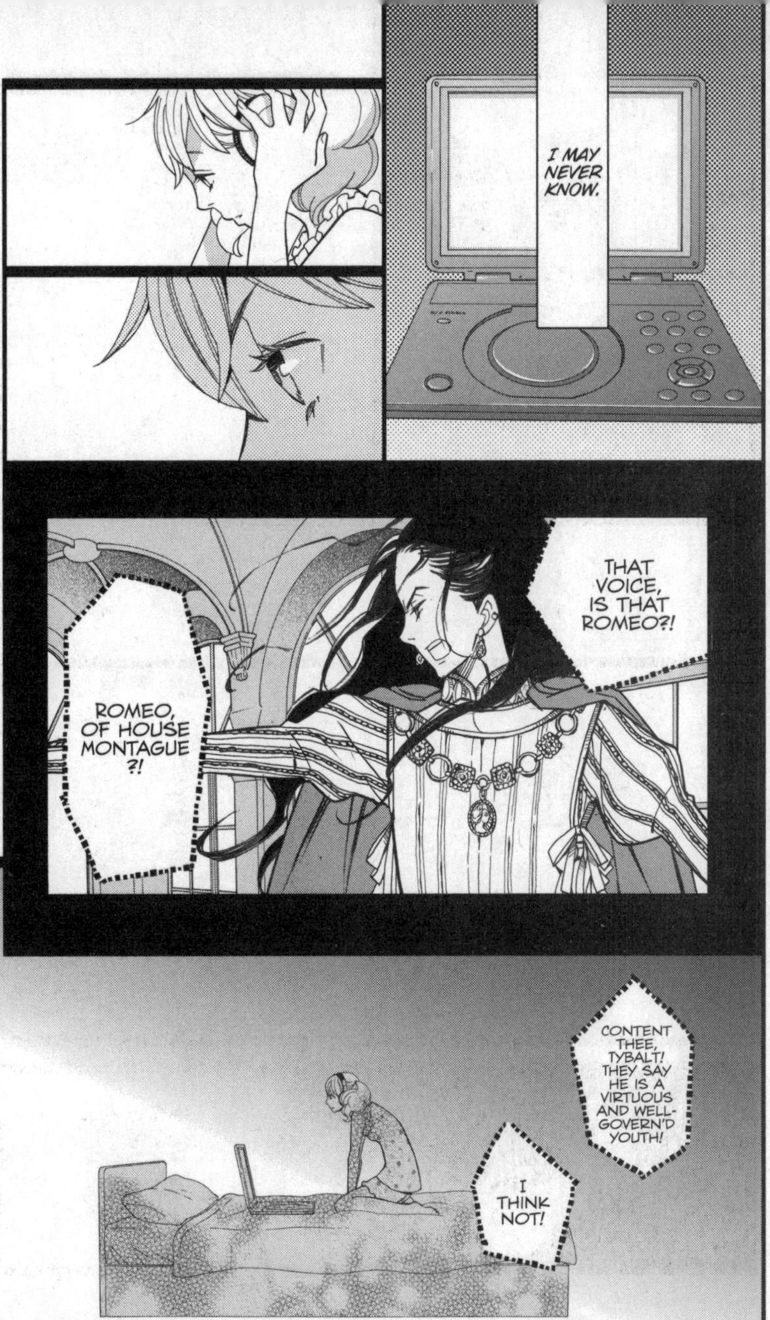
I MAY NEVER KNOW.
THAT VOICE, IS THAT ROMEO?!
ROMEO, OF HOUSE MONTAGUE ?!
CONTENT THEE, TYBALT! THEY SAY HE IS A VIRTUOUS AND WELL-GOVERN'D YOUTH!
I THINK NOT!

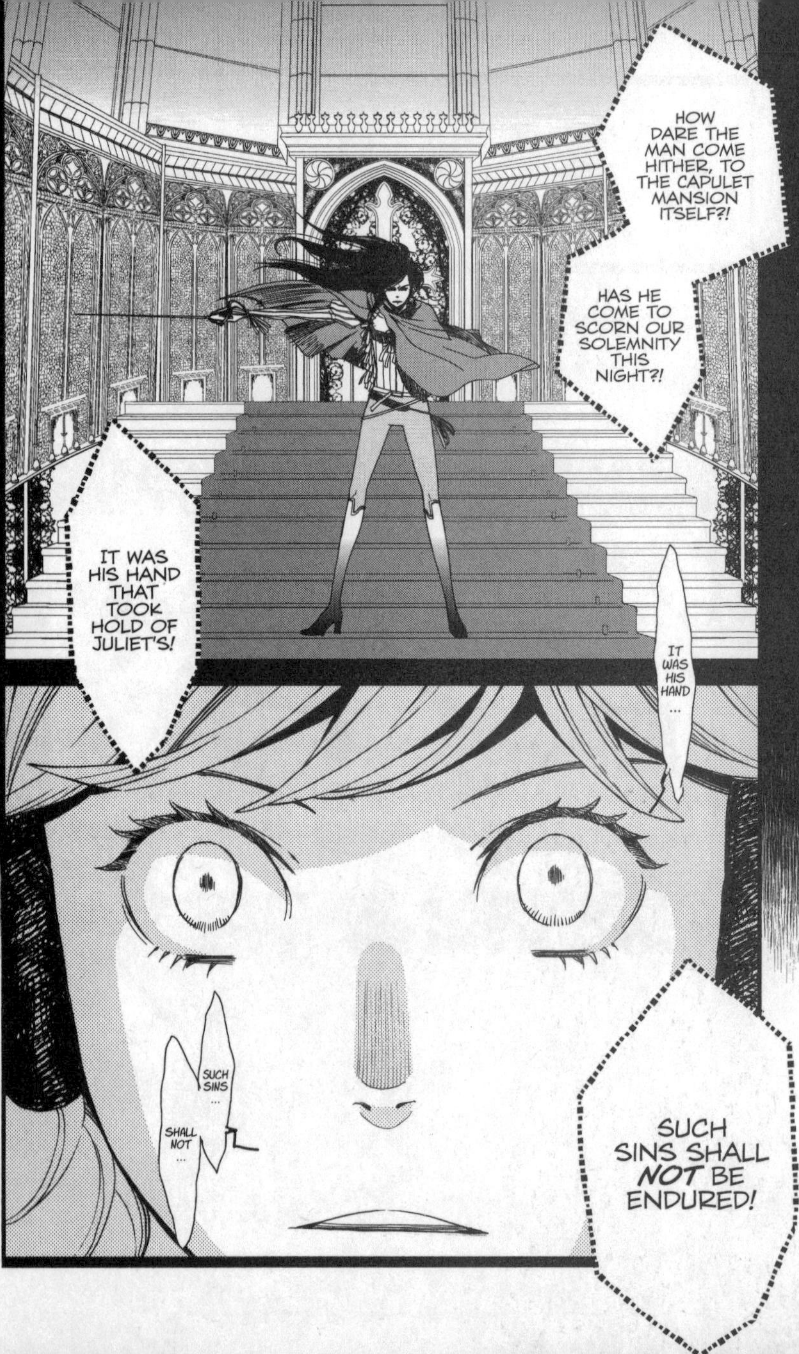
HOW DARE THE MAN COME HITHER, TO THE CAPULET MANSION ITSELF?!
HAS HE COME TO SCORN OUR SOLEMNITY THIS NIGHT?!
IT WAS HIS HAND THAT TOOK HOLD OF JULIET'S!
IT WAS HIS HAND...
SUCH SINS...
SHALL NOT...
SUCH SINS SHALL *NOT* BE ENDURED!

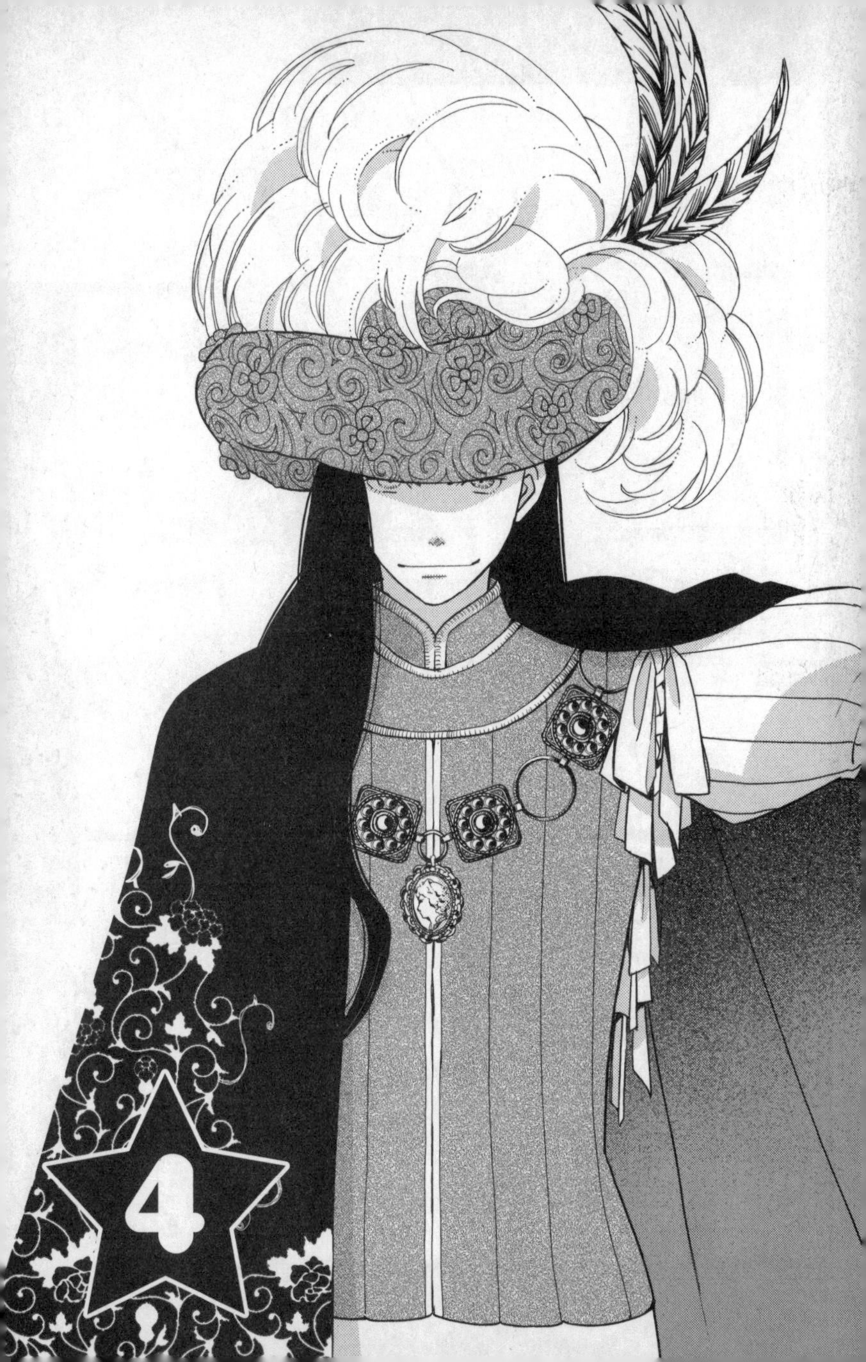
4

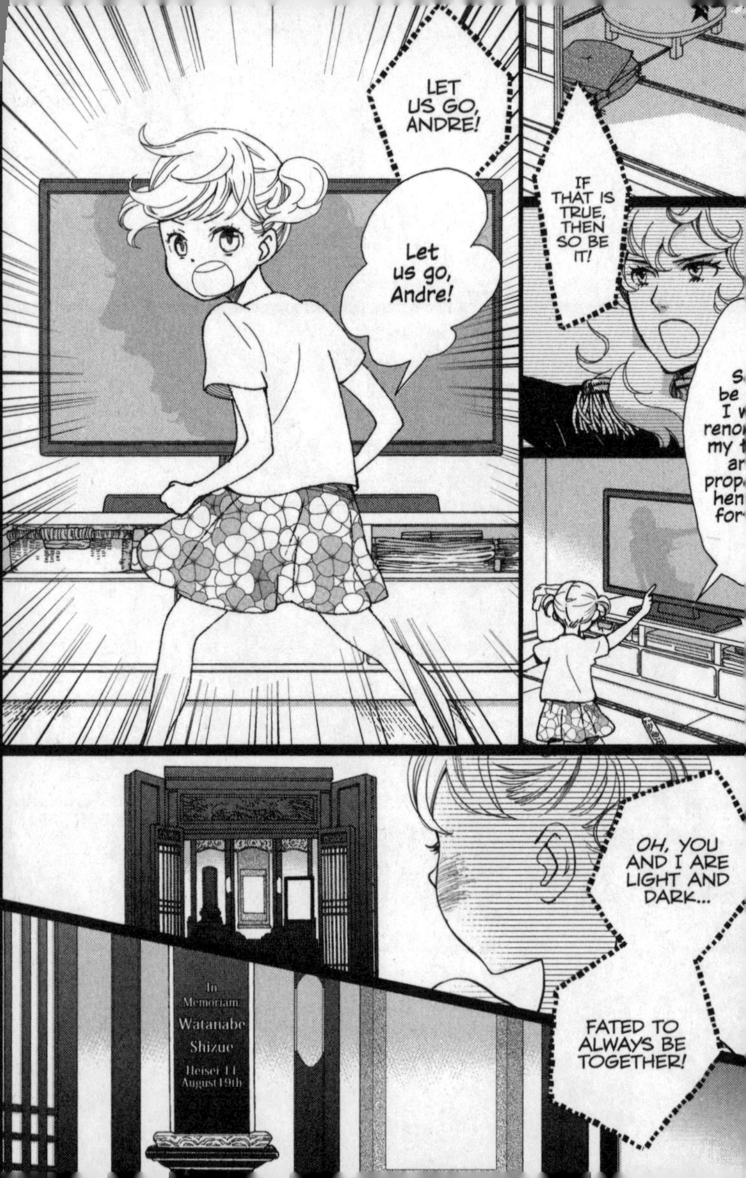
IF THAT IS TRUE, THEN SO BE IT!
LET US GO, ANDRE!
Let us go, Andre!
OH, YOU AND I ARE LIGHT AND DARK...
FATED TO ALWAYS BE TOGETHER!
In Memoriam: Watanabe Shizue Heisei 11 August 19th

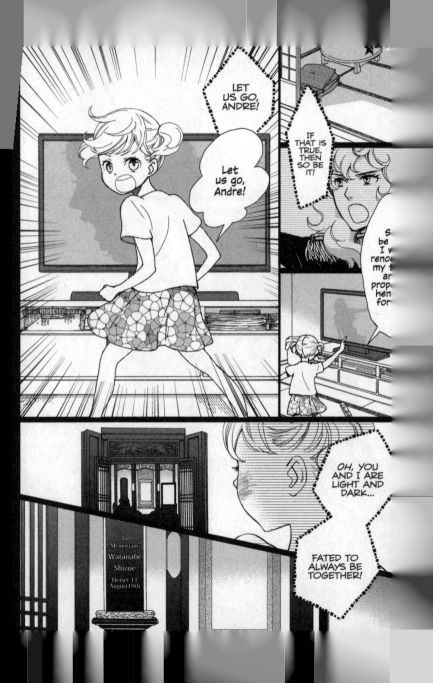

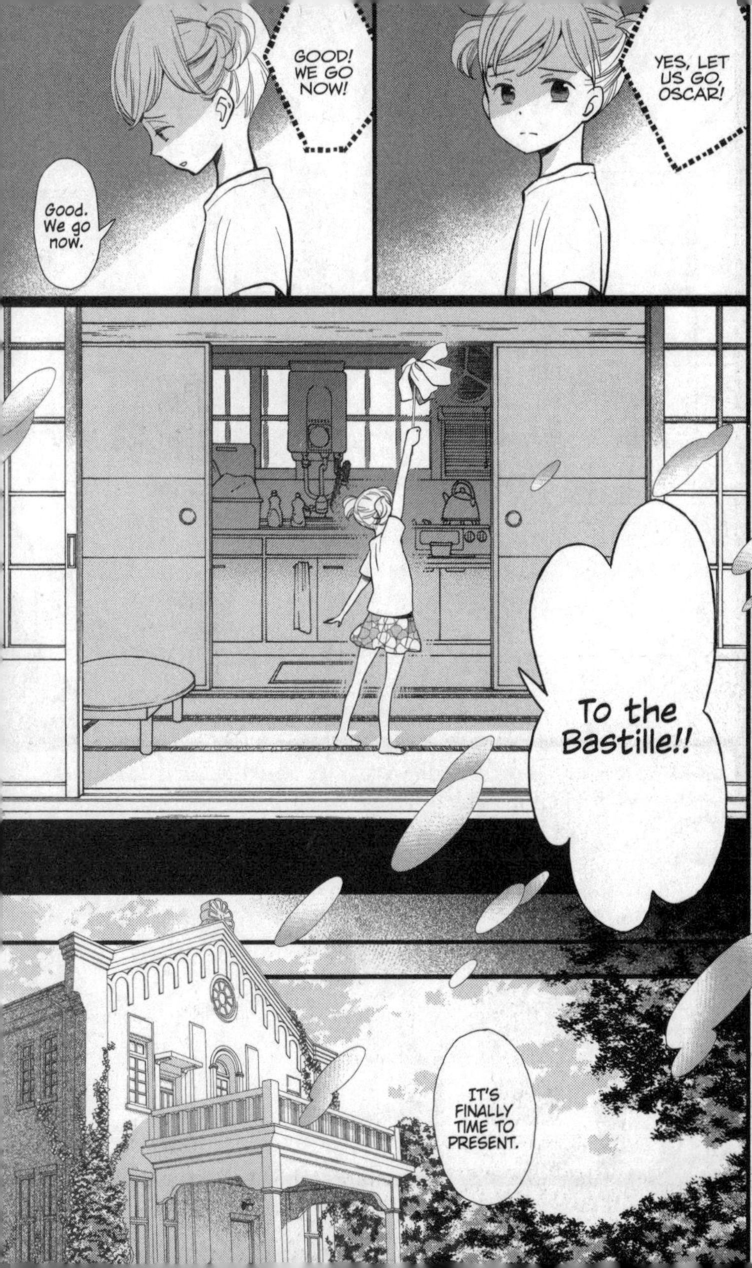
YES, LET US GO, OSCAR!
GOOD! WE GO NOW!
Good. We go now.
To the Bastille!!
IT'S FINALLY TIME TO PRESENT.

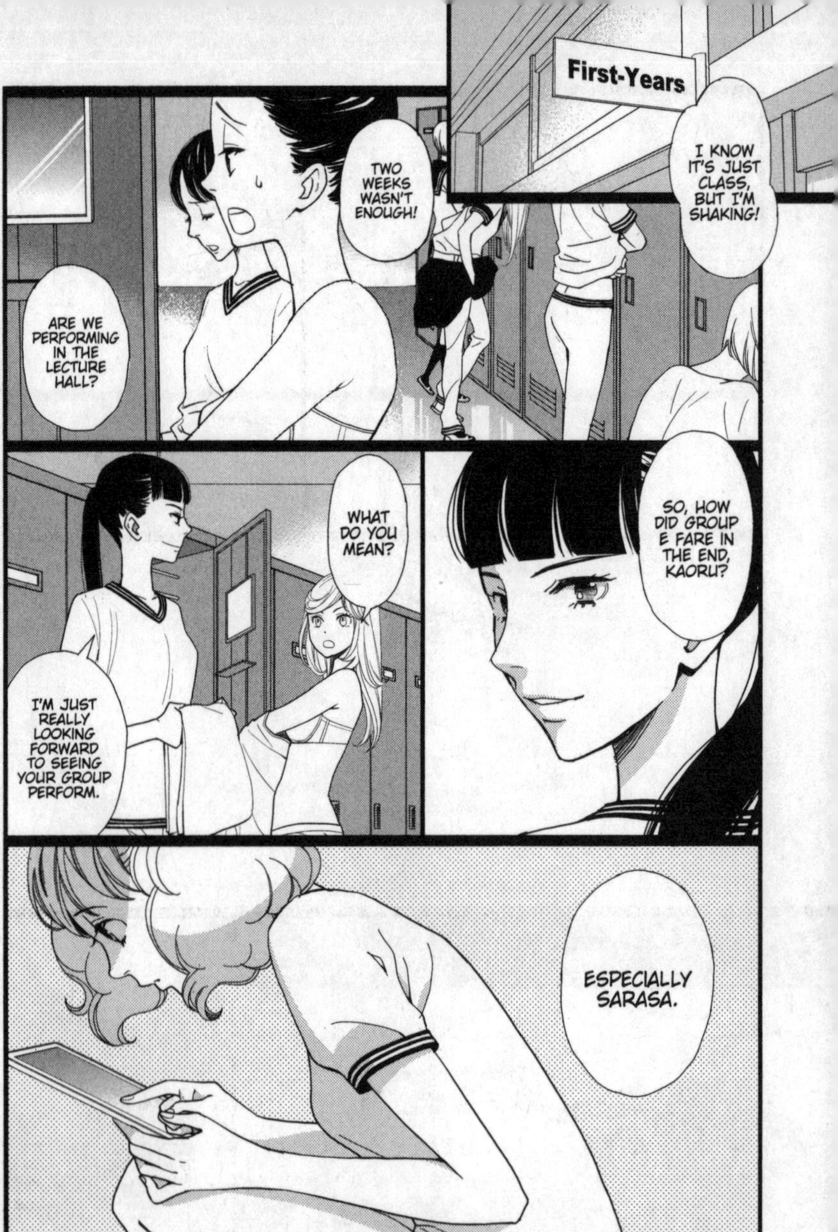
First-Years
I KNOW IT'S JUST CLASS, BUT I'M SHAKING!
TWO WEEKS WASN'T ENOUGH!
ARE WE PERFORMING IN THE LECTURE HALL?
SO, HOW DID GROUP E FARE IN THE END, KAORU?
WHAT DO YOU MEAN?
I'M JUST REALLY LOOKING FORWARD TO SEEING YOUR GROUP PERFORM.
ESPECIALLY SARASA.

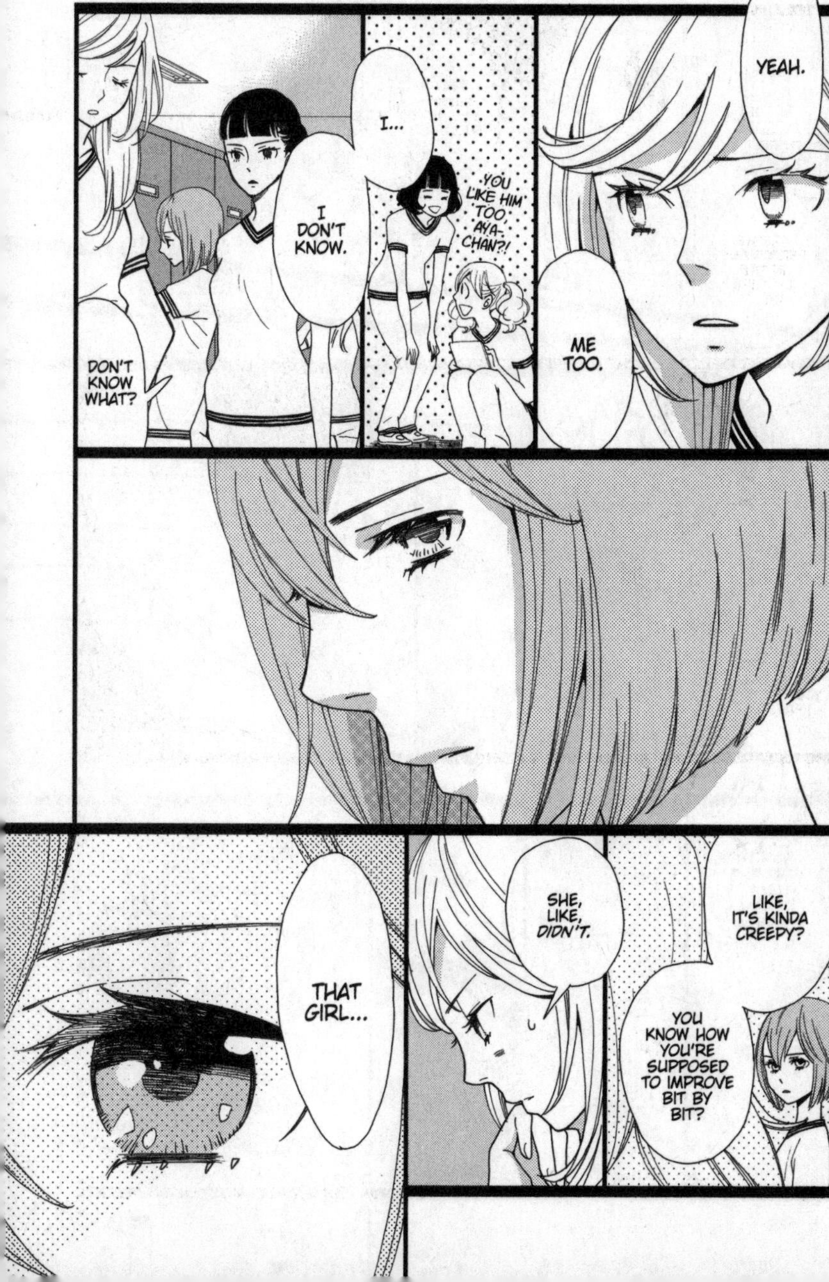
YEAH.
ME TOO.
YOU LIKE HIM TOO, AYA-CHAN?!
I...
I DON'T KNOW.
DON'T KNOW WHAT?
LIKE, IT'S KINDA CREEPY?
YOU KNOW HOW YOU'RE SUPPOSED TO IMPROVE BIT BY BIT?
SHE, LIKE, DIDN'T.
THAT GIRL...

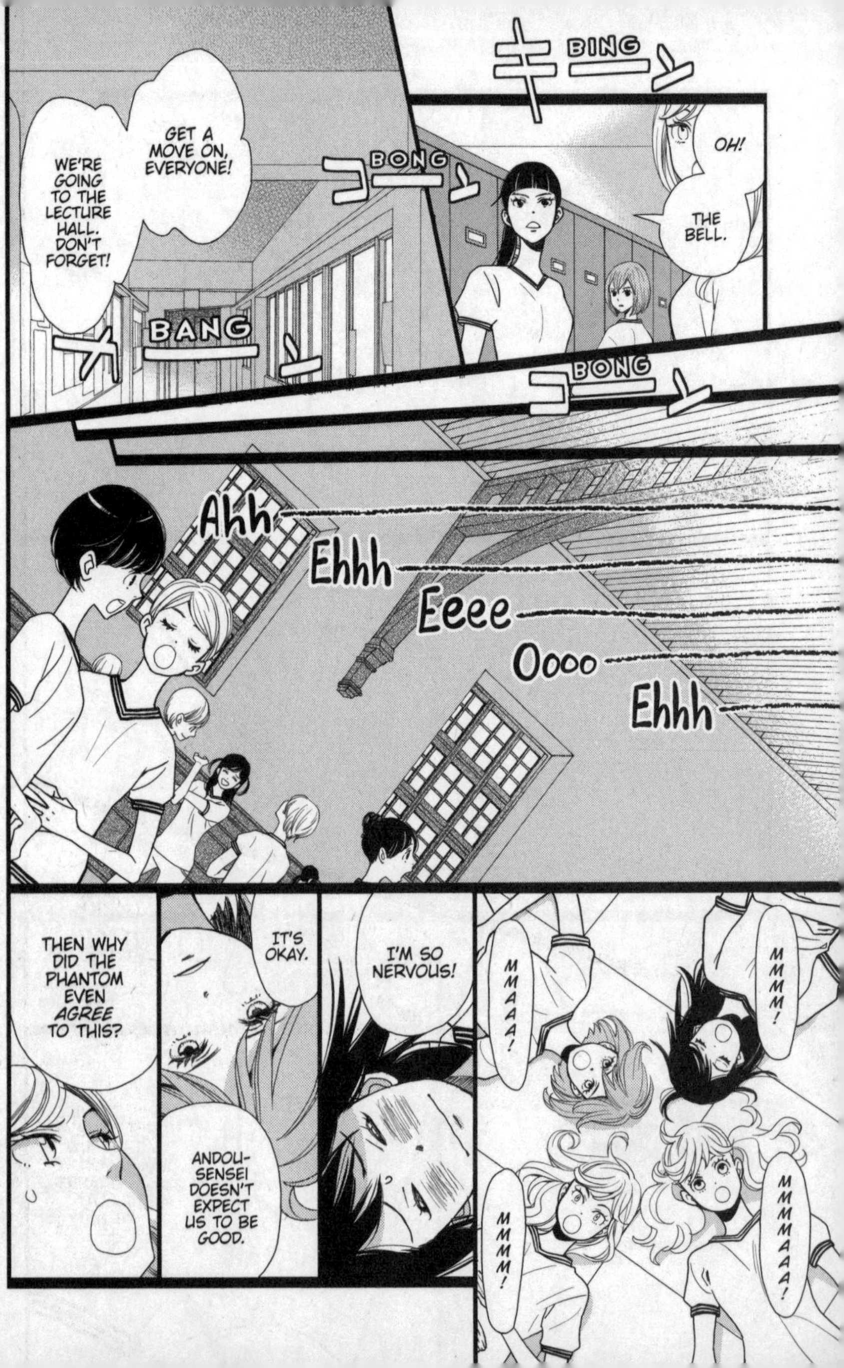
BING
OH!
THE BELL.
BONG
GET A MOVE ON, EVERYONE!
WE'RE GOING TO THE LECTURE HALL. DON'T FORGET!
BANG
BONG
Ahh
Ehhh
Eeee
Oooo
Ehhh
MMMM!
MMAAA!
MMMMAAA!
MMMM!
I'M SO NERVOUS!
IT'S OKAY.
ANDOU-SENSEI DOESN'T EXPECT US TO BE GOOD.
THEN WHY DID THE PHANTOM EVEN *AGREE* TO THIS?

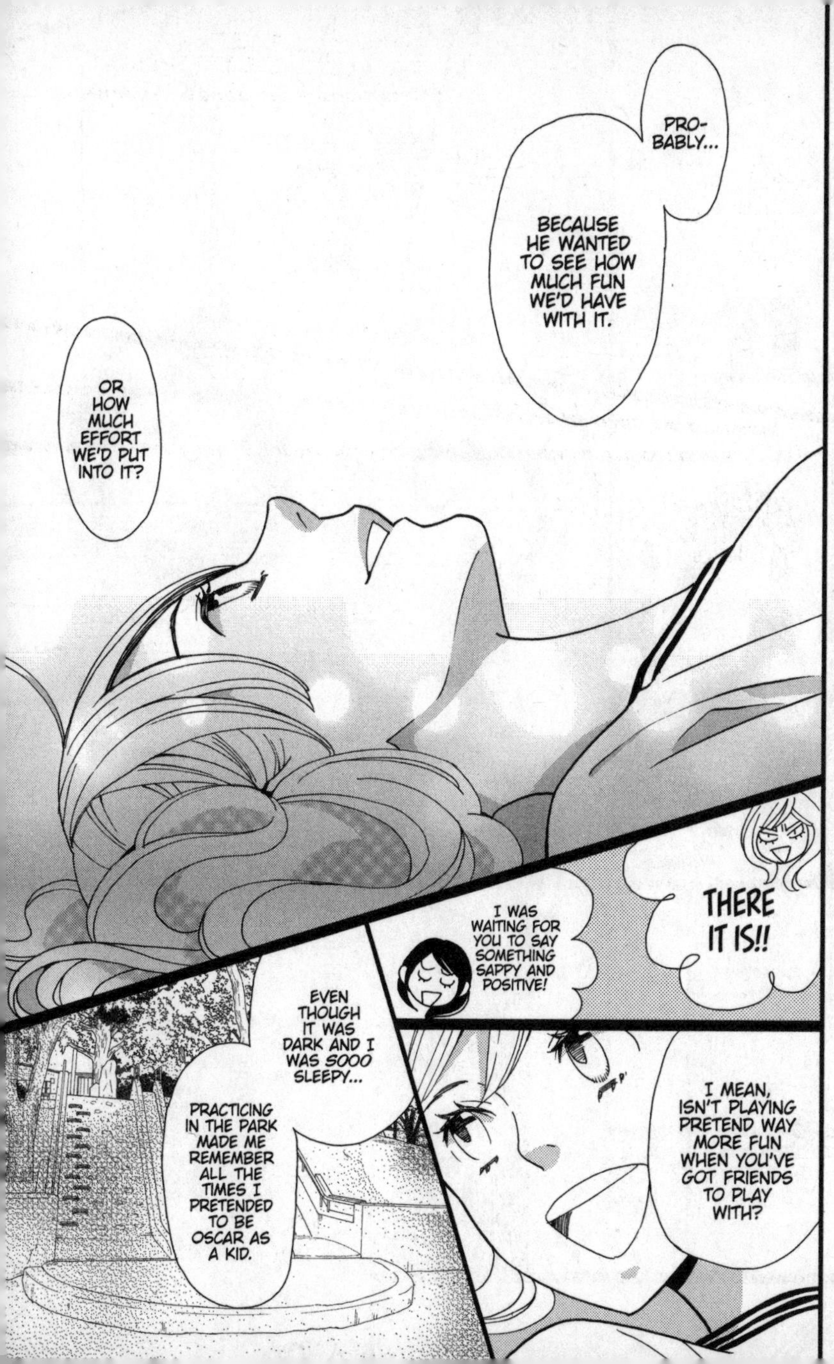
PRO-BABLY...
BECAUSE HE WANTED TO SEE HOW MUCH FUN WE'D HAVE WITH IT.
OR HOW MUCH EFFORT WE'D PUT INTO IT?
THERE IT IS!!
I WAS WAITING FOR YOU TO SAY SOMETHING SAPPY AND POSITIVE!
I MEAN, ISN'T PLAYING PRETEND WAY MORE FUN WHEN YOU'VE GOT FRIENDS TO PLAY WITH?
EVEN THOUGH IT WAS DARK AND I WAS *SOOO* SLEEPY...
PRACTICING IN THE PARK MADE ME REMEMBER ALL THE TIMES I PRETENDED TO BE OSCAR AS A KID.

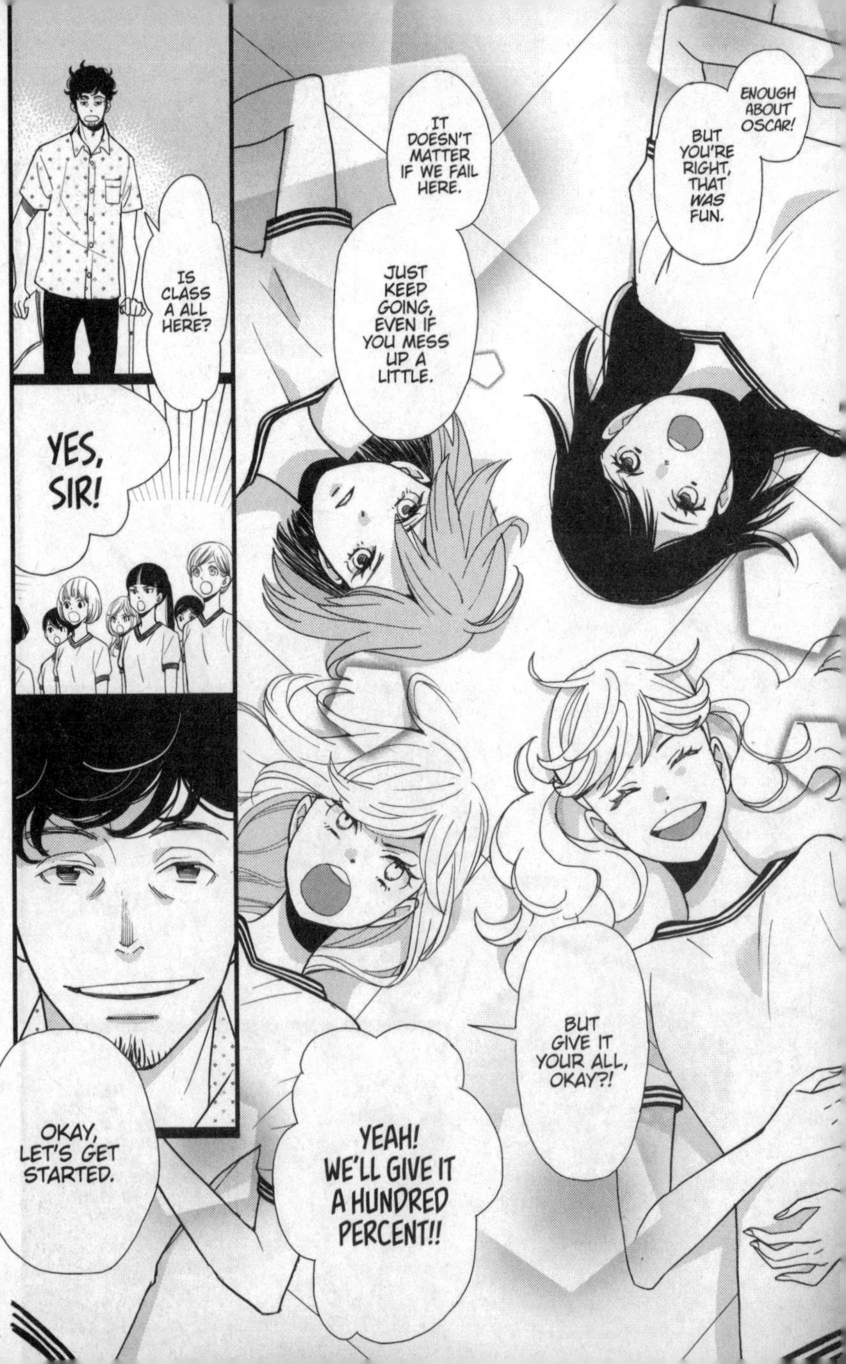
ENOUGH ABOUT OSCAR!
BUT YOU'RE RIGHT, THAT *WAS* FUN.
IT DOESN'T MATTER IF WE FAIL HERE.
JUST KEEP GOING, EVEN IF YOU MESS UP A LITTLE.
BUT GIVE IT YOUR ALL, OKAY?!
YEAH! WE'LL GIVE IT A HUNDRED PERCENT!!
IS CLASS A ALL HERE?
YES, SIR!
OKAY, LET'S GET STARTED.

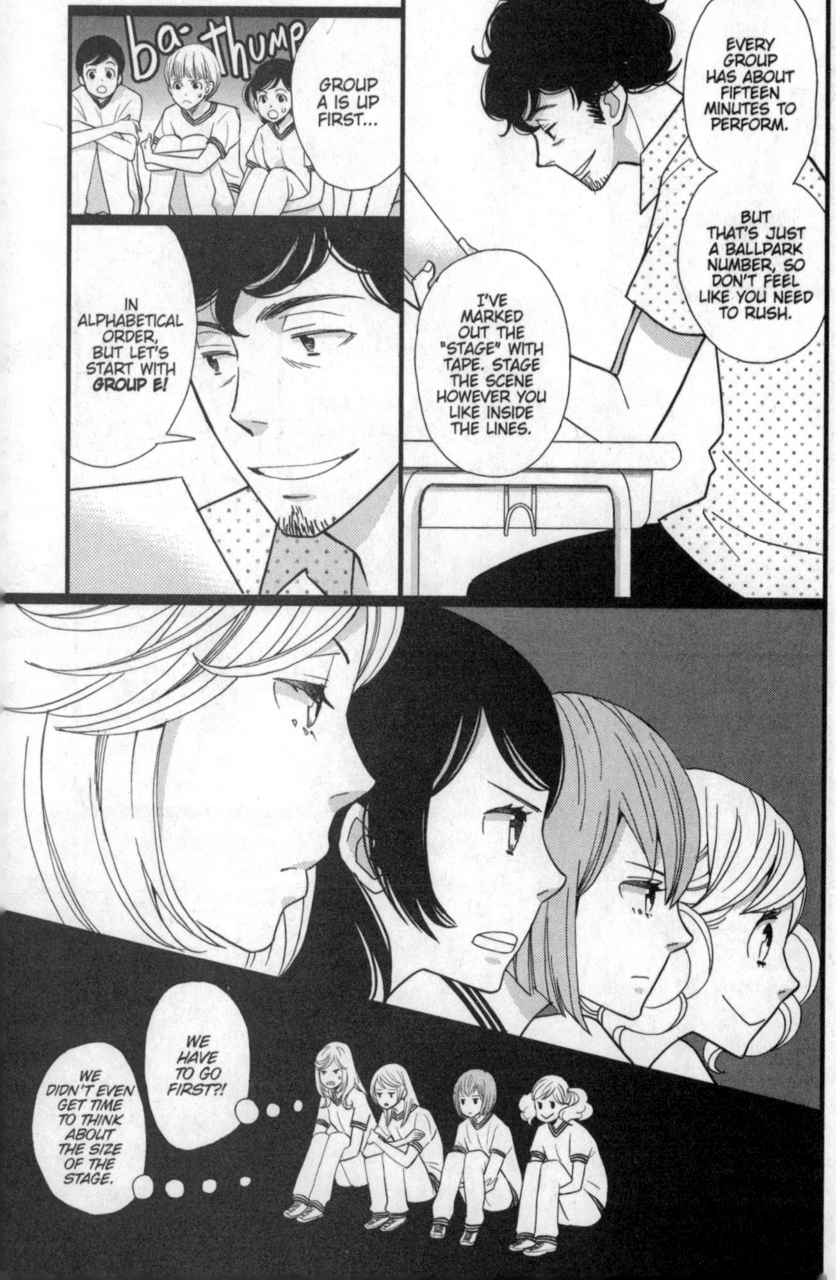
EVERY GROUP HAS ABOUT FIFTEEN MINUTES TO PERFORM.
BUT THAT'S JUST A BALLPARK NUMBER, SO DON'T FEEL LIKE YOU NEED TO RUSH.
I'VE MARKED OUT THE "STAGE" WITH TAPE. STAGE THE SCENE HOWEVER YOU LIKE INSIDE THE LINES.
ba-thump
GROUP A IS UP FIRST...
IN ALPHABETICAL ORDER, BUT LET'S START WITH **GROUP E!**
WE HAVE TO GO FIRST?!
WE DIDN'T EVEN GET TIME TO THINK ABOUT THE SIZE OF THE STAGE.

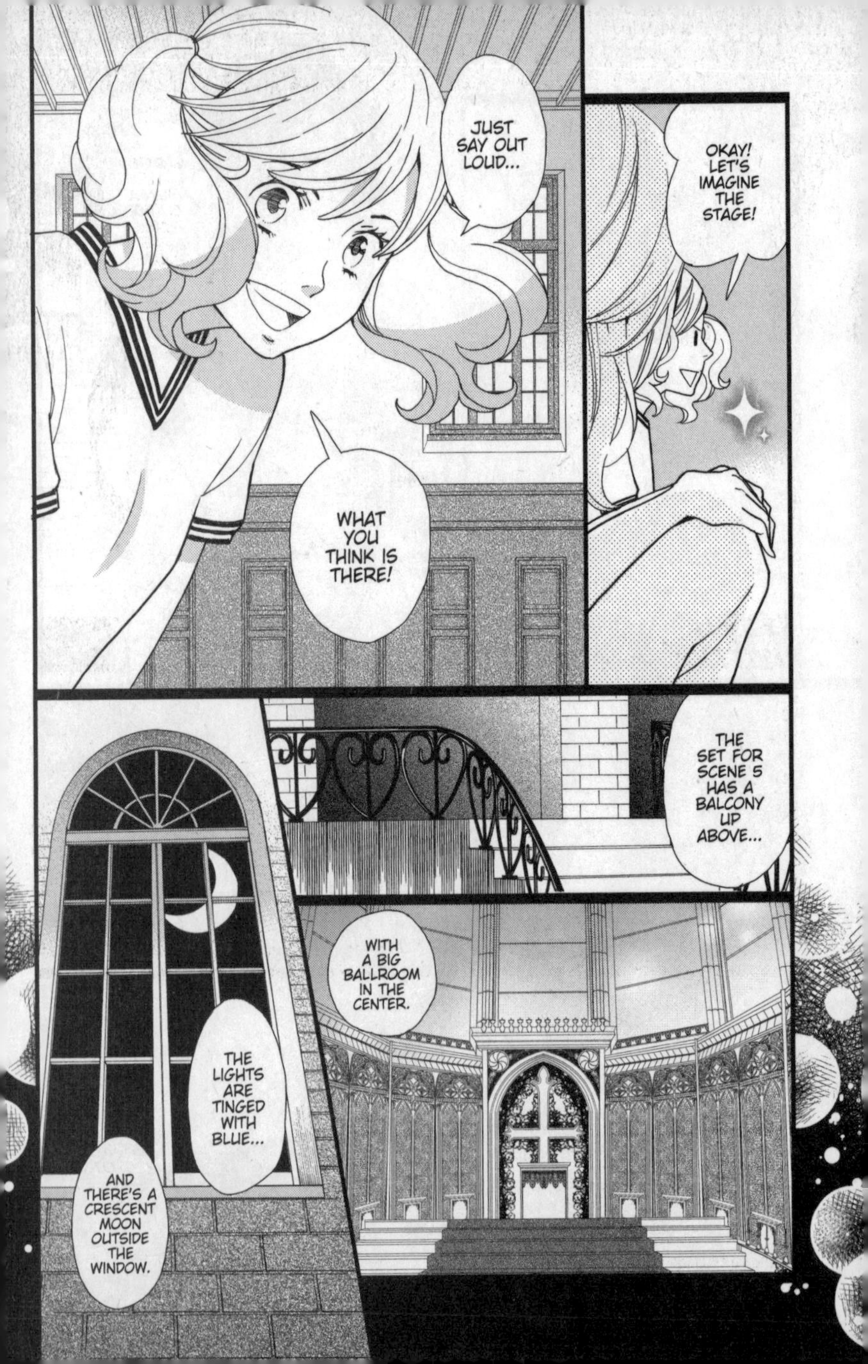
OKAY! LET'S IMAGINE THE STAGE!
JUST SAY OUT LOUD...
WHAT YOU THINK IS THERE!
THE SET FOR SCENE 5 HAS A BALCONY UP ABOVE...
WITH A BIG BALLROOM IN THE CENTER.
THE LIGHTS ARE TINGED WITH BLUE...
AND THERE'S A CRESCENT MOON OUTSIDE THE WINDOW.

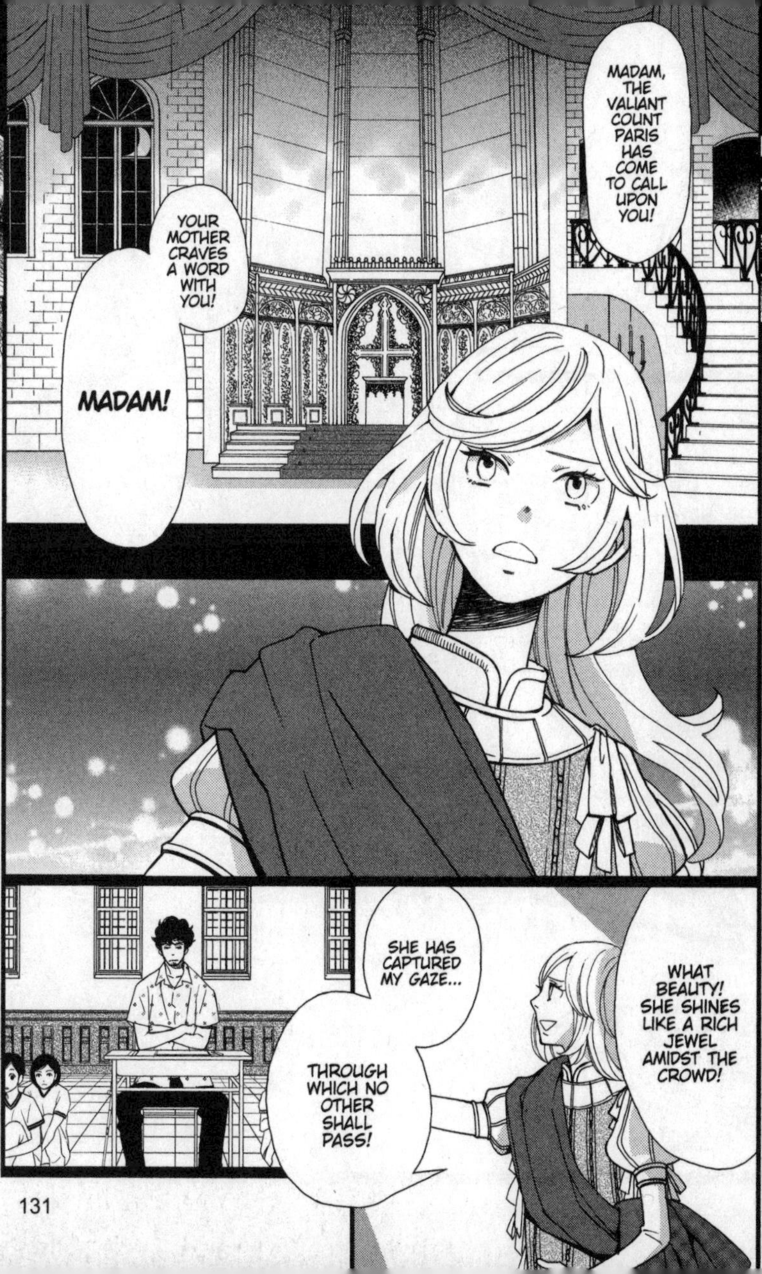
MADAM, THE VALIANT COUNT PARIS HAS COME TO CALL UPON YOU!
YOUR MOTHER CRAVES A WORD WITH YOU!
MADAM!
WHAT BEAUTY! SHE SHINES LIKE A RICH JEWEL AMIDST THE CROWD!
SHE HAS CAPTURED MY GAZE...
THROUGH WHICH NO OTHER SHALL PASS!

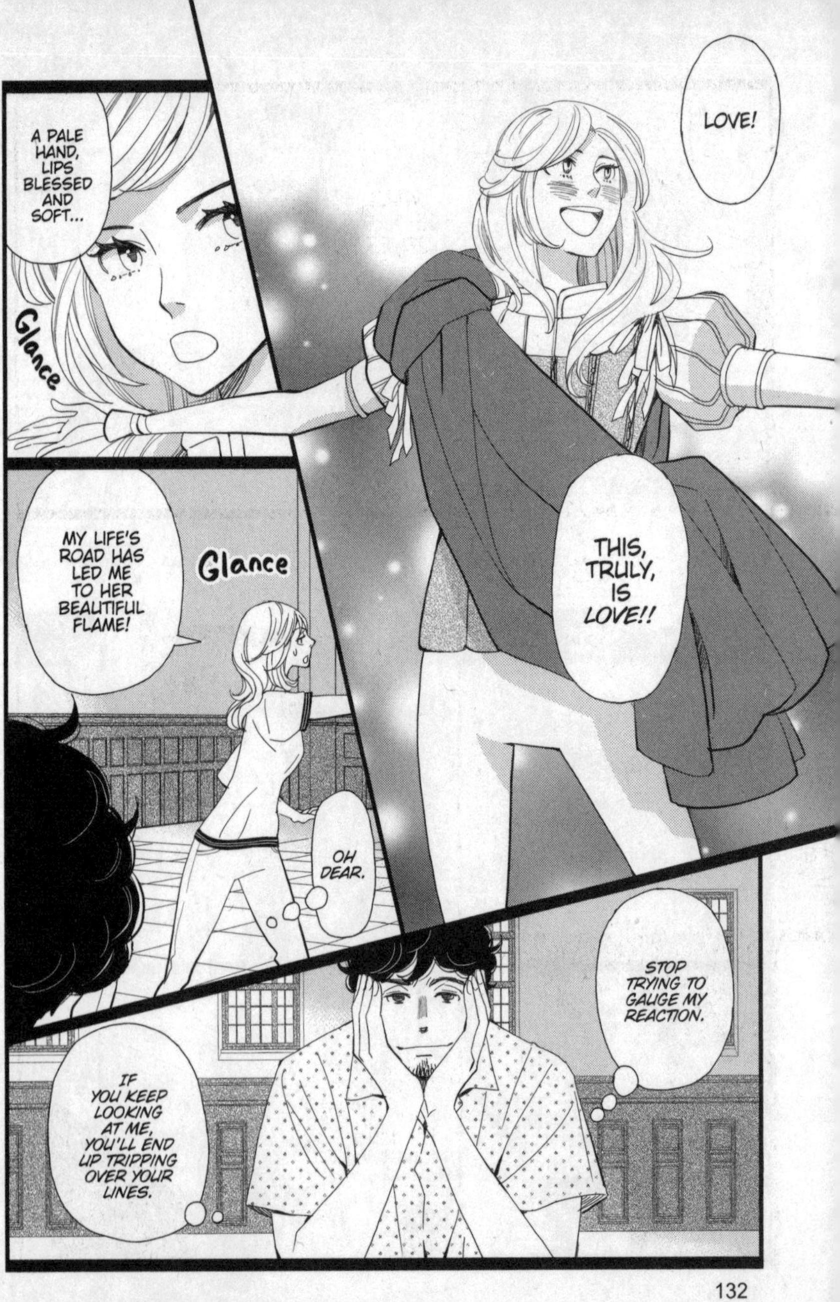
LOVE!
THIS, TRULY, IS LOVE!!
A PALE HAND, LIPS BLESSED AND SOFT...
Glance
MY LIFE'S ROAD HAS LED ME TO HER BEAUTIFUL FLAME!
Glance
OH DEAR.
STOP TRYING TO GAUGE MY REACTION.
IF YOU KEEP LOOKING AT ME, YOU'LL END UP TRIPPING OVER YOUR LINES.

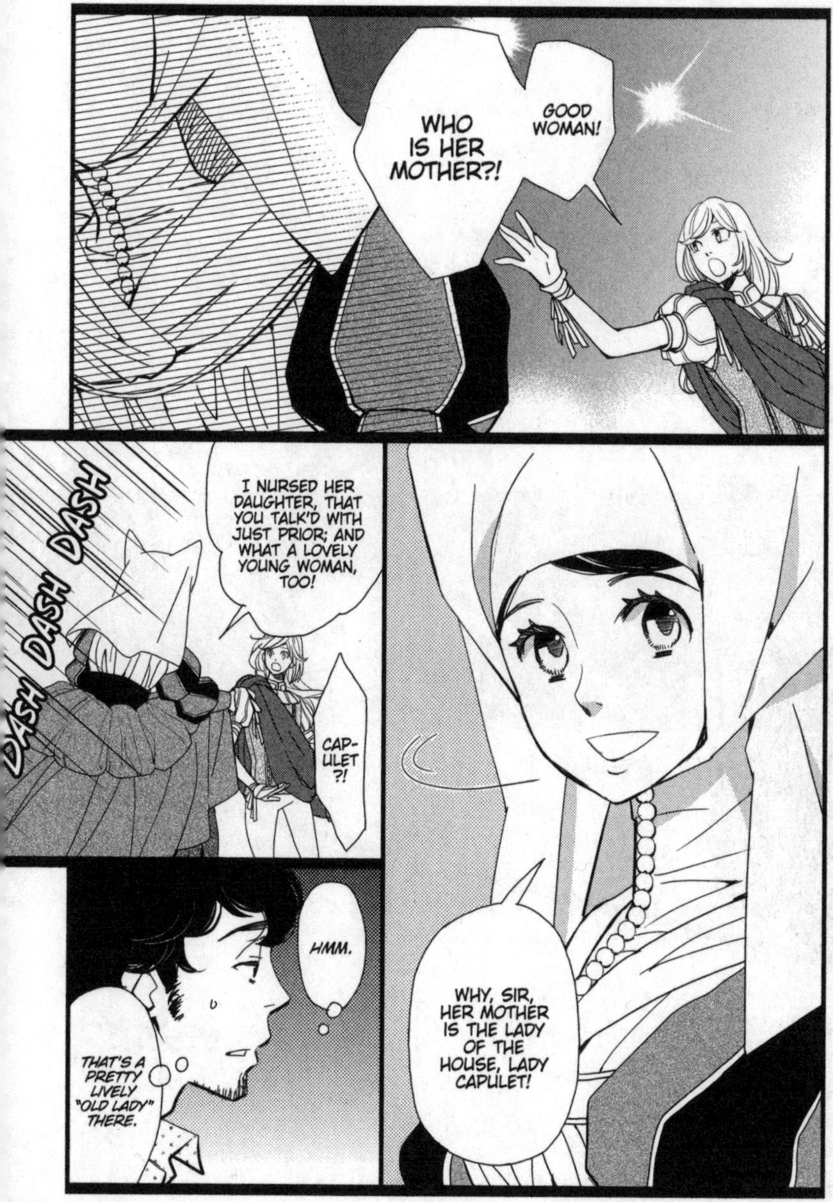
GOOD WOMAN!
WHO IS HER MOTHER?!
WHY, SIR, HER MOTHER IS THE LADY OF THE HOUSE, LADY CAPULET!
I NURSED HER DAUGHTER, THAT YOU TALK'D WITH JUST PRIOR; AND WHAT A LOVELY YOUNG WOMAN, TOO!
CAP-ULET ?!
DASH DASH DASH
HMM.
THAT'S A PRETTY LIVELY "OLD LADY" THERE.

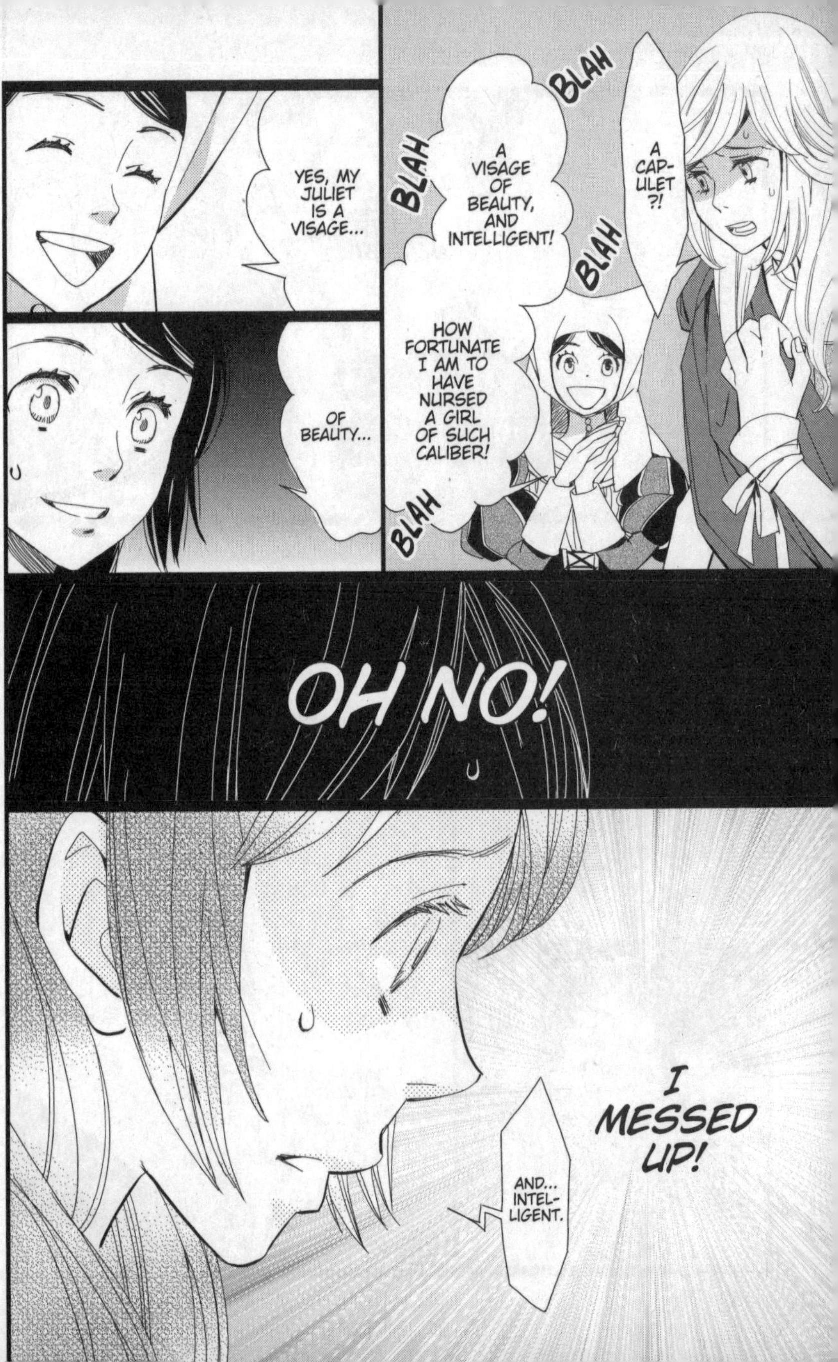

A CAP-ULET?!
BLAH
A VISAGE OF BEAUTY, AND INTELLIGENT!
BLAH
BLAH
HOW FORTUNATE I AM TO HAVE NURSED A GIRL OF SUCH CALIBER!
BLAH
YES, MY JULIET IS A VISAGE...
OF BEAUTY...
OH NO!
I MESSED UP!
AND... INTEL-LIGENT.

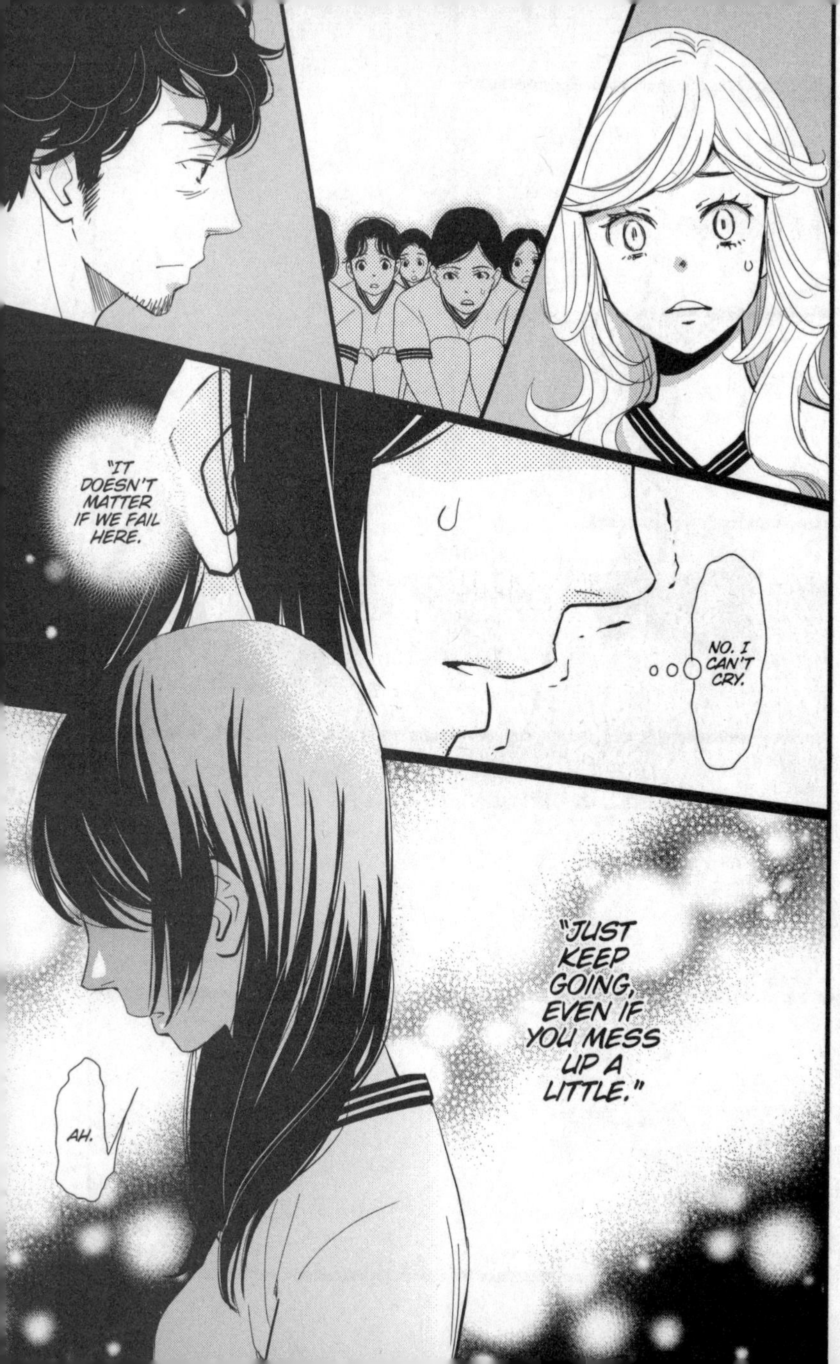
NO. I CAN'T CRY.
"IT DOESN'T MATTER IF WE FAIL HERE.
"JUST KEEP GOING, EVEN IF YOU MESS UP A LITTLE."
AH.

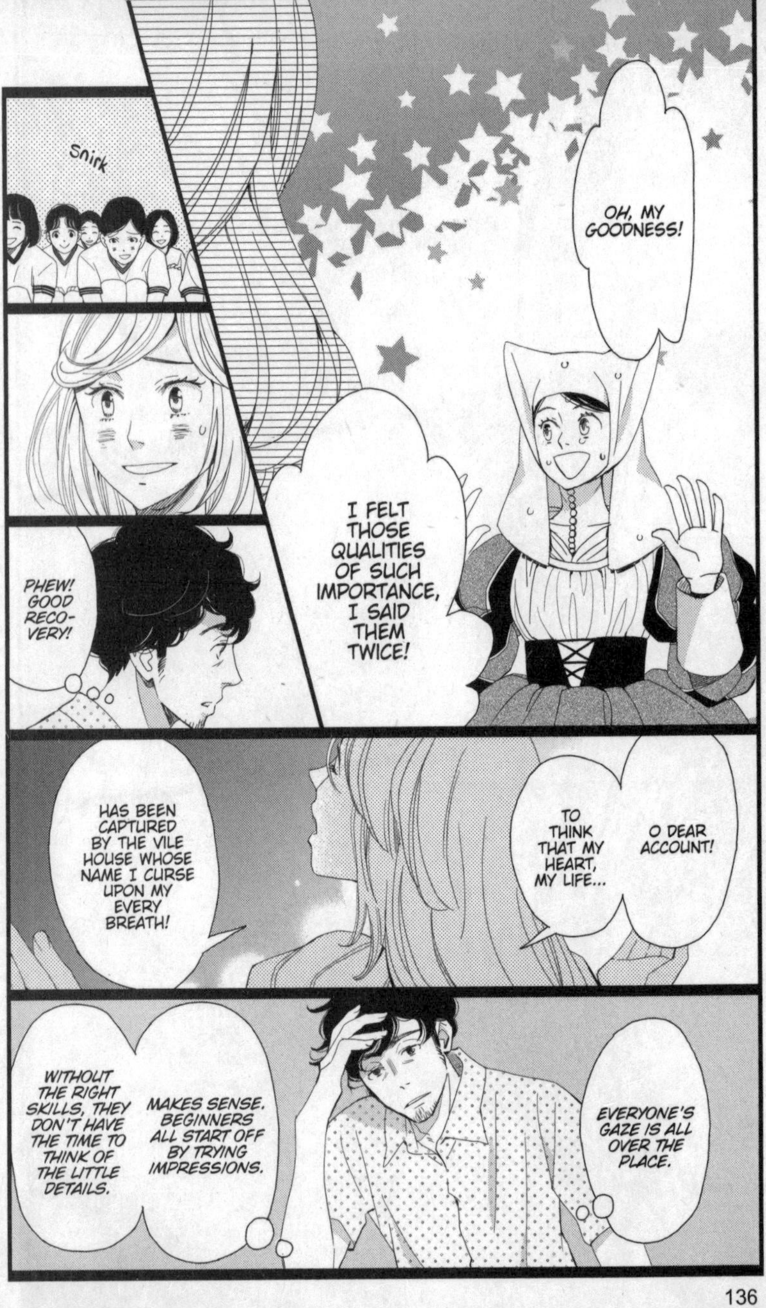
OH, MY GOODNESS!
I FELT THOSE QUALITIES OF SUCH IMPORTANCE, I SAID THEM TWICE!
Snirk
PHEW! GOOD RECO-VERY!
O DEAR ACCOUNT!
TO THINK THAT MY HEART, MY LIFE...
HAS BEEN CAPTURED BY THE VILE HOUSE WHOSE NAME I CURSE UPON MY EVERY BREATH!
EVERYONE'S GAZE IS ALL OVER THE PLACE.
MAKES SENSE. BEGINNERS ALL START OFF BY TRYING IMPRESSIONS.
WITHOUT THE RIGHT SKILLS, THEY DON'T HAVE THE TIME TO THINK OF THE LITTLE DETAILS.

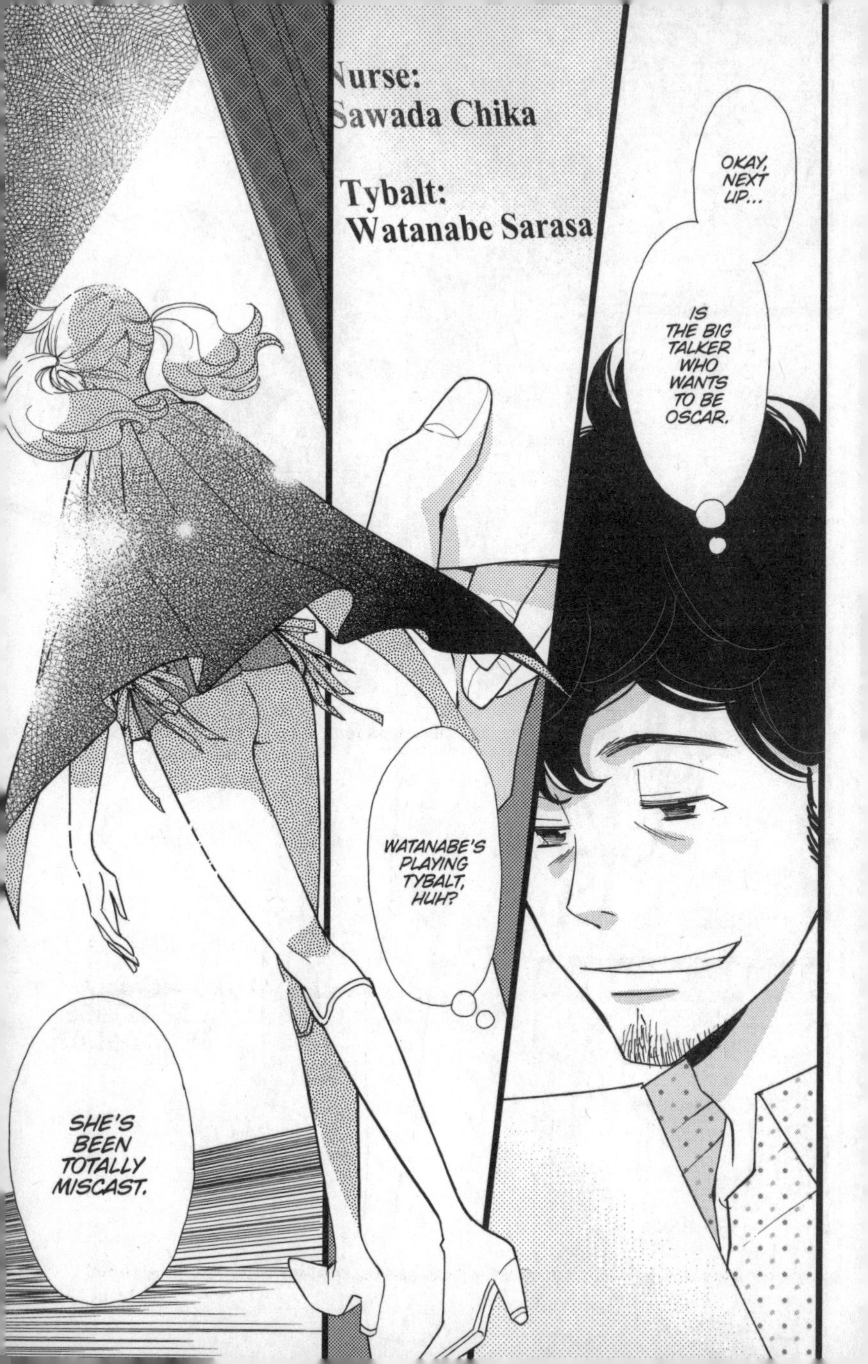
OKAY, NEXT UP...
IS THE BIG TALKER WHO WANTS TO BE OSCAR.
Nurse: Sawada Chika
Tybalt: Watanabe Sarasa
WATANABE'S PLAYING TYBALT, HUH?
SHE'S BEEN TOTALLY MISCAST.

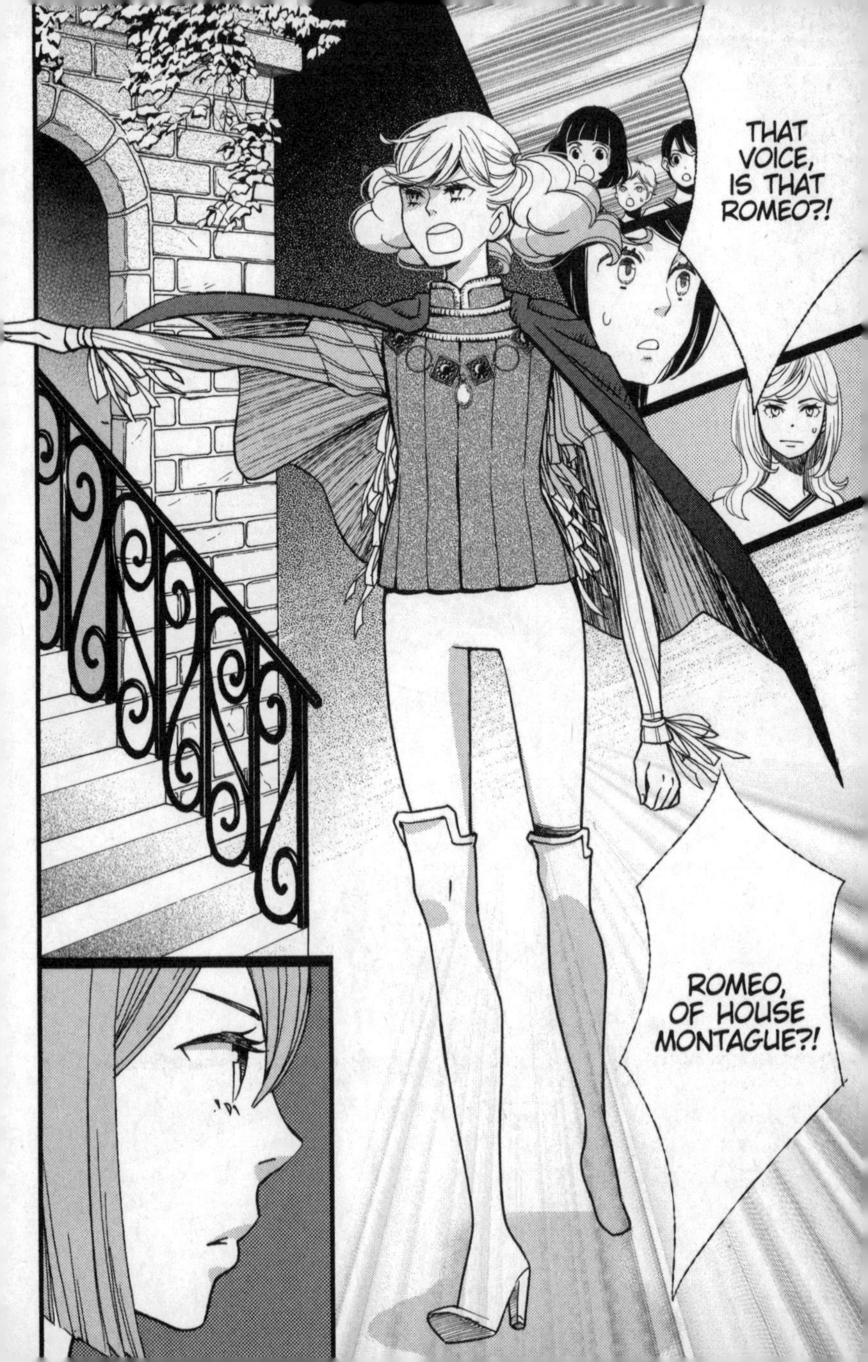
THAT VOICE, IS THAT ROMEO?!
ROMEO, OF HOUSE MONTAGUE?!

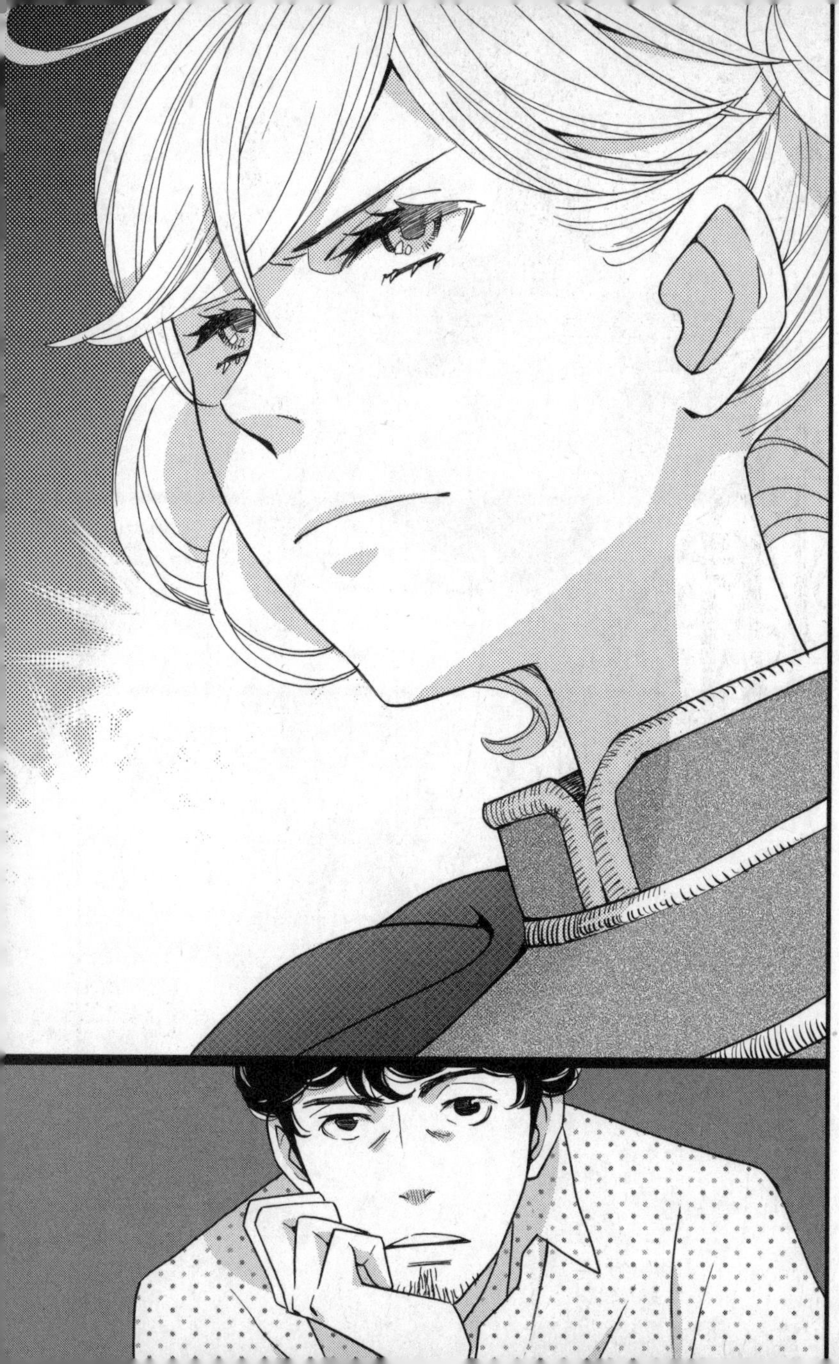

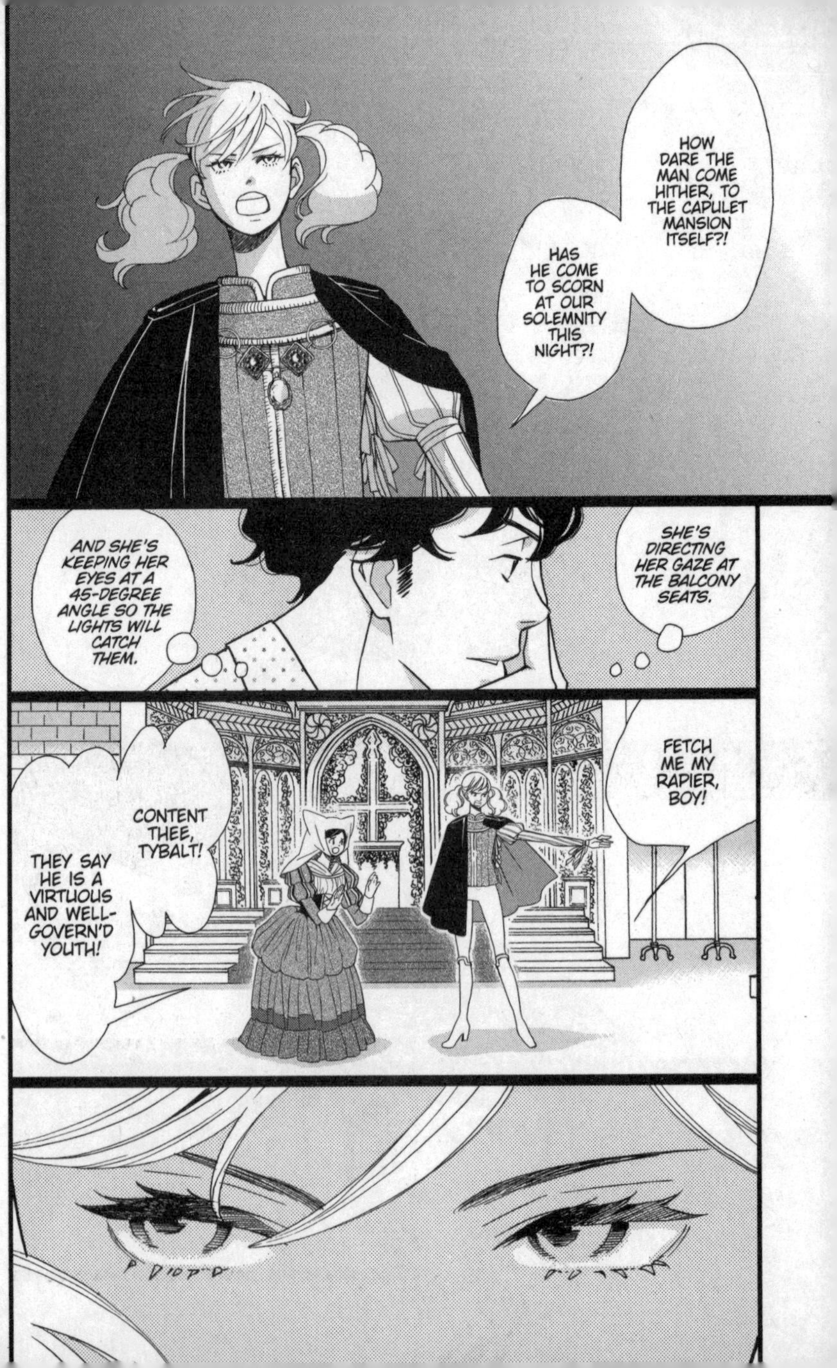
HOW DARE THE MAN COME HITHER, TO THE CAPULET MANSION ITSELF?!
HAS HE COME TO SCORN AT OUR SOLEMNITY THIS NIGHT?!
SHE'S DIRECTING HER GAZE AT THE BALCONY SEATS.
AND SHE'S KEEPING HER EYES AT A 45-DEGREE ANGLE SO THE LIGHTS WILL CATCH THEM.
FETCH ME MY RAPIER, BOY!
CONTENT THEE, TYBALT!
THEY SAY HE IS A VIRTUOUS AND WELL-GOVERN'D YOUTH!

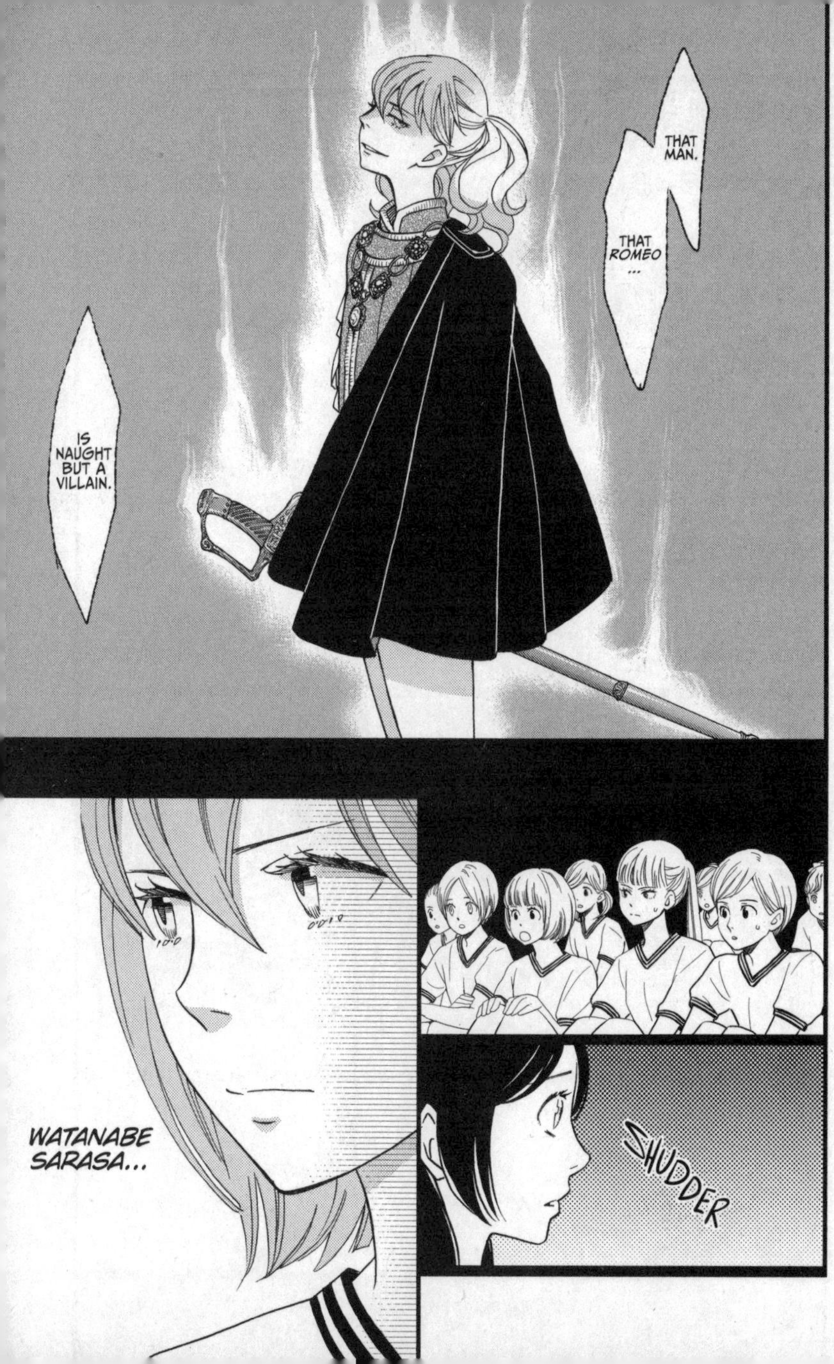
THAT MAN.
THAT ROMEO ...
IS NAUGHT BUT A VILLAIN.
SHUDDER
WATANABE SARASA...

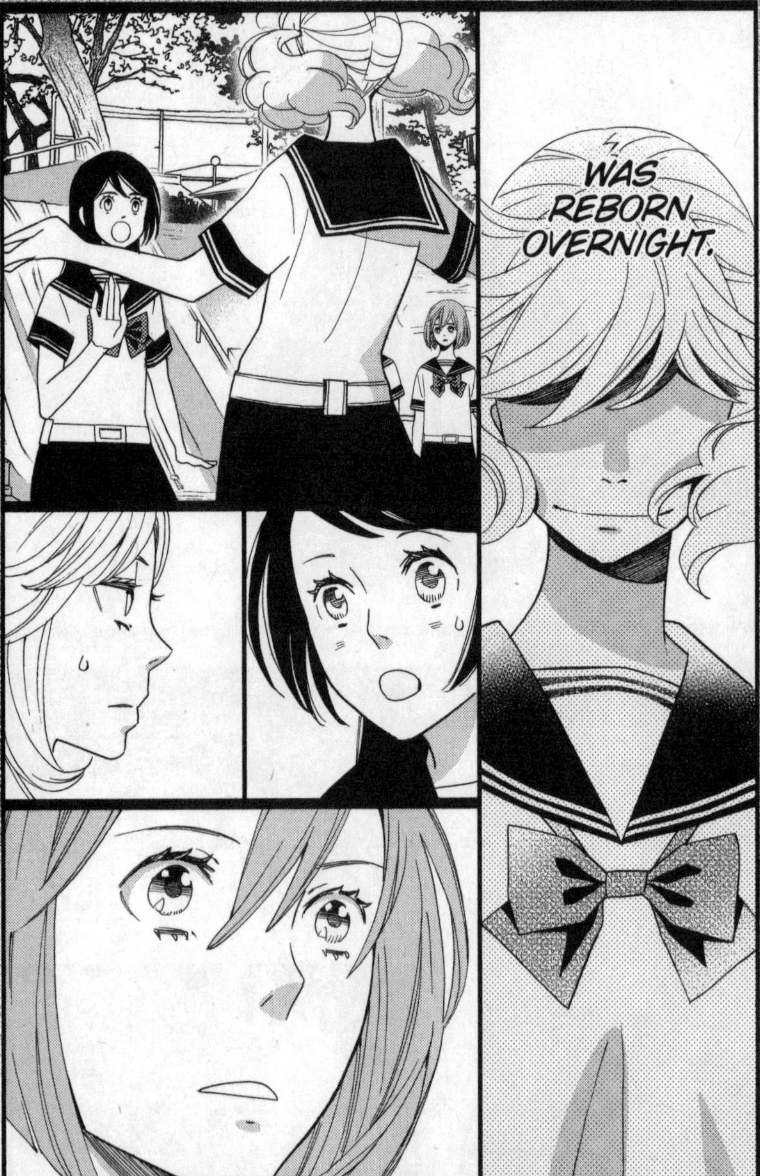
WAS REBORN OVERNIGHT.

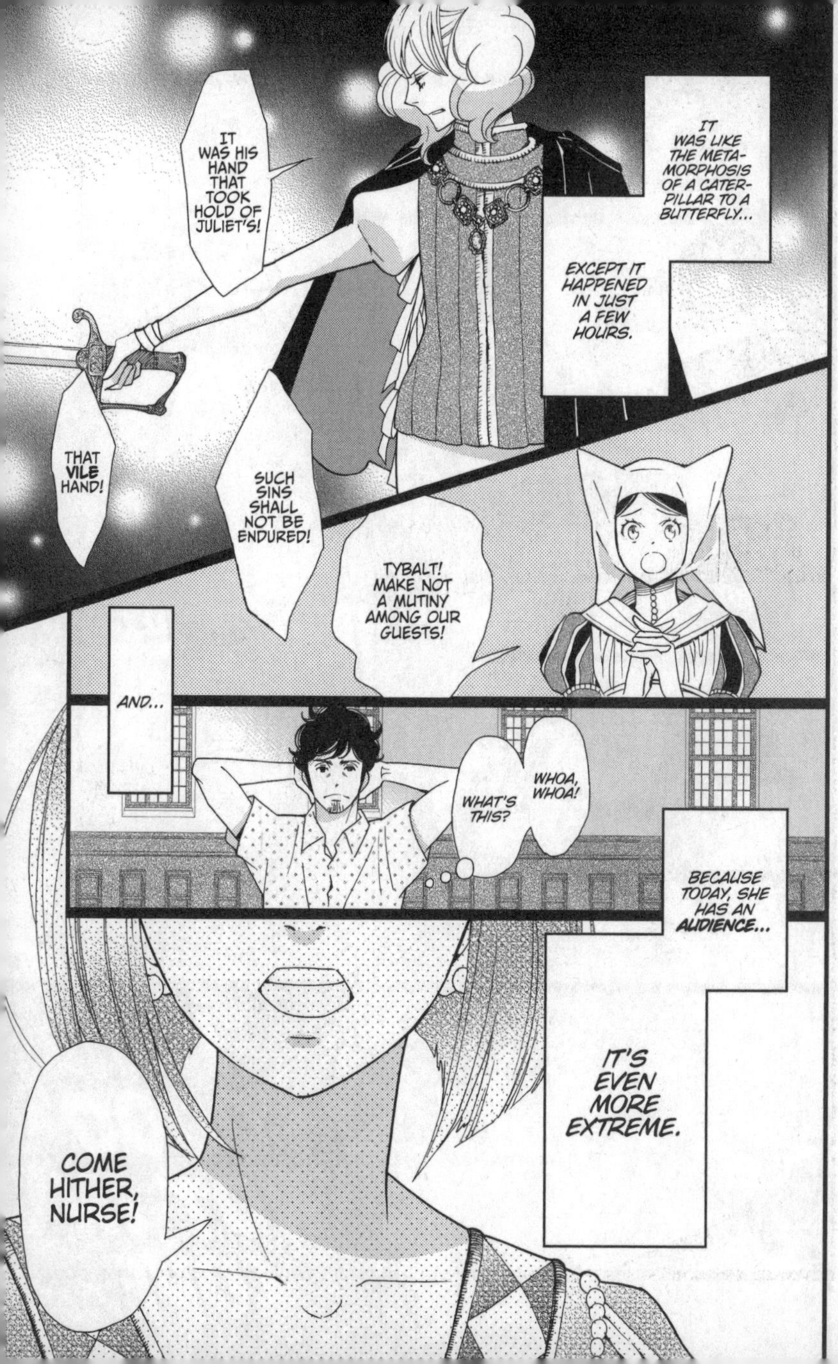
IT WAS LIKE THE METAMORPHOSIS OF A CATERPILLAR TO A BUTTERFLY...
EXCEPT IT HAPPENED IN JUST A FEW HOURS.
IT WAS HIS HAND THAT TOOK HOLD OF JULIET'S!
THAT **VILE** HAND!
SUCH SINS SHALL NOT BE ENDURED!
TYBALT! MAKE NOT A MUTINY AMONG OUR GUESTS!
AND...
WHOA, WHOA!
WHAT'S THIS?
BECAUSE TODAY, SHE HAS AN **AUDIENCE**...
IT'S EVEN MORE EXTREME.
COME HITHER, NURSE!

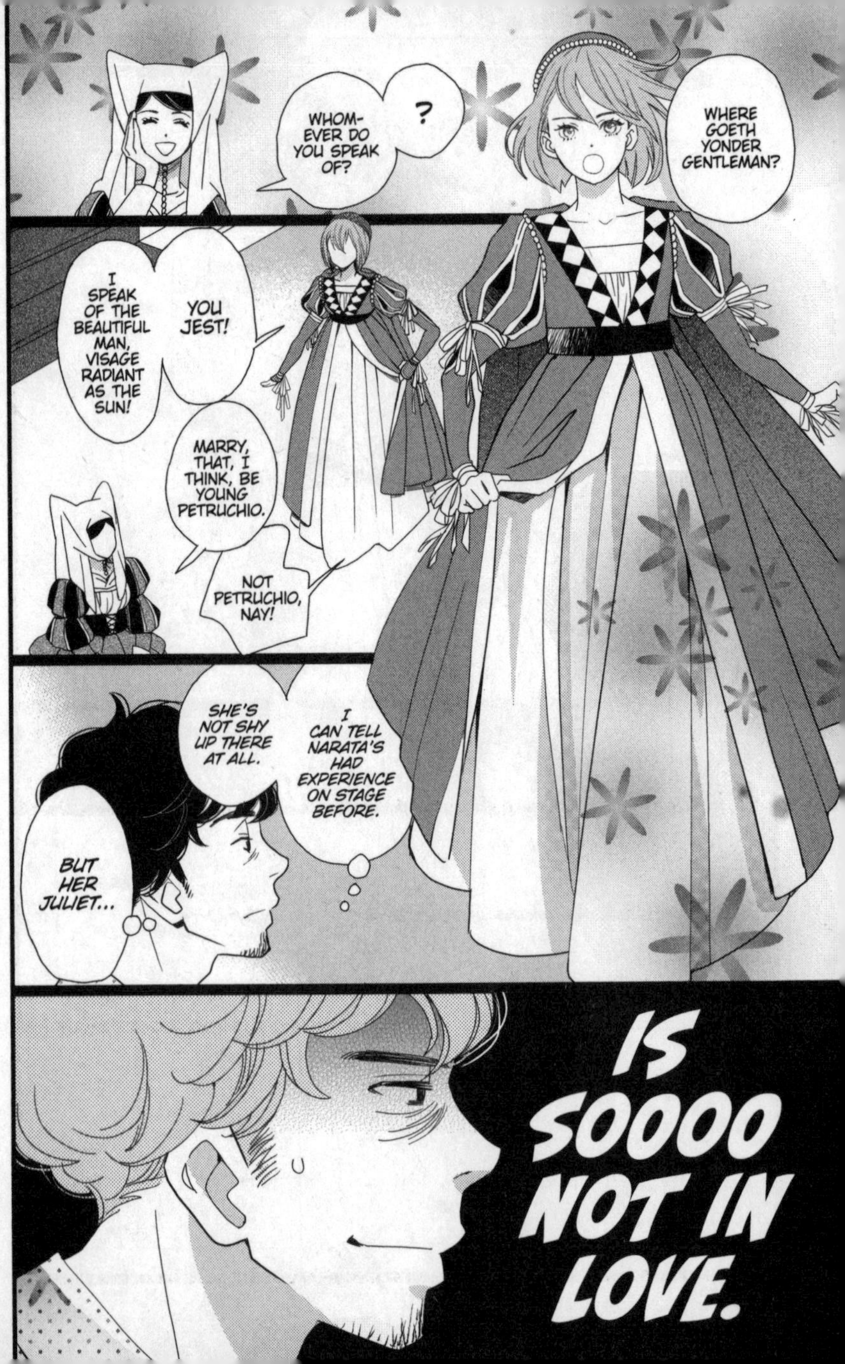
WHERE GOETH YONDER GENTLEMAN?
?
WHOM-EVER DO YOU SPEAK OF?
YOU JEST!
I SPEAK OF THE BEAUTIFUL MAN, VISAGE RADIANT AS THE SUN!
MARRY, THAT, I THINK, BE YOUNG PETRUCHIO.
NOT PETRUCHIO, NAY!
I CAN TELL NARATA'S HAD EXPERIENCE ON STAGE BEFORE.
SHE'S NOT SHY UP THERE AT ALL.
BUT HER JULIET...
IS SOOOO NOT IN LOVE.

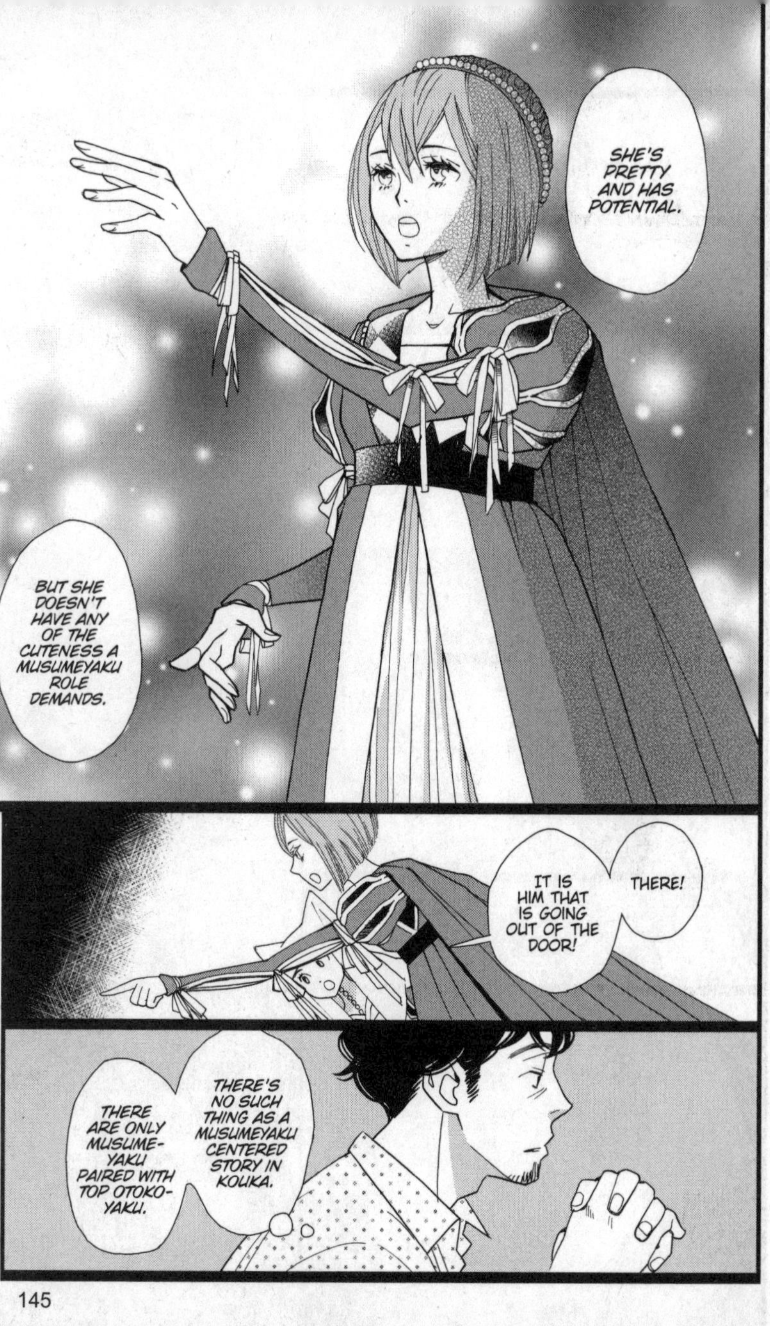
SHE'S PRETTY AND HAS POTENTIAL.
BUT SHE DOESN'T HAVE ANY OF THE CUTENESS A MUSUMEYAKU ROLE DEMANDS.
THERE!
IT IS HIM THAT IS GOING OUT OF THE DOOR!
THERE'S NO SUCH THING AS A MUSUMEYAKU CENTERED STORY IN KOUKA.
THERE ARE ONLY MUSUME-YAKU PAIRED WITH TOP OTOKO-YAKU.

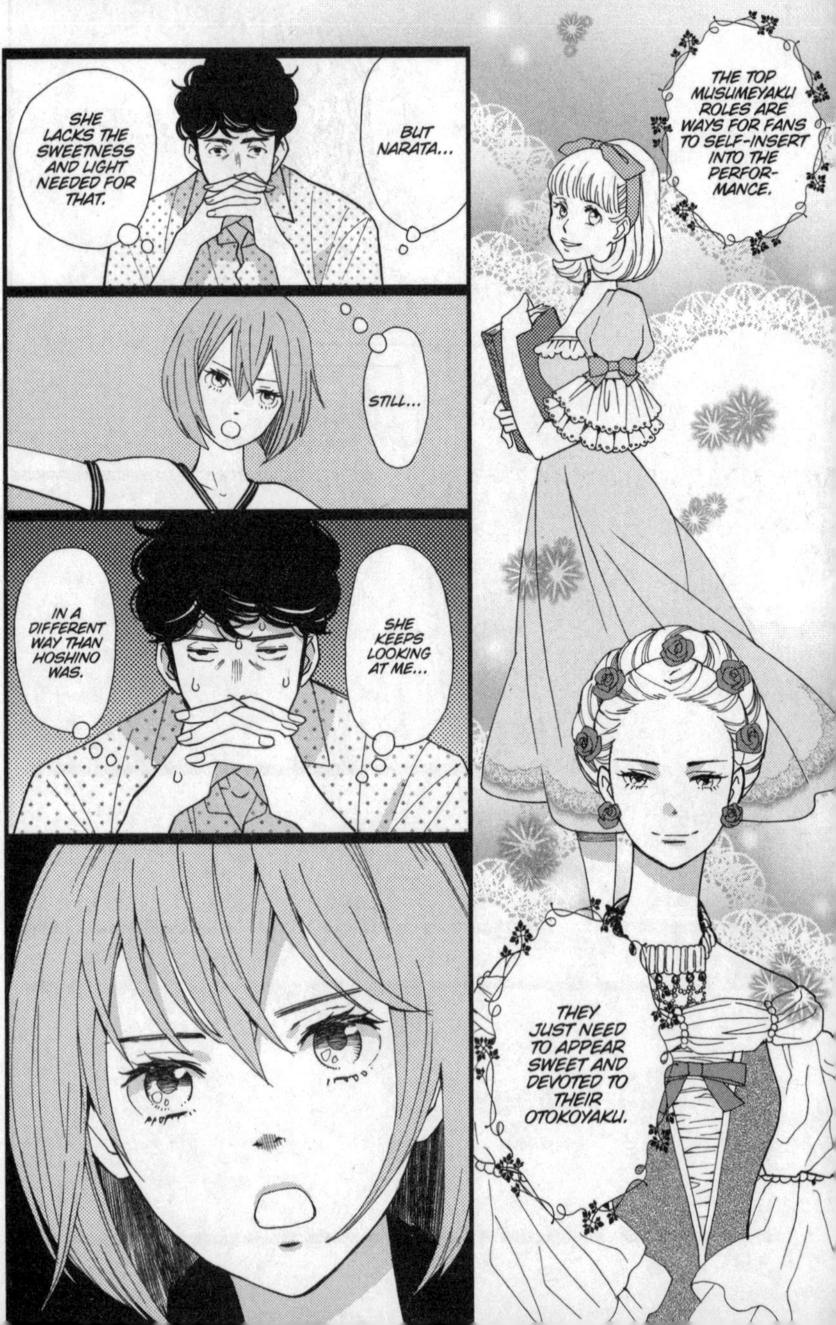
THE TOP MUSUMEYAKU ROLES ARE WAYS FOR FANS TO SELF-INSERT INTO THE PERFORMANCE.
THEY JUST NEED TO APPEAR SWEET AND DEVOTED TO THEIR OTOKOYAKU.
BUT NARATA...
SHE LACKS THE SWEETNESS AND LIGHT NEEDED FOR THAT.
STILL...
SHE KEEPS LOOKING AT ME...
IN A DIFFERENT WAY THAN HOSHINO WAS.

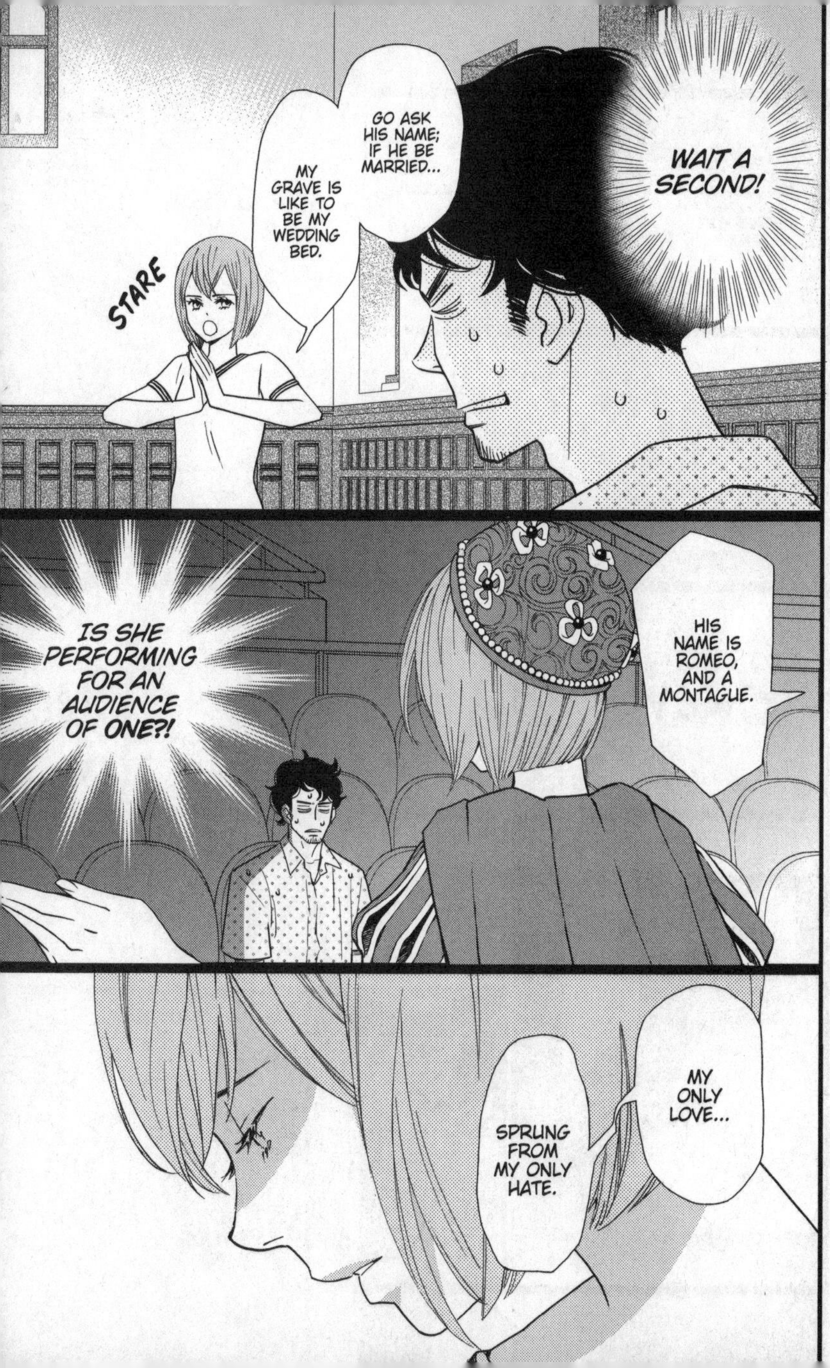
WAIT A SECOND!
GO ASK HIS NAME; IF HE BE MARRIED...
MY GRAVE IS LIKE TO BE MY WEDDING BED.
STARE
HIS NAME IS ROMEO, AND A MONTAGUE.
IS SHE PERFORMING FOR AN AUDIENCE OF ONE?!
MY ONLY LOVE...
SPRUNG FROM MY ONLY HATE.

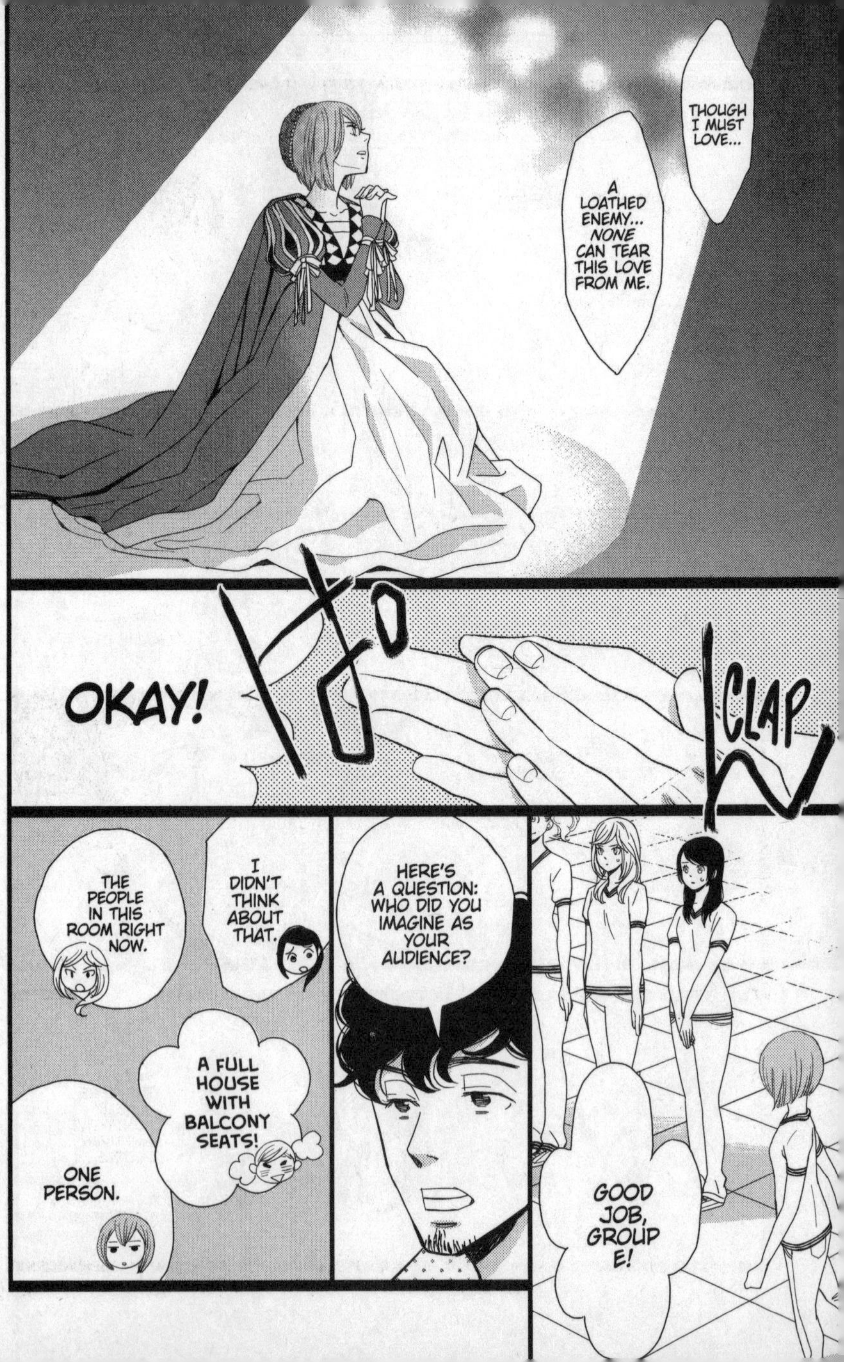
THOUGH I MUST LOVE...
A LOATHED ENEMY... *NONE* CAN TEAR THIS LOVE FROM ME.
CLAP
OKAY!
GOOD JOB, GROUP E!
HERE'S A QUESTION: WHO DID YOU IMAGINE AS YOUR AUDIENCE?
I DIDN'T THINK ABOUT THAT.
THE PEOPLE IN THIS ROOM RIGHT NOW.
A FULL HOUSE WITH BALCONY SEATS!
ONE PERSON.

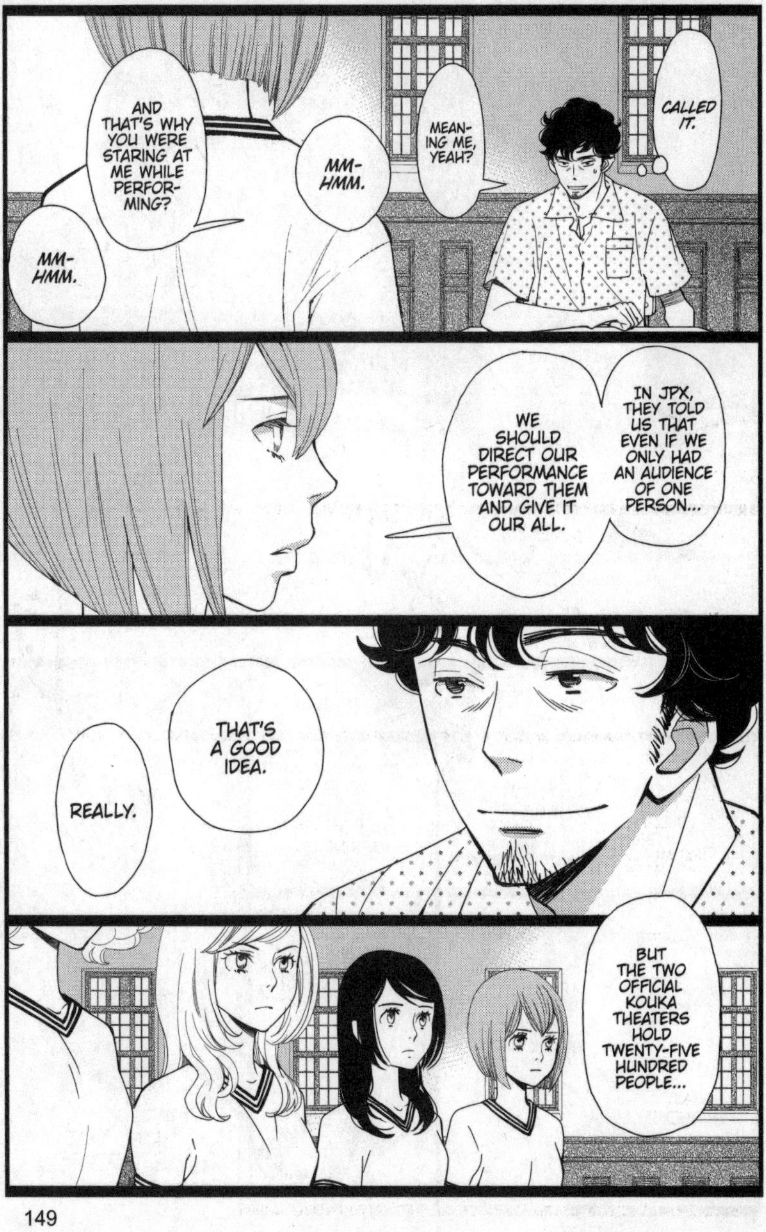
CALLED IT.
MEAN-ING ME, YEAH?
MM-HMM.
AND THAT'S WHY YOU WERE STARING AT ME WHILE PERFORM-ING?
MM-HMM.
IN JPX, THEY TOLD US THAT EVEN IF WE ONLY HAD AN AUDIENCE OF ONE PERSON...
WE SHOULD DIRECT OUR PERFORMANCE TOWARD THEM AND GIVE IT OUR ALL.
THAT'S A GOOD IDEA.
REALLY.
BUT THE TWO OFFICIAL KOUKA THEATERS HOLD TWENTY-FIVE HUNDRED PEOPLE...

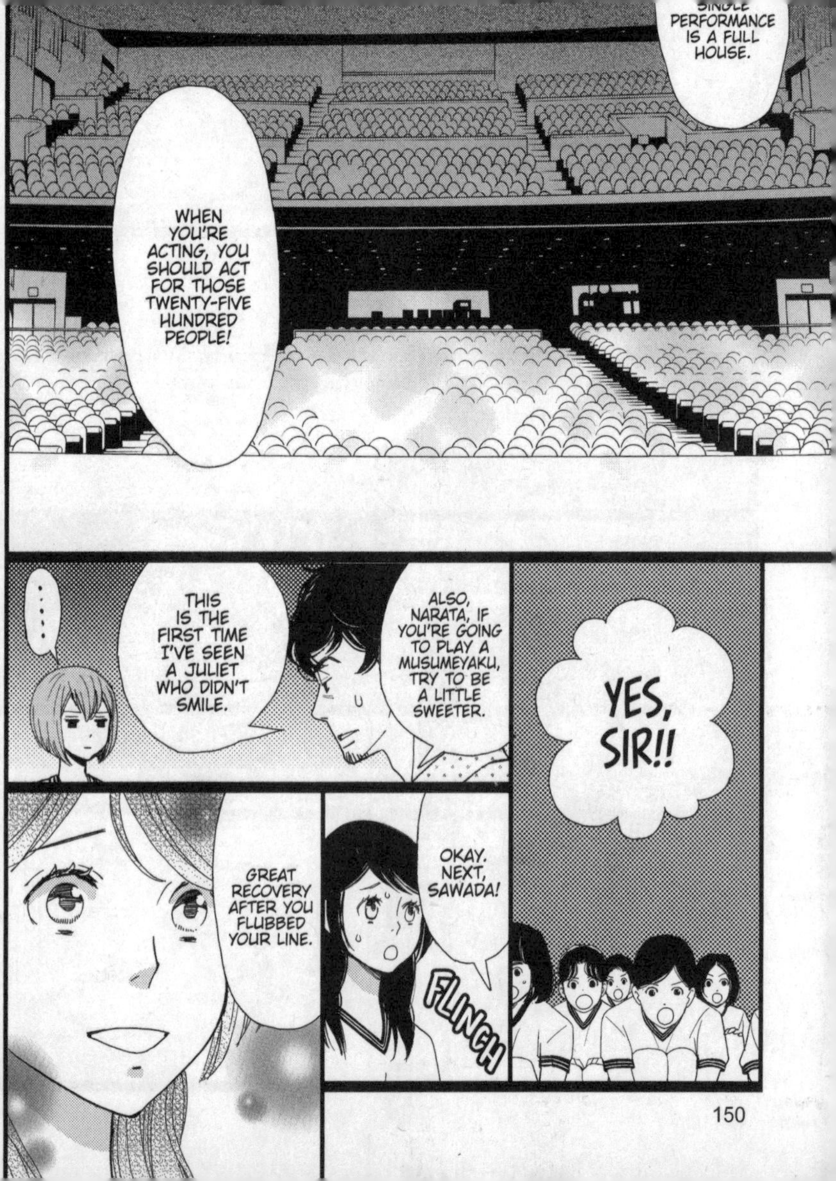
SINGLE PERFORMANCE IS A FULL HOUSE.
WHEN YOU'RE ACTING, YOU SHOULD ACT FOR THOSE TWENTY-FIVE HUNDRED PEOPLE!
ALSO, NARATA, IF YOU'RE GOING TO PLAY A MUSUMEYAKU, TRY TO BE A LITTLE SWEETER.
THIS IS THE FIRST TIME I'VE SEEN A JULIET WHO DIDN'T SMILE.
.....
YES, SIR!!
OKAY. NEXT, SAWADA!
FLINCH
GREAT RECOVERY AFTER YOU FLUBBED YOUR LINE.

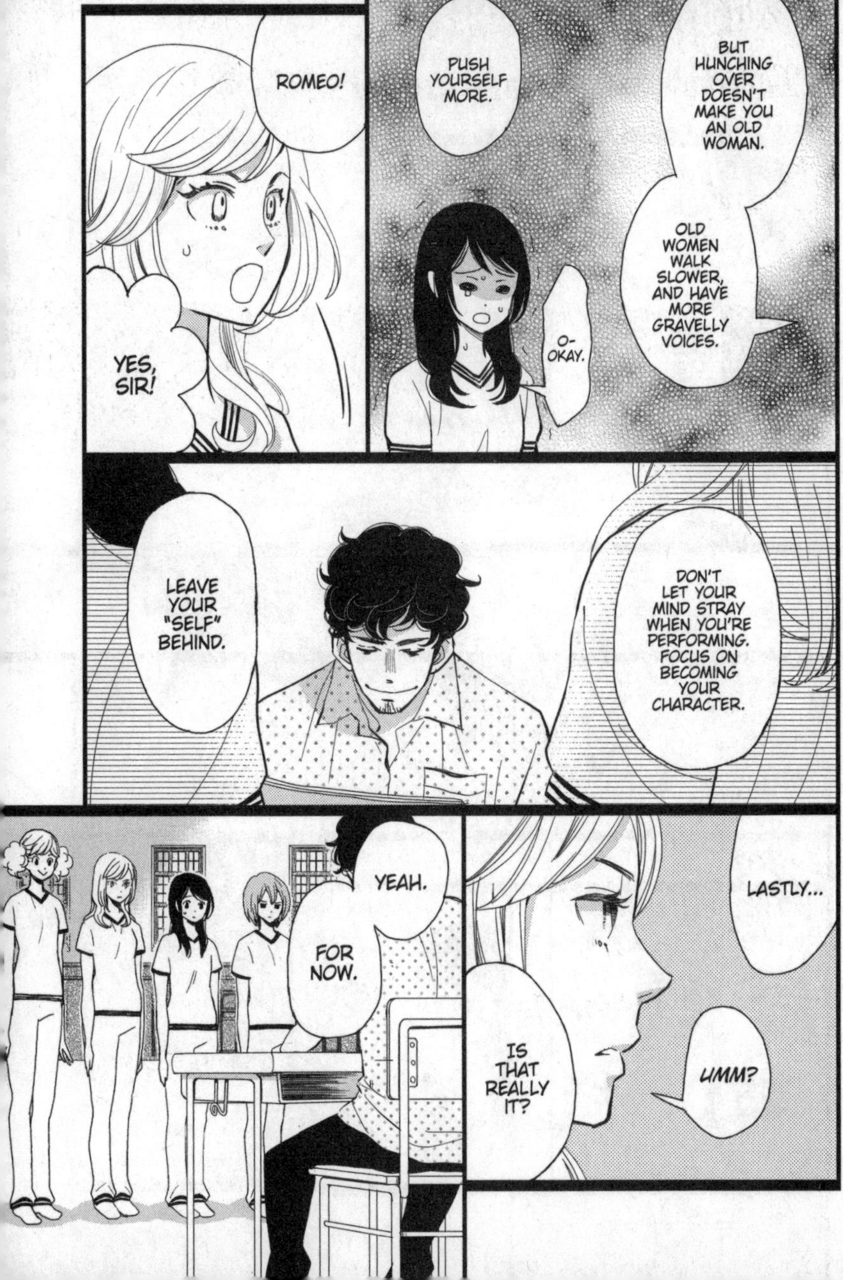
BUT HUNCHING OVER DOESN'T MAKE YOU AN OLD WOMAN.
OLD WOMEN WALK SLOWER, AND HAVE MORE GRAVELLY VOICES.
PUSH YOURSELF MORE.
O-OKAY.
ROMEO!
YES, SIR!
DON'T LET YOUR MIND STRAY WHEN YOU'RE PERFORMING. FOCUS ON BECOMING YOUR CHARACTER.
LEAVE YOUR "SELF" BEHIND.
LASTLY...
UMM?
IS THAT REALLY IT?
YEAH.
FOR NOW.

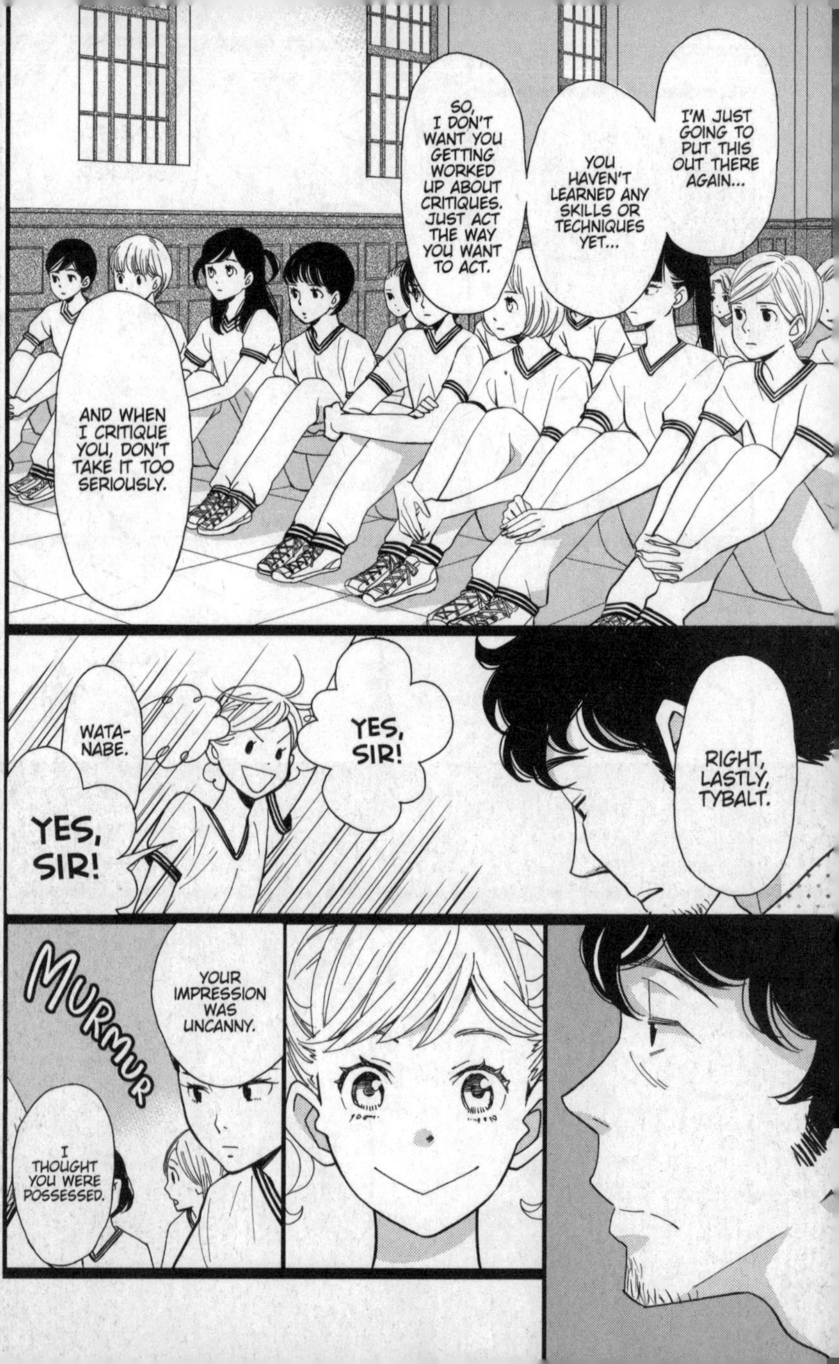
I'M JUST GOING TO PUT THIS OUT THERE AGAIN...
YOU HAVEN'T LEARNED ANY SKILLS OR TECHNIQUES YET...
SO, I DON'T WANT YOU GETTING WORKED UP ABOUT CRITIQUES. JUST ACT THE WAY YOU WANT TO ACT.
AND WHEN I CRITIQUE YOU, DON'T TAKE IT TOO SERIOUSLY.
RIGHT, LASTLY, TYBALT.
YES, SIR!
WATA-NABE.
YES, SIR!
YOUR IMPRESSION WAS UNCANNY.
MURMUR
I THOUGHT YOU WERE POSSESSED.

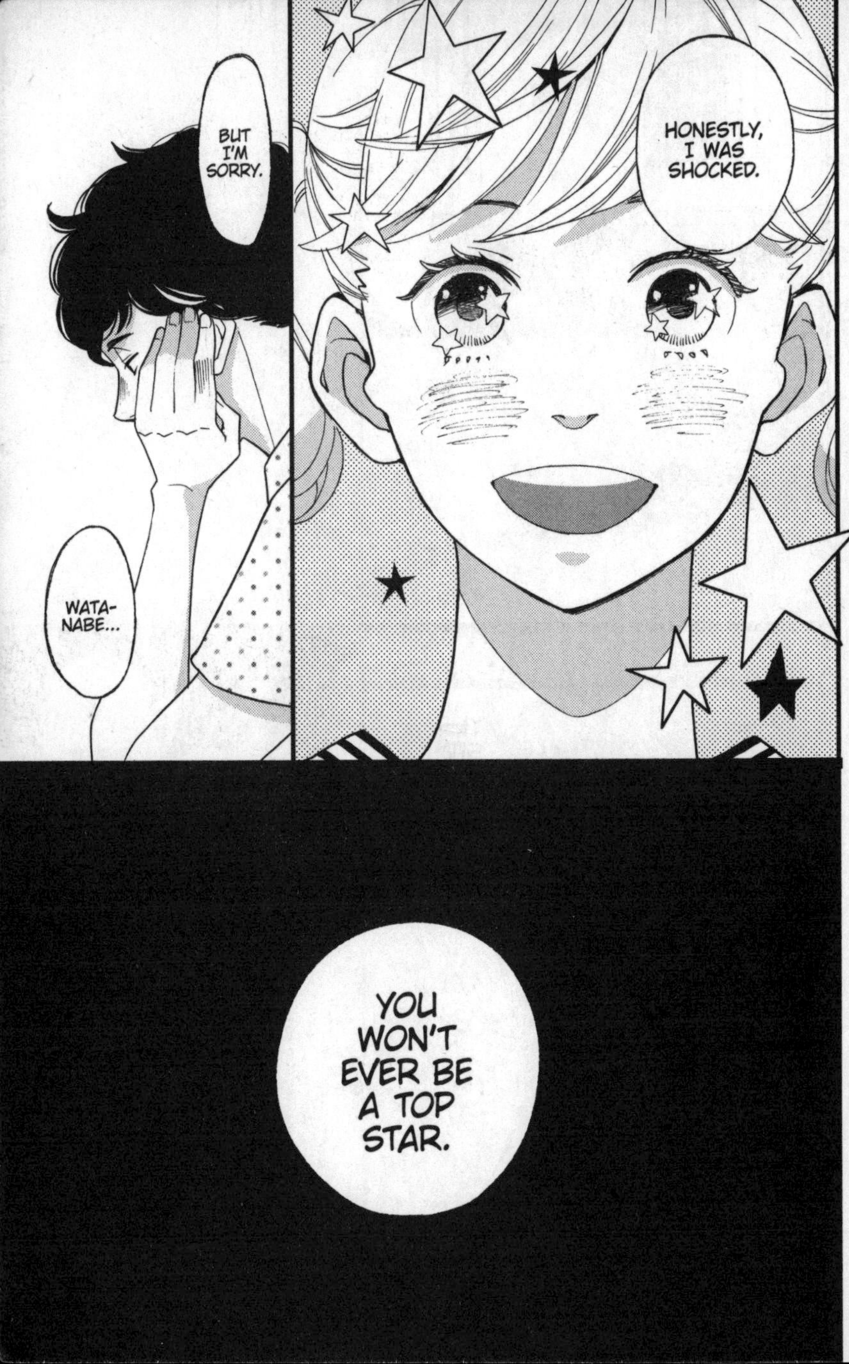
HONESTLY, I WAS SHOCKED.
BUT I'M SORRY.
WATA-NABE...
YOU WON'T EVER BE A TOP STAR.

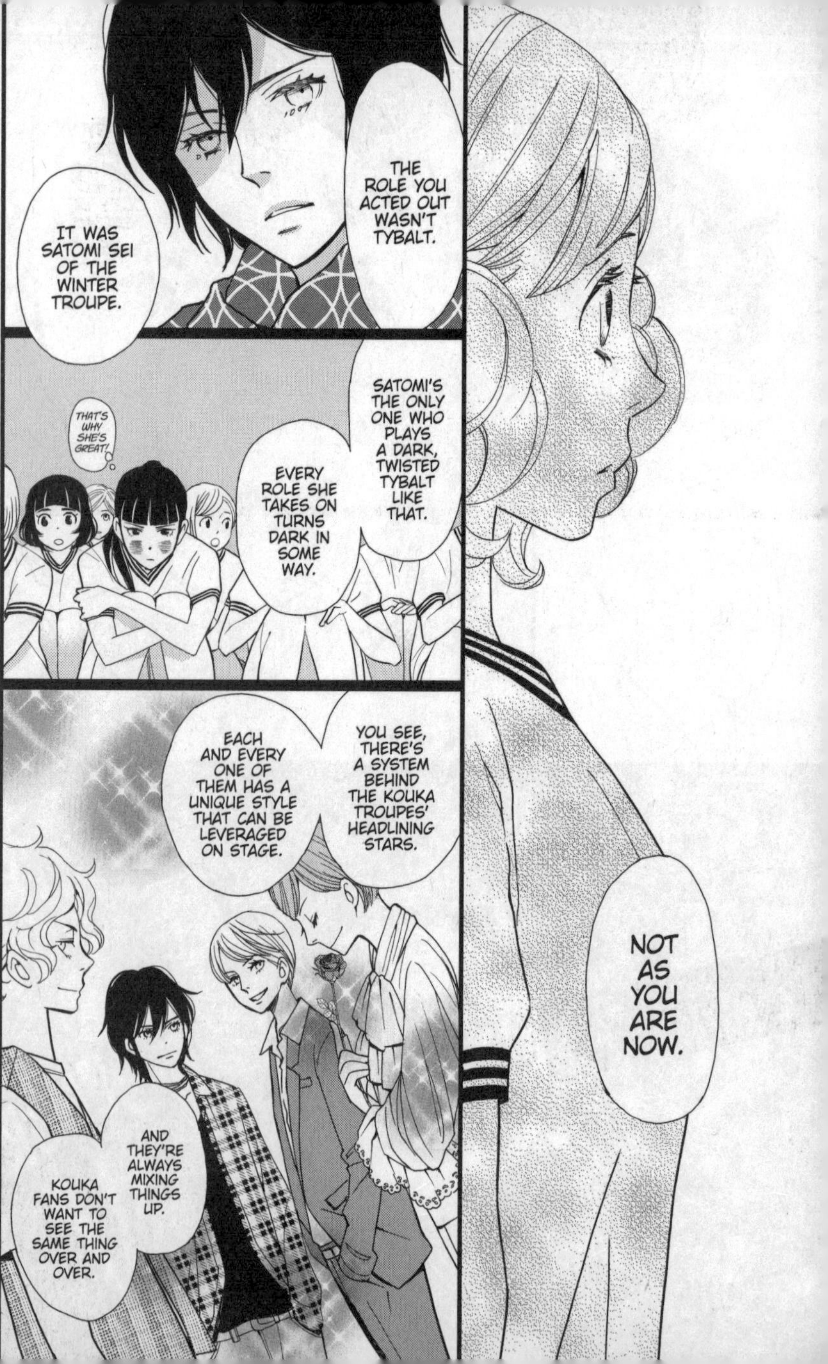
NOT AS YOU ARE NOW.
THE ROLE YOU ACTED OUT WASN'T TYBALT.
IT WAS SATOMI SEI OF THE WINTER TROUPE.
SATOMI'S THE ONLY ONE WHO PLAYS A DARK, TWISTED TYBALT LIKE THAT.
EVERY ROLE SHE TAKES ON TURNS DARK IN SOME WAY.
THAT'S WHY SHE'S GREAT!
YOU SEE, THERE'S A SYSTEM BEHIND THE KOUKA TROUPES' HEADLINING STARS.
EACH AND EVERY ONE OF THEM HAS A UNIQUE STYLE THAT CAN BE LEVERAGED ON STAGE.
AND THEY'RE ALWAYS MIXING THINGS UP.
KOUKA FANS DON'T WANT TO SEE THE SAME THING OVER AND OVER.

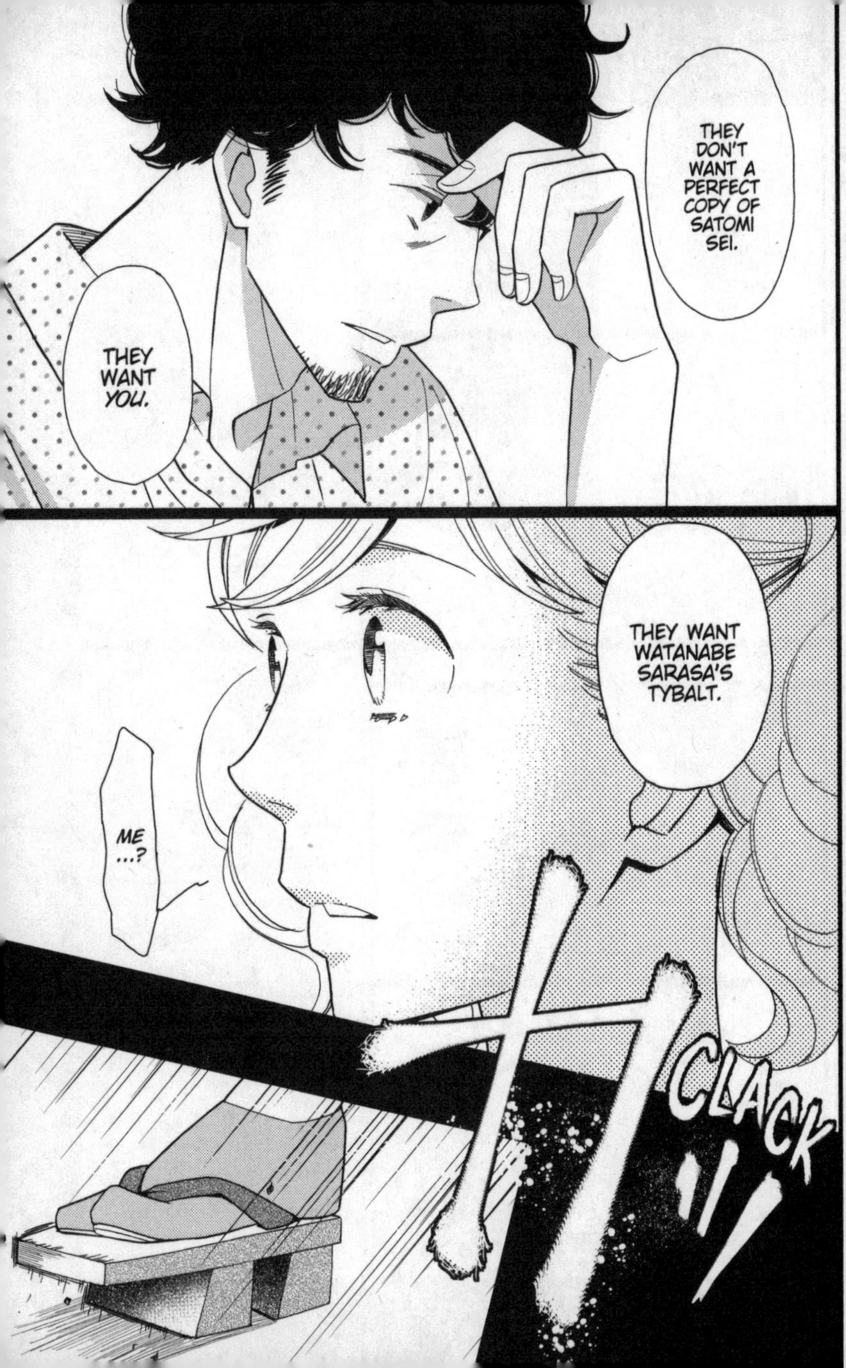
THEY DON'T WANT A PERFECT COPY OF SATOMI SEI.
THEY WANT YOU.
THEY WANT WATANABE SARASA'S TYBALT.
ME ...?
CLACK

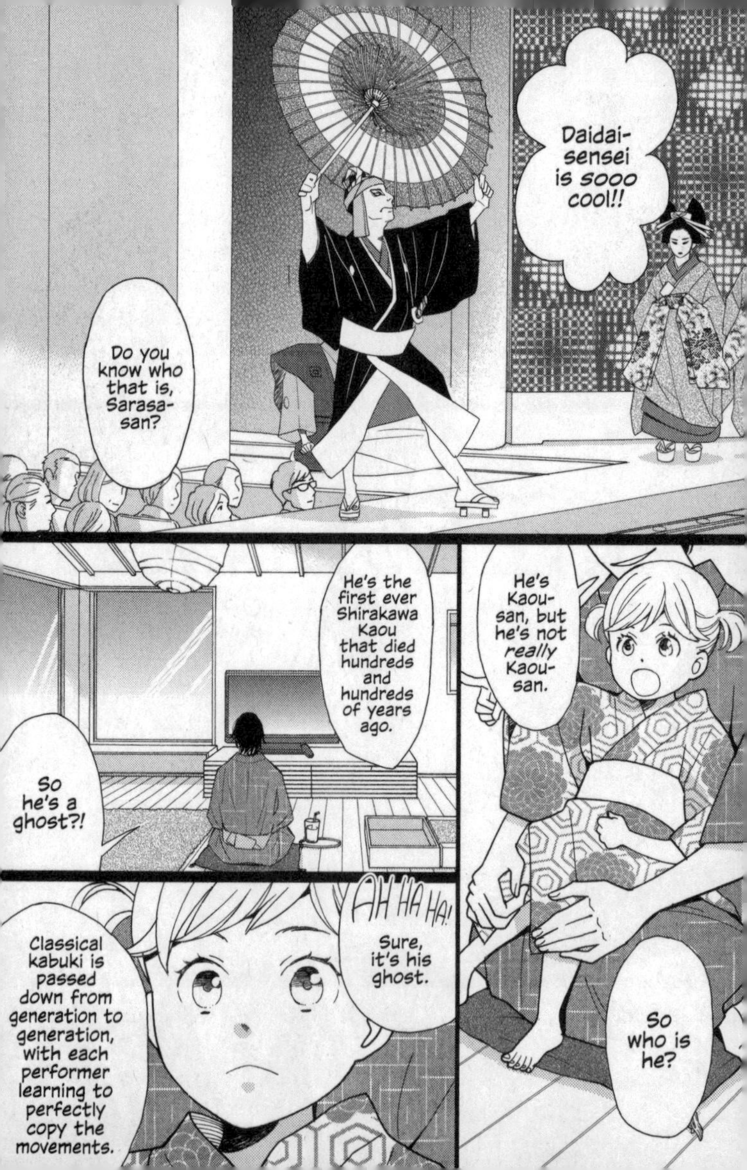
Daidai-sensei is sooo cool!!
Do you know who that is, Sarasa-san?
He's Kaou-san, but he's not *really* Kaou-san.
So who is he?
He's the first ever Shirakawa Kaou that died hundreds and hundreds of years ago.
So he's a ghost?!
AH HA HA!
Sure, it's his ghost.
Classical kabuki is passed down from generation to generation, with each performer learning to perfectly copy the movements.

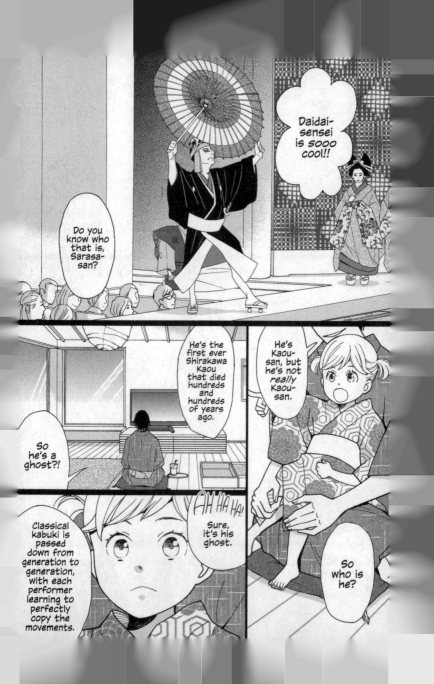

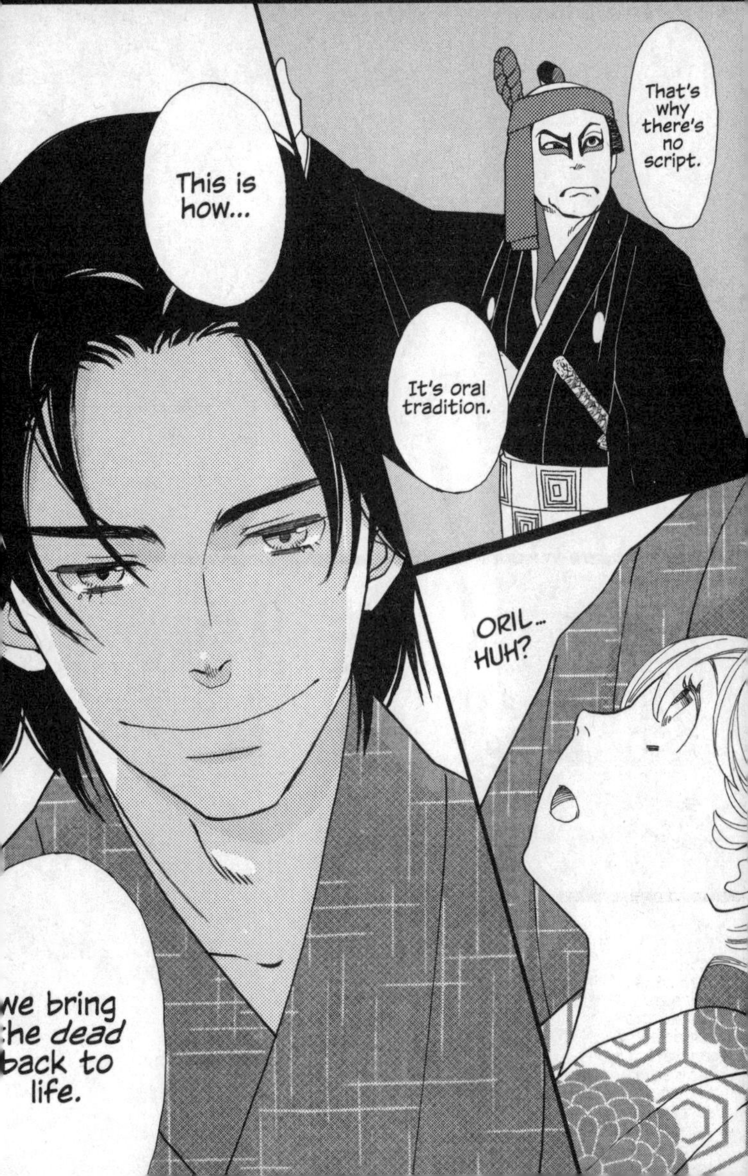
That's why there's no script.
It's oral tradition.
ORIL... HUH?
This is how...
we bring the dead back to life.

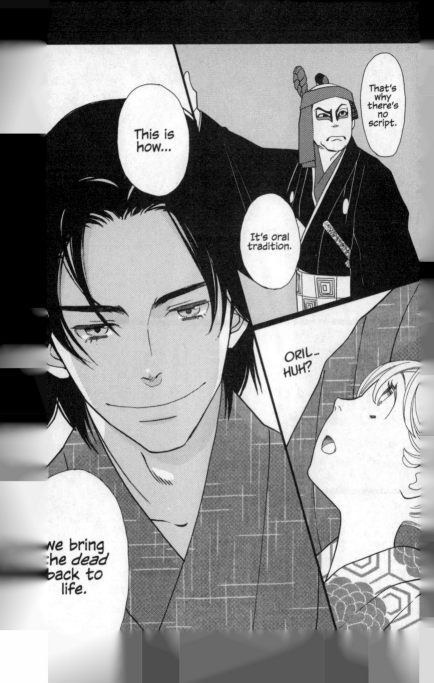

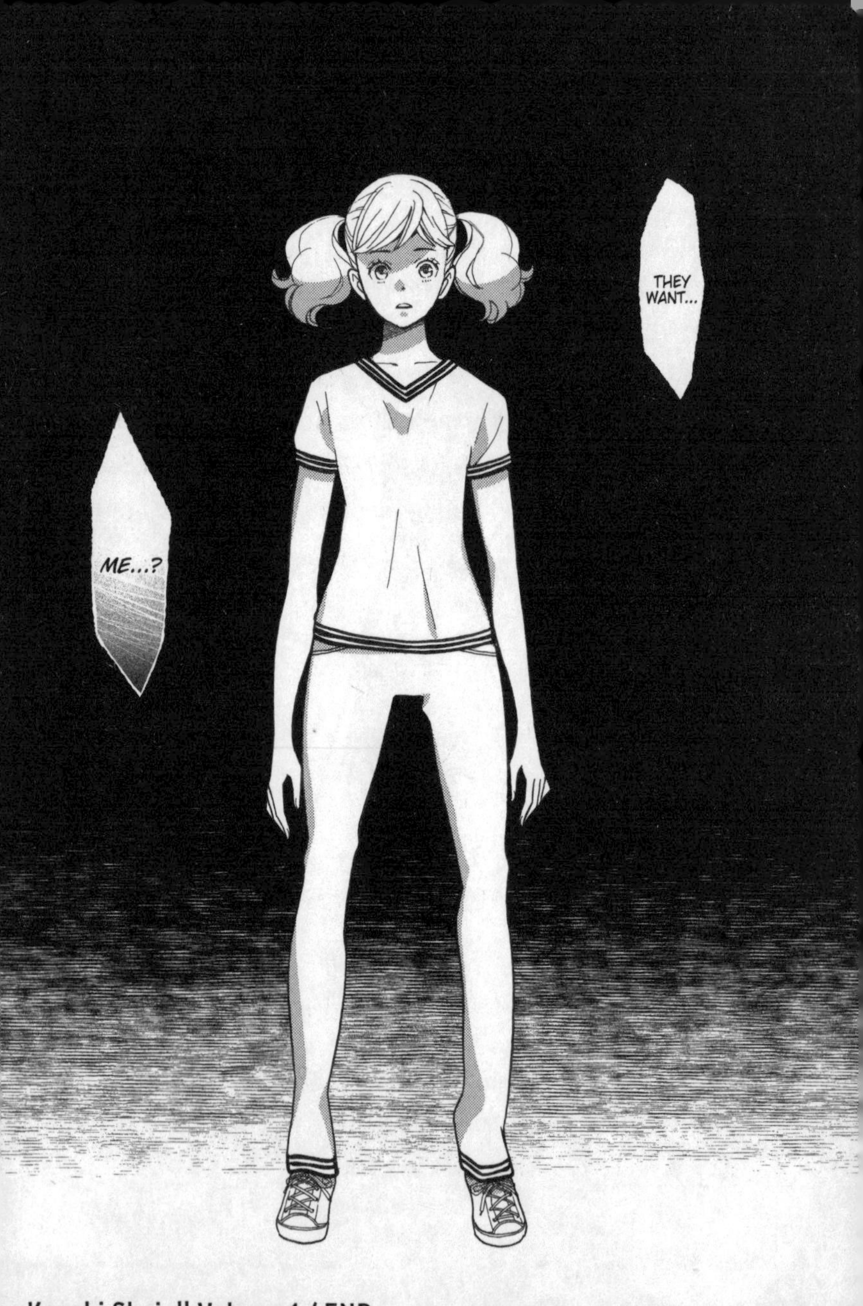
THEY WANT...
ME...?

Kageki Shojo!! Volume 1 / END

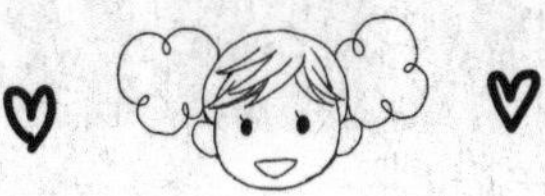

Hello again, and to you new readers, hello! \(^o^)/

I'm Watanabe Sarasa, the main character of this story.

I'm sure you're already *loving* our story in *Kageki Shojo!!*,

but if you want to enjoy more of the Kouka School bunch,

you should read our prequel, *Kageki Shojo!!: The Curtain Rises!*

You get to see Ai-chan with her super cute short hair! (^o^)

And if your bookstore doesn't have it, please...

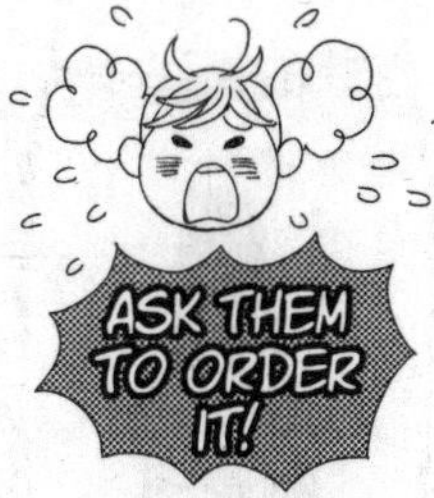
ASK THEM TO ORDER IT!

Let's meet again in volume two! (^_^)/¯

☆Special Thanks*

Pochi-chan, Tara-chan, Koizumi-san,

Yoshida-san, Andou-san, Kouta-san,

Ishigaki-sama, Kuroki-sama,

all my readers

with love from

Kumiko Saiki

斉木久美子

SEVEN SEAS ENTERTAINMENT PRESENTS

KAGEKI SHOJO!!

Vol. 1

story and art by **KUMIKO SAIKI**

TRANSLATION
Katrina Leonoudakis

LETTERING
Aila Nagamine

COVER DESIGN
Hanase Qi

LOGO DESIGN
Courtney Williams

PROOFREADER
Rebecca Schneidereit

COPY EDITOR
Dawn Davis

EDITOR
Shannon Fay

PREPRESS TECHNICIAN
hiannon Rasmussen-Silverstein

PRODUCTION ASSOCIATE
Christa Miesner

PRODUCTION MANAGER
Lissa Pattillo

MANAGING EDITOR
Julie Davis

ASSOCIATE PUBLISHER
Adam Arnold

PUBLISHER
Jason DeAngelis

First published in Japan in 2015 by HAKUSENSHA, INC., Tokyo.
English language translation rights in U.S.A. arranged with HAKUSENSHA, INC., Tokyo through TOHAN CORPORATION, Tokyo.

Seven Seas press and purchase enquiries can be sent to Marketing Manager Lianne Sentar at press@gomanga.com. Information regarding the distribution and purchase of digital editions is available from Digital Manager CK Russell at digital@gomanga.com.

ISBN: 978-1-64827-585-2
Printed in Canada
First Printing: July 2021
10 9 8 7 6 5 4 3 2 1

READING DIRECTIONS

This book reads from ***right to left***, Japanese style. If this is your first time reading manga, you start reading from the top right panel on each page and take it from there. If you get lost, just follow the numbered diagram here. It may seem backwards at first, but you'll get the hang of it! Have fun!!

1
2
3
4
5
6
7
8
9

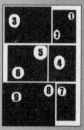

Follow us online: www.SevenSeasEntertainment.com